THE ROAD TO OREGON

*The Santa Fé Trail being first established, a
signboard was later set up to show where the
Oregon Trail branched off. It bore the simple
legend "Road to Oregon." . . . Surely so
unostentatious a sign never before nor since
announced so long a journey.*
—H. M. Chittenden: *The American
Fur Trade of the Far West*

EMIGRANT TRAIN IN THE ROCKY MOUNTAINS

From a rare print of an engraving by F. F. Palmer (1866) in the Collection formerly owned by Norman James

THE ROAD TO OREGON

*A Chronicle of the Great
Emigrant Trail*

by
W. J. GHENT

With 32 illustrations and a map

TUDOR PUBLISHING CO.
NEW YORK
1934

INTRODUCTION

IT is singular that no comprehensive historical treatment of the Oregon Trail has until now been attempted. The subject is of wide interest; the material is abundant, and it has long been available; for of the great wealth of recently discovered material that compels the rewriting of much of the history of the Far West, little has been added to the early documentation of the Trail. Historical essays, such as Professor F. G. Young's " The Oregon Trail," Mr. W. E. Connelley's " National Aspects of the Old Oregon Trail " and H. M. Chittenden's brief and compact sketch in *The American Fur Trade of the Far West,* have outlined the subject; and more recently has appeared the excellent study of some of its phases, *Opening a Highway to the Pacific,* 1838–1846, by Mr. James Christy Bell, Jr.; but the writing of an extended history with the Trail as its central theme has somehow been neglected.

In 1848 Francis Parkman published *The Oregon and California Trail.* It is a book that has had its hundreds of thousands of readers, and doubtless will always be popular. To students, however, it is disappointing by reason of what it omits. Of the Trail itself the book gives little information. Parkman was ill; he was young, and he had not yet developed that first essential of a historian — the spirit of inquiry. On matters that especially interested him he writes with an engaging charm; on all other matters he seems to show the incuriousness of an Indian. He disliked and shunned the emigrants; that constantly renewing company of pioneers that included such men as Bidwell, Burnett, the Applegates, Nesmith, Belden, and hundreds of others that could be named, he found uncouth, intrusive, dour, and unfriendly; and those who invaded Fort Laramie, shortly after his arrival, " totally devoid of any sense of delicacy or propriety." He seems, moreover, not to have had the slightest notion of the significance of the emigration movement.

He talks with a trader whom, most ineptly, he calls " old Vaskiss," apparently not knowing that the man is Colonel Louis Vasquez, noted mountain man and partner of James Bridger. Of Bridger he seems not to have heard, and of the famous fort he knows only that it is " a remote post in the mountains." A little inquiry might have disclosed to him that it was not remote except in the sense that it was four hundred miles from Fort Laramie, since it was on the main line of the Trail; and that it was not " in the mountains," but in a pleasant dell in the great Green Valley. He repeats a story of James P. Beckwourth's daredevil storming of a Blackfoot fort, not knowing that the story was identical with one that had been told of Edward Rose years before Beckwourth saw the frontier; and he gives an ill character to Beckwourth that is quite without warrant.

He talks and rides with Paul Dorion, son of the interpreter of Hunt's Astoria expedition of 1811. One would think that at the sound of the name Dorion his imagination had taken fire. For this Paul was one of the two living sons of that Sioux girl-mother who accompanied the expedition all the way from St. Louis to Astoria; who shared uncomplainingly every hardship that befell that ill-starred company, and who was later, with her two infants, the heroine of a thrilling escape quite unmatched in the annals of the western frontier. Wih-munke Wakan (Holy Rainbow) was her name, as Mr. Doane Robinson gives it, and she holds a place among women of the western tribes second only to that of Sacagawea, the Bird Woman of the Lewis and Clark expedition. Parkman had read all about her in *Astoria*. What questions he might have asked concerning her! Was she beautiful, after the Sioux fashion? Was she tall? Did she bear herself, as Dr. Elijah White attests, with a noble dignity? Did she, as some say, live out her days in far-away Oregon, or, as others say, contrive to return to her people? But the nascent historian apparently asked no questions; he was not interested.

In 1897 Major Henry Inman and Colonel William F. Cody published *The Great Salt Lake Trail*. What they meant by the term was, for the greater part of its length, the Oregon Trail. They were, however, apparently unaware that this Trail was ever used by emigrants on the way to Oregon. Of this remarkable work Professor F. G. Young has written:

The body of the book touches upon topics ranging in time from Jonathan Carver's explorations in 1766–'68 to the building of the Union Pacific Railroad. Its map lays "The Old Salt Lake Trail" exactly on the route of the Oregon trail as far as Fort Bridger, in Southwestern Wyoming. But the Oregon migrations are not hinted at by a single word in the body of the book. The authors' account of them could not

have been crowded out by more weighty matters, as all the dis-
jointed fragments of Indian hunting and fighting and drunken
carousal, whether happening on the line of the trail or not, are
crowded in. Either the story of the Oregon movement during
the thirties, forties and fifties was absolutely unknown to
Colonels Inman and Cody, or, if known, thought worthy of
relegation to oblivion by them.*

It is obvious that neither of these books can be considered as a serious historical treatment of the Oregon
Trail.

The sources for the present work are largely the
journals and travel-books of the trapper era (which
over a period of many years has been a favorite field of
the author's) and the diaries and reminiscences of the
emigrants published in the *Transactions* of the Oregon
Pioneer Association, the *Quarterly* of the Oregon Historical Society, the *Washington Historical Quarterly*
and various California publications. In the treatment
of the stage-coach and mail services Professor LeRoy
R. Hafen's *The Overland Mail* and Messrs. F. A. Root
and W. E. Connelley's *The Overland Stage to California* have been freely drawn upon — the former for
its exact data and the latter for its lively depiction of the
times and the people. The tracing of the Trail follows
mainly the authority of Professor Archer Butler Hulbert, of the Stewart Commission on Western History,
whose four volumes on the central trails in the *Crown
Collection of Maps* have proved invaluable. Reports
of Indian Commissioners and the files of the Indian, the
Engineers' and the Adjutant General's Offices have

* "The Oregon Trail," *Quarterly* of the Oregon Historical Society,
Vol. I, No. 4 (December 1900).

been consulted. Of many secondary sources found helpful special mention should be made of the work by James Christy Bell, Jr., already referred to; Joseph R. Wilson's resumé of the diplomatic negotiations regarding Oregon, in the *Quarterly* of the Oregon Historical Society for June and September 1900; Frederic L. Paxson's *The Last American Frontier;* J. Cecil Alter's *James Bridger;* Cardinal Goodwin's *The Trans-Mississippi West;* Professor Joseph Schafer's *History of the Pacific Northwest;* Professor Grace Raymond Hebard and Mr. E. A. Brininstool's *The Bozeman Trail* (not always accurate in detail, but containing much original matter of great value), and the Rev. Myron Eells' *Marcus Whitman, Pathfinder and Patriot,* a book that has been somewhat roughly handled by the anti-Whitmanites, but that is, though unskilfully and sometimes blunderingly written, an honest attempt to outline a period and to portray a great character.

It is sometimes asserted that the main business of a historical writer is interpretation. In the view of the author the main business is accuracy. He has sought to be exact; and he here echoes the prayer of the conscientious Elliot Coues that every error committed, " whether in ignorance or by inadvertence, may be exposed and corrected."

Grateful acknowledgments for information or criticism received are due to Professor Allan Nevins; to Mr. W. E. Connelley, secretary of the Kansas State Historical Society; to Miss Stella M. Drumm, librarian of the Missouri Historical Society; to Mrs. Clarence S. Paine, secretary of the Mississippi Valley Historical Association; to Professor Grace Raymond Hebard, of the University of Wyoming; to Mr. Charles L. Camp, of the University of California; to Mr. David Hilger, librarian of the Historical Society of Montana; to Professor Ralph P. Bieber, of Washington University, St. Louis; to Mr. T. C. Elliott, of Walla Walla, Washington; to the Hon. Charles L. McNary, United States Senator from Oregon; to the Hon. Robert G. Simmons, Representative from the Sixth District of Nebraska; to Mr. Frederick S. Dellenbaugh; to Major H. H. Stickney, Corps of Engineers, United States Army, Washington, D. C.; to Mr. Herbert S. Auerbach, of Salt Lake City; to Mr. Walter E. Meacham, of Baker, Oregon; to Messrs. H. E. Mills and Charles Jackson, of Atlantic City, Wyoming, and to President Stephen B. L. Penrose, of Whitman College.

W. J. GHENT

WASHINGTON, D. C.

CONTENTS

LIST OF ILLUSTRATIONS

THE ROAD TO OREGON

The Road to
OREGON

CHAPTER I

THE PATHMAKERS

WILD animals made the first trails. The buffalo
moved in such great masses that on open ground he was
a destroyer, rather than a maker, of trails; but the deer,
the elk, and the antelope left pathways over the plains
and along the valleys and among the foothills, and the
loftiest heights showed the track of the bighorn sheep.
The Indian followed, and he also made paths of his own
— peace trails to the villages of his friends, war trails
to the country of his enemies, hunting trails that inter-
cepted the herds on their migrations or struck them
in their winter retreats. Wild animal and Indian alike
chose the easiest way — the route with the fewest
obstacles.

When the fur-trappers invaded the West they found
a criss-cross pattern of many trails. Some of these for
a time they followed, but oftener they made their way
through an untracked wilderness. They were hunting
for beaver, and far and wide they searched wherever
beaver might be found. Perhaps none of them ever trod
the floor of the Grand Canyon of the Colorado, but
elsewhere they seem to have penetrated to every niche
and cranny of the rugged West. Long before the Gov-

1

ernment undertook any general exploration of this vast region, virtually all of it had become known, in minute detail, to the hardy and indomitable trappers.

This early exploration was largely financed by the plug hat of our forefathers. The dauntless spirits who in the face of every peril kept to their quest could hardly have indulged their passion for adventure but for the good money commanded by the beaver pelt. Fashion decreed the high hat of prime beaver fur, and even the unfashionable accepted the decree. Assuredly the beaver fur had many other uses: the Chinese, for instance, who were never addicted to high hats, were its eager buyers; but its steady demand as material for headgear gave stability to the trade. In 1832 came the silk hat, with the result that by another seven years the price of beaver fur in London fell to one-eighth of its former level. For a time American fashion resisted the innovation. As late as 1846 Oliver Wendell Holmes could write the impressive counsel to men who wished to dress both modishly and well:

Have a good hat; the secret of your looks
Lives with the beaver in Canadian brooks —

some years after the silk hat had won a certain favor in Europe and the beaver had virtually disappeared from the brooks of Wyoming and Montana. The drop in the price of fur, along with the gradual exhaustion of the supply, had paralyzed the trapping industry and driven the trappers from the mountains.

These trapper-explorers, or " mountain men," who broke the trails that opened up the West, were a unique breed of men. They had no forerunners, and their like can never again appear on the earth. Irving's familiar tribute, based on the word of Bonneville, tells what toils they endured and what perils they faced:

There is, perhaps, no class of men on the face of the earth, . . . who lead a life of more continued exertion, peril and excitement, and who are more enamoured of their occupations, than the free trappers of the West. No toil, no danger, no privation can turn the trapper from his pursuit. His passionate excitement at times resembles a mania. In vain may the most vigilant and cruel savages beset his path; in vain may rocks, and precipices, and wintry torrents oppose his progress; but let a single track of beaver meet his eye, and he forgets all dangers and defies all difficulties. At times he may be seen with his traps on his shoulder, buffeting his way across rapid streams, amidst floating blocks of ice: at other times, he is to be found with his traps swung on his back clambering the most rugged mountains, scaling or descending the most frightful precipices, searching, by routes inaccessible to the horse, and never before trodden by white man, for springs and lakes unknown to his comrades, and where he may meet with his favorite game. Such is the mountaineer, the hardy trapper of the West.

The English traveler, Lieutenant George Frederick Ruxton, has entertainingly stressed the peculiarities of dress, manner, conduct and speech which set the trapper apart from other men. Perhaps his account is a bit overdrawn, or at best not wholly representative; for he wrote in the twilight of the trapper era, when none but the most eccentric of all that adventurous brotherhood were left in the mountains. Osborne Russell, himself a trapper, in his journal for April 1838, gives us an authentic picture of a party of Bridger's men setting out for their labors in the Bighorn country:

Early next morning about thirty of us were armed, equipped and mounted, as circumstances required. A trapper's equipment in such cases is generally one animal upon which is placed one or two epishemores [apishamores, saddle blankets], a riding saddle and bridle, a sack containing six beaver traps, a blanket with an extra pair of mocassins, his powder horn and bullet pouch, with a belt to which is attached a butcher knife, a wooden box containing bait for beaver, a tobacco sack with a pipe and implements for making fire, with sometimes a hatchet fastened to the pommel of his saddle. His personal dress is a flannel or cotton shirt (if he is fortunate enough to obtain one, if not antelope skin answers the purpose of over and undershirt), a pair of leather breeches with blanket or smoked buffalo skin leggings, a coat made of blanket or buffalo robe, a hat or cap of wool, buffalo or other skin, his hose are pieces of blanket wrapped around his feet, which are covered with a pair of mocassins made of dressed deer, elk or buffalo skins, with his long hair falling loosely over his shoulders, completes his uniform. He then mounts and places his rifle before him on his saddle. Such was the dress equipage of the party, myself included, now ready to start.[1]

Not all the men who trapped for beaver were of this independent and daring class. Far lower in the social scale of the mountains were the *engagés,* or contract men, of the fur companies, whose business it was to do what they were told, to go where they were ordered and to subsist on the standard rations of bread and bacon. " Pork-eaters " or even " lard-eaters," they were disdainfully called by the aristocracy of the profession, who fed on game when they could find it and at other times went hungry. Yet there was no hard-and-fast line in this social cleavage. To the hardy and bold the pork-eating period was but a time of apprenticeship, and when their contracts expired they joined the free trappers; while, on the other hand, among those who had started independently, the lazy, the un-enterprising and those into whose souls the fear of the Indian had taken lodgment were glad to exchange their freedom for security and rations.

The trapper-explorers wanted and expected to get rich. When the incomparable John Colter, as a reward for his faithful services with the Lewis and Clark expedition, obtained his release at the Mandan villages, his companion, Sergeant John Ordway, thus recorded the episode:

[August 17, 1806] John Colter one of our party asks leave of our officers to go back with Mᴿ Dixon a trapping, which permission was granted him so our officers Settled with him and fitted him out with powder lead and a great number of articles which compleated him for a trapping voiage of two years which they are determined to Stay untill they make a fortune, &C. &C.

A competence, or perhaps a fortune, was the dream of most of them. Yet for all their high hopes, their industry and their contempt of danger, they made not even a decent living. The trading companies saw well to *that,* and many were the fortunes built up from the toils of the trappers. Improvident the trappers were, as a rule; but even had they been thriftier their share of the product was too small to promise a fit reward for saving; and those who survived the rigors of the life and the assaults of the savages found themselves no better off than when they began. Their time has been called the *romantic* period of the frontier, and again, more appropriately, the *heroic* period. They were, however, for all their bold hardihood, a short-sighted folk.

They thought only of beaver. They might have done better in a material way to vary their search for it with a search for gold. Many of the icy streams they waded were rich in the precious metal, though the fact did not become known until years after they had scattered to other scenes.

The trails that later became useful to the emigrants were the paths along which the trappers carried their furs to the frontier capital, St. Louis, or made their way — as some of them occasionally did — between the Columbia and the Green. The valley of this Green River — the Rio Verde of the Spaniards and the Seedskeedee of the Crow Indians — just west of the main ridge of the Rockies, in the present Wyoming, was the strategic center of all the activities of the trappers; and the low gap by which it was entered from the east — South Pass — became the chief gateway to the Pacific and so remained until the building of the railroad. Out of the most practicable of these various travel-stretches, linked end to end, slowly evolved the Oregon Trail. Its course was dictated by the contour of the country, the drainage, herbage, and forestation. For the pack-train, as for the later emigrant wagon train, the necessary conditions were much the same. Ridges must be surmounted on their easiest grades, streams crossed at their safest fords, and at distances averaging from fifteen to twenty-five miles there must be fuel for camp-fires, grass for the livestock and pure water for both man and beast. For one long stretch of the Trail — from Grand Island, on the Platte, to near Fort Laramie — there was little or no wood; but the plains were covered with " buffalo chips " (the dried dung of the bison), which trappers and emigrants alike used and which proved an excellent fuel.

This route to the Pacific in time bore many names. To some persons it was the Platte Trail, or even the Great Platte Trail; to others the Emigrant Road or the Road to Oregon. James Clyman, trapper and emigrant, in his diary for 1844, calls it the Oregon Trace. To Francis Parkman, in 1848, it was the Oregon and California Trail. In later years its southern detour from Julesburg to Fort Bridger came to be known as the Overland Trail. With varying and usually inappropriate meanings the names of the Mormon Trail and the Great Salt Lake Trail were also applied to it. To the Indians generally, according to Father de Smet, it was the Great Medicine Road of the Whites, while to Washakie's band of Eastern Shoshones it was the White-Topped Wagon Road.

Its original course (which farther along will be traced in detail) was from Independence, Missouri, to the mouth of the Walla Walla, in Washington. From this frontier town, ten miles east of the present Kansas City, it followed the Santa Fé Trail through the nearby town of Westport, past the Shawnee Mission and on to a point near the present town of Gardner, Kansas, forty-one miles from the starting place. Here the roads parted. The Oregon Trail ran to the northwest, crossed the Kansas, and continuing in a northwestward course reached the Platte in the vicinity of Grand Island. Thence it followed the south bank of the Platte to the forks, ascended the South Platte for some miles, crossed it and ran to the North Platte. Along the south bank of this stream it continued to Fort Laramie. From here

it diverged somewhat from the river, but reached it
again near the present city of Casper, Wyoming. Crossing the river, it ran southwest to the Sweetwater, which
it ascended to the main range of the Rocky Mountains.
It traversed South Pass, crossed the Green River and
(from the year 1843) turned southward to Fort Bridger.
From there its general course was northwestward to
Soda Springs, Idaho, and then northward to old Fort
Hall, whence it followed the south bank of the Snake
to the present Glenn's Ferry, in Owyhee County.
Crossing the Snake, it ran to the neighborhood of the
present Boisé, then down the Boisé River to its mouth,
where it again crossed the Snake. From there it ran
northwestward to the present La Grande, Oregon, then
to Whitman's Mission, near the present Walla Walla,
and on to the mouth of the Walla Walla River. Properly
speaking, this point was, until 1843, the end of the Trail,
since the remainder of the journey was by boat and
portage. In that year wagons broke a roadway along
the south bank of the Columbia as far as the Dalles,
and in the following year another roadway to the Dalles
was made by the caravans turning northwestward from
La Grande. The Trail in time was to have new starting
points and new feeders in the East and many new terminal lines in the West, but the main route, except for two
important cut-offs frequently used and a number of
minor detours, was to remain unaltered to the end.

The first party of whites known to have journeyed
along any section of what was to become the Oregon
Trail was that of Wilson Price Hunt's overland Astorians in 1811–12, and the section was in the remote West.
The Lewis and Clark expedition of 1804–06, though it

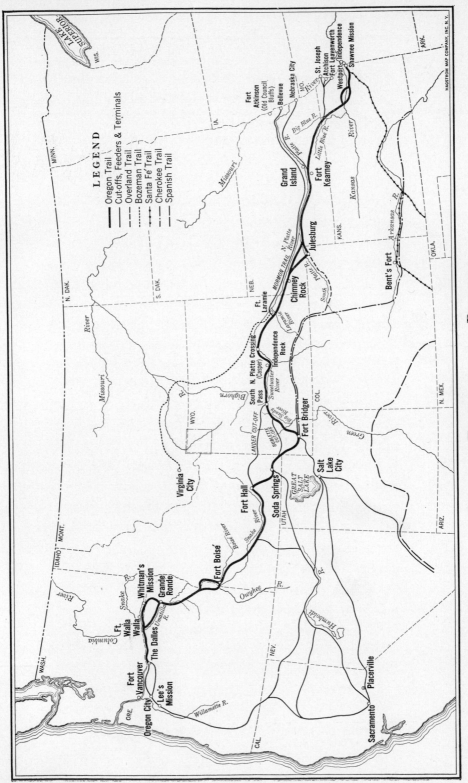

CENTRAL TRAILS TO THE PACIFIC

twice passed the mouth of the Walla Walla, traveled no part of the Trail. It was in the early spring of 1811 that Hunt started out, with sixty men, one woman (the Indian wife of the interpreter, Dorion), and two children, on his memorable journey through the western wilderness. John Jacob Astor had determined upon his magnificent venture of setting up an establishment at the mouth of the Columbia; to this projected Astoria he had sent one expedition by sea, and he had chosen Hunt to lead another by land. Up the Missouri in boats went the leader with his company, pressing his boatmen to the utmost exertions, for he was eager to keep ahead of the trader, Manuel Lisa, who with a trapping party was frantically endeavoring to overtake him. The early annals of the river bear no record of another such race as this one, which lasted for more than two months and covered a distance of more than a thousand miles. Lisa won; on the upper borders of the Sioux country he caught up with Hunt, and a bit farther on, near the present boundary between the two Dakotas, the two companies rested at the villages of the Arikaras.

These Arikaras (later commonly known as Rees), though they lived remote from the region of the future Trail, were a factor in its opening, as we shall see later on, and a word of introduction may be given them here. Cousins of the Pawnees, they had many of the undesirable qualities of their kinsmen; but their outstanding distinction was their capriciousness. One never knew which to expect from them — peace or war. Friendly to one party of white visitors, they would treacherously attack the next. This time they were peaceful, though the fact that the two companies numbered more than eighty well-armed men may have had something to do with their attitude. They were not merely peaceful, but indulgent; and they reaped a rich harvest by renting out their women to the voyagers. The young traveler, Henry M. Brackenridge, who was with Lisa, tells us that " fathers brought their daughters, husbands their wives, brothers their sisters, to be offered for sale at this market of indecency and shame." Continuing he writes:

> Seeing the chief one day in a thoughtful mood, I asked him what was the matter. " I was wondering," said he, " whether you white people have any women amongst you." I answered him in the affirmative. " Then," said he, " why is it that your people are so fond of our women, one might suppose they had never seen any before."

A dozen years later these Arikaras were to launch an unprovoked attack on a party of trappers making for the mountains by the customary river route and thereby so to obstruct the route as to turn the course of travel to a direct penetration of the mid-west region overland from St. Louis. About the middle of July Hunt's party left them, and traveling through what is now Wyoming to where the Wind River turns north and becomes the Bighorn, ascended the Wind, crossed the two ranges westward and reached the abandoned fort which Major Andrew Henry had established on Henry's Fork of the Snake the previous fall. Here, by a tragic blunder, the horses were loosed, and the party attempted to descend the unnavigable Snake in canoes. Disasters multiplied, such of the canoes as were not wrecked were abandoned, and the party, broken into several detachments, began its long and weary walk to the Columbia. North of the present Pocatello, Idaho, in the neighborhood of the town of Fort Hall (where the trading post of that name was established twenty-three years later), some of this company reached ground that thirty-two years afterward was to be tracked by the wheels of the emigrants' wagons; and thence on to near the end of their pitiful journey they approximated from time to time the future course of the Oregon Trail.

The small party of Astorians, under Robert Stuart, that set out from the Columbia for St. Louis on June 29, 1812, traveled or paralleled the line of the Trail from the mouth of the Walla Walla as far as the Fort Hall region, and may again have struck it at the western approach to South Pass, but more probably near the junction of the Sweetwater and the North Platte. From there, descending the North Platte, the party reached the Missouri in the spring of 1813; and if it followed the south bank its journey was along a part of the future Trail. The remote western section was further followed or paralleled by the two Snake expeditions of the North West Company from Fort Nez Percés (later Fort Walla Walla) in 1818–20, and by the four expeditions of the Hudson's Bay Company, under Peter Skene Ogden, in 1824–29.

Thus the western end of the Trail had been well traveled before the eastern end was even broken. The middle section was also earlier traveled, for the first approaches to western Wyoming were by northern routes. Who first blazed the meandering trail between Grand Island and the bend of the Missouri, at the present Kansas

City, is not known. Parties of hunters and trappers had traversed the plains of Nebraska and may have reached the foothills of Wyoming before the middle of the second decade. The company that included the noted Ezekiel Williams, sent out by Manuel Lisa from Fort Mandan in 1809, of whose experiences D. H. Coyner, in *The Lost Trappers,* made so absurd a mess, was one of these; and the rescue party under Charles Sanguinet, dispatched in the fall of 1812, was another. There was also, among others, the mysterious Jacques Laramie, about whom much has been written, who with a few companions is supposed to have entered eastern Wyoming in 1820 and who was probably killed by Indians in the following year. It may be that some of these fearless wanderers broke paths that later became included in the Oregon Trail, but we have little knowledge of them or their movements.

The first American trappers known to have made trails later used in crossing the continent were Ashley's men, and so were the first trappers known to have crossed South Pass. William Henry Ashley was a Virginian who settled in Ste. Geneviève, in what is now Missouri, probably in the year of the Louisiana purchase. He became a surveyor, a land speculator, a merchant and a manufacturer of gunpowder. His affairs prospered, and in 1819, seeking a wider field for his activities, he moved to St. Louis. On the outskirts of the town he built what was called a mansion, where he entertained his friends and acquaintances with profuse hospitality. A cultivated man, able and ambitious, he soon attained prominence in the affairs of the frontier community. He was made brigadier-general of the territorial militia, and in 1821 was elected the first lieutenant-governor of the state. During the following winter he determined to enter the fur trade. In the light of conditions in the trade at that period his resolution must be regarded as a bold, and even a reckless one. The two British organizations, the North West and the Hudson's Bay Companies, after a prolonged, vicious and expensive struggle against each other, had combined in 1821 and were soon to fasten an unbreakable hold on the Oregon country. What was left of Lisa's old Missouri Fur Company, though constantly hampered by the maneuvers of the Hudson's Bay Company farther north, held the upper Missouri; the middle Missouri was controlled by the Columbia Fur Company, and Astor, with his American Fur Company, was making the final negotiations which resulted, a few months later, in giving him a secure lodgment in St. Louis.

But Ashley believed in his lucky star and went defiantly onward with his preparations. For his field captain he chose Major Andrew Henry, who in the early spring of 1810 had led a brigade of the St. Louis Missouri Fur Company to the perilous Three Forks of the Missouri, and who, driven away by the implacable Blackfeet, had penetrated the Idaho wilderness and set up the first stockade erected west of the Rocky Mountains. In the *Missouri Republican* of St. Louis of March 20, 1822, appeared this most historic of all " Help Wanted " advertisements:

To enterprising young men. The subscriber wishes to engage one hundred young men to ascend the Missouri River to its source, there to be employed for one, two or three years. For particulars enquire of Major Andrew Henry, near the lead mines in the county of Washington, who will ascend with and command the party; or of the subscriber near St. Louis.

Signed, WILLIAM H. ASHLEY.

From the motley gathering that answered the call Ashley selected his company. It is well to note that the chosen included an eighteen-year-old boy named James Bridger, later to become (with the exception of Kit Carson) the most noted of all the mountain men. From St. Louis, on April 22, the expedition started, and after five months of labor against the heady current of the Missouri reached the mouth of the Yellowstone. Here a fort was built, whereupon Ashley, leaving Henry in charge, returned home. In the following spring he organized another expedition, which included at least three men whose names are inseparably connected with the history of the Far West. One of these was Thomas Fitzpatrick, an Irish youth of twenty-four, who eight years before had come to America. " Broken Hand " and " Bad Hand " the Indians at a later time were to call him, because of an injury suffered through the bursting of a gun; and also " White Hair," because of the premature graying of his locks through a terrible experience with the Blackfeet. No man in all the West (unless it be Carson) lived through a more varied experience. In his thirty-one years on the frontier he was in turn trapper, Indian fighter, a partner in the Rocky Mountain Fur Company, an employee of the American Fur Company, guide to the party of Father de Smet in 1841, to that of Dr. Elijah White in the following year, to the second Frémont expedition and to Kearny's southwestern expedition as far as Socorro, N. M.; and at his death in February 1854, he had been for nearly eight years agent for the Cheyennes, the Arapahos and the Kiowas on the Upper Platte and the Arkansas.

Then there was Jedediah Strong Smith, an upstate New Yorker, twenty-five years old, who on reaching St. Louis had eagerly joined the company in order to get a sight of the remoter frontier. It is possible that he may have been, as some assert, a member of the expedition of the previous year, but the matter is uncertain. He was to become Ashley's right-hand man, to lead the first expedition across country to South Pass and to be a partner in the firm of Smith, Jackson, and Sublette, which in the summer of 1826 succeeded Ashley. He was a student and an intimate observer of nature, and his thirst for knowledge of the unbroken wilds was quenchless. With his Bible and his rifle and a few companions he made journeys that covered thousands of miles, through many perils and extreme hardships. Though of a religious turn, and perhaps something of a zealot, he seems not to have obtruded his views on others, and all the testimony shows him to have been affable in manner and singularly generous and helpful in disposition. Twice he escaped a general massacre of his men, but at last he, too, fell (May 27, 1831), at the hands of Comanches, near the Santa Fé Trail.

There was also William L. Sublette, later to become one of the leading figures in the fur trade, at one time a partner with Smith and David E. Jackson and later a partner with Robert Campbell, that " pork-eating " trapper who became one of the wealthiest and most honored merchants of St. Louis. And there was James Clyman, who by a freak of history has had to wait the better part of a century for any general recognition of his worth. He was not only a trapper but a writer, and though innocent of spelling or grammar, a good one. His diaries and reminiscences, published in book form in 1928, add greatly to our knowledge of both the trapper and the emigrant periods.

With his company Ashley set forth on the second expedition in the spring of 1823. Near the present boundary between the two Dakotas he was attacked by the Arikaras (June 2), and after suffering heavy losses was compelled to retreat. For just such an emergency as this the Government had established, four years earlier, its farthest outpost, Fort Atkinson, sixteen miles north of the present Omaha. Soldiers under Colonel Henry Leavenworth and trappers of the Missouri Fur Company under Joshua Pilcher came up from the fort, and with them a large party of Sioux. On August 9 the battle was renewed, but the Arikaras, with few losses, were permitted to escape from their village. The whole affair turned out a fiasco; the Arikaras, unpunished, remained as hostile as before, and Ashley found the northern route seriously obstructed. Some of his men who, under Henry, had come down from the Yellowstone fort to render help, now returned, but the remainder retreated to a trading post known as Fort Kiowa, near the present Chamberlain, South Dakota, whence most of them, with all the experience of Indian warfare they wanted, sought their homes back in the settlements.

From Fort Kiowa, about the last of September, a party of eleven men, headed by Smith, with Fitzpatrick as second in command, was detailed to strike due west

JAMES CLYMAN (1792–1881)
*From Charles L. Camp's "James Clyman
American Frontiersman" (1928)*

JAMES BRIDGER (1804–1881)
As he appeared about 1866

for the mountains. Rounding the southern slope of the Black Hills, the men reached the Wind River and wintered with the Crows. From these Indians they learned of an easy way to reach Green River. They started in February 1824, passed south along the Popo Agie, crossed the intervening ridge to the Sweetwater, turned west, and early in March traversed South Pass and on either the 19th or 20th of the month reached the Green.[2]

The other party of Ashley men, headed by Henry and including Etienne Provot and young Bridger, had given up their fort at the mouth of the Yellowstone, ascended that river and wintered at the mouth of the Bighorn. With the opening of spring they moved south, following the Smith-Fitzpatrick party through South Pass and in various detachments traversed the Green Valley, the eastern part of the Great Basin, and the Bear Valley. By the winter of 1824–25 a wide region that included parts of the present Wyoming, Colorado, Utah, and Idaho had been well explored.

That there were gaps in the lofty chain of the Rocky Mountains through which it could be easily crossed in wagons had been common report in St. Louis for more than a decade. Brackenridge, talking with Colter in the summer of 1810, heard of them and in the fall of 1811 heard of them again from Henry. They were, he said, " considerably south of the source of the Jefferson river." He mentioned two, which seem likely to have been, as Chittenden suggests, Bozeman (though this one is *not* south of the source of the Jefferson) and either Union or Two-gwo-tee, near the head of Wind River. Mr. John G. White, who has studied this matter with care and has traveled over much of the region, believes

that Colter crossed South Pass going west in the winter
of 1807–08 and that the " Colter's River " of General
William Clark's map, published in 1814, is really the
Big Sandy.[3]   Robert Stuart's returning Astorians, in
November 1812, probably also traversed it, as Ramsay
Crooks, a member of the party, vigorously asserted in
a letter written forty-four years later. It is a broad
pass, twenty miles from side to side, and though we may
be certain that they did not journey along the Indian
trail which subsequently became the trappers' and the
emigrants' roadway, we are warranted in believing that
they crossed the range somewhere north of the southern
wall of the pass, Table Mountain. In the *Missouri Ga-
zette* (St. Louis), of May 15, 1813, is a report of the
return of Stuart's company in which occurs this statement:

> By information received from these gentlemen, it appears
> that a journey across the continent of N. America, might be
> performed with a waggon, there being no obstruction in the
> whole route that any person would dare to call a mountain.

Stuart's manuscript journal shows him to have
crossed in the vicinity of Table Mountain, and there is
no other passage across the range within many miles of
this point of which the foregoing statement could possibly have been made. It is difficult to believe that those
hardy and daring adventurers, John Hoback, Edward
Robinson, and Jacob Reasoner (or Rezner) did not also
find the pass. They had been with Henry at his fort
on Henry's Fork in the winter of 1810–11, and with
Hunt's expedition, from which they were detached at
the fort to remain in the country and trap and explore.

It is possible that the Spanish trading party that visited the Green in 1818 may have found it, and that it may also have been revealed to members of the North West Company, who are said to have trapped the Green in the same year.

But the movements of all these early adventurers bore no enduring results. The *effective* discovery of the gap that opened the West to the wagons of the trappers and the emigrants was made by the Smith-Fitzpatrick party. One of the members of this party, Clyman, became separated from his companions on the Sweetwater, and not knowing what else to do, trudged all the six hundred perilous miles back to the Missouri, arriving at Fort Atkinson, eighty days later, almost dead from hunger and exhaustion. A little later Fitzpatrick, with two others, also came in. The course they followed was probably along the north bank of the Platte, thus approximating what later became known as the Mormon Trail. They had cached a valuable stock of furs at Independence Rock, and they now sought means of recovering and bringing it in.[4] From Fort Atkinson Fitzpatrick communicated with Ashley at St. Louis, and the General immediately set out with an expedition for the mountains. It came up the Missouri to the fort, and in November started overland along the north bank of the Platte, crossing the river in the neighborhood of the forks. From here it followed the South Fork to the vicinity of the present Fort Collins and then turned up into Wyoming, arriving on the Green about the middle of April 1825. The general course of Ashley's journey from the mouth of Lodge Pole Creek (at the present Julesburg) is that which

later became known as the Overland Trail. In July, at
the mouth of Henry's Fork of the Green (not to be confused with the far-away Henry's Fork of the Snake),
Ashley held a rendezvous of trappers, the first of a
series of annual mountain fairs that was to continue for
sixteen years.

Henry, who in the summer of 1824 brought back the
first cargo of furs from the Green, made the long water
journey by way of the Bighorn, the Yellowstone, and
the Missouri, successfully evading the Arikaras; and
Ashley, in the following year, though he had entered
the mountains by the overland route, followed the water-
way home, escorted from the mouth of the Yellowstone
by the military command of General Atkinson. Thence-
forth, however, all the journeys to and from the Wyoming country were made by land. There now came
to be two or three expeditions each year, and, both eastbound and westbound, they seem to have followed an
approximate course between the bend of the Missouri
and Grand Island. Clyman, going out as an emigrant
in 1844, found at a point north of the Kansas and near
to the then well-marked Trail, the track of a trapping
party he had led from the mountains in the fall of 1827.

The most important of these early expeditions following the discovery of South Pass was that of Ashley's
immediate successors in 1830. Ashley had grown
wealthy from his few years of gathering furs in the mid-
land region, and in the summer of 1826 he had sold his
business to three of his employees, Smith, Jackson, and
Sublette. This expedition was important because it
marked the beginning of wheeled traffic on the Oregon
Trail, for till then the only wheels the Trail had known

were those attached to a four-pounder cannon taken to the present Ogden in the summer of 1827. The train, composed of ten loaded wagons, drawn by five mules each, and two Dearborn carriages, drawn by one mule each, left St. Louis on April 10. It was led by Sublette, for the other partners were then in the mountains. Doubtless it passed through the infant towns of Lexington and Independence. It followed the Santa Fé Trail " about forty miles," then went " some degrees north of west," crossing the Kansas and reaching the Platte, which it followed " to the Rocky Mountains and to the head of Wind River where it issues from the mountains " (the scene of the rendezvous of that year). Most likely it left the Trail at the commonly used crossing near the present Casper, Wyoming. It arrived on July 16, and here the partners, perhaps satisfied that they had skimmed the cream of the mountain fur trade, sold their business to the Rocky Mountain Fur Company, composed of Fitzpatrick, Milton G. Sublette (a brother of William's), Bridger and two others. Three weeks after the arrival the train started on its return, and on October 10 it reached St. Louis.

The partners were justly proud of their feat, and they wrote a long letter about it to the Hon. John H. Eaton, Jackson's Secretary of War.[5] It is a letter of exceptional value for its revelation not only of the existence of a trail to the mountains, but of what was then thought and felt about access to the Western Coast. " The ease and safety with which it [the taking of wagons] was done proved the facility of communicating overland with the Pacific Ocean," they say. " The route from the Southern Pass, where the wagons stopped [an obvious

error, since the trappers' rendezvous was north and east
of South Pass], to the Great Falls of the Columbia, being easier and better than on their side of the mountains,
with grass enough for horses and mules, but a scarcity
of game for the support of men." They knew of an
" Oregon question," and they had strong views about it.
They protested against the privileges being given to the
Hudson's Bay Company and argued that the convention of 1818 should be terminated and that each nation
should be confined to its own territories. Primarily
their standpoint was that of fur hunters who had been
worsted in a duel with the powerful British company,
but their mention of wagons suggests that they also had
a thought about the future of colonization.

A new record for the Trail was made by the picturesque Captain B. L. E. Bonneville in 1832, when he
took the first wagons through South Pass and across
the Green to the mouth of Horse Creek. In the same
year Nathaniel Jarvis Wyeth, a merchant of Cam-
bridge, Massachusetts, with a pack-train and eleven
men, reopened the western end of the Trail by journeying from the Portneuf to the mouth of the Walla
Walla, whence he went on to the Hudson's Bay Company post of Fort Vancouver. With him was John
Ball, of New Hampshire, an early enthusiast about
Oregon, who remained there, the first permanent American settler in the Oregon country.

There was thus by 1832, nine years before the first
emigrant train set out for the Pacific, a continuous trail
— part of it marked by wheels and all of it stamped with
the hoofprints of mules and horses — all the way from
the bend of the Missouri to the mouth of the Walla

Walla. Franklin, two hundred miles from the mouth of the Missouri, had been the first point of departure (by way of the ferry at Arrow Rock) for the Santa Fé traders; but it had been washed away about the time travel began on the eastern end of the Oregon Trail. It was succeeded for a short time by Boonville, across the river, and then by Lexington, founded in 1822, which served as the starting place for both trails. But the apex of the moving wedge of frontier settlement, pointed along the Missouri River, soon passed beyond Lexington. In March 1827, Independence — only a few miles east of the bend of the river — was begun; and in May of the same year the Government, realizing that the penetration of the Great Plateau was not to be by the upper Missouri, established a new post, Fort Leavenworth, about thirty miles beyond Independence, and thereupon abandoned Fort Atkinson forever.

By at least 1832 Independence had taken the lead as the jumping-off place for all westward expeditions. It was to have a rival, Westport, eight miles farther on, founded in 1833; and after 1843 it was to have other rivals farther up the Missouri. But Westport, in spite of its frequent mention in the early chronicles, developed slowly; Clyman, as late as 1846, characterizes it as " a small ordinary village "; and for all the early years Independence remained the nominal (though not always the actual) point of departure. Occasionally in these early years, as steamboat transit developed, an expedition would be transported as far as the new trading post of Bellevue, at the mouth of the Platte. Lucien Fontenelle's trapping party of 1835, with which the Rev. Samuel Parker and Dr. Marcus Whitman traveled to the Green River rendezvous, followed this route; and so did Fitzpatrick's party of the next year, taking with it the Whitmans and the Spaldings on the first leg of their long journey to Oregon. But these were rare exceptions. Nearly all the early expeditions started from the vicinity of Independence.

The route from Independence to the mouth of the Walla Walla was the original Oregon Trail, parent of all the central routes to the Pacific. To it were to be added new feeders from the many towns farther up the Missouri; extensive detours, such as the Sublette and the Lander Cut-offs, were to be made; in the Green Valley, beginning with 1843, it was to run farther south, in order to pass Bridger's newly built trading post; and toward its western end it was to break up into a maze of radial lines to Utah, California, and Oregon. This great highway ran through a wilderness. From Independence to Fort Walla Walla there was nowhere along its line, at the beginning of 1832, even a cabin. Shaped gradually by the trappers, this road was now to be traveled by the missionaries, and in a few years by thousands of emigrants seeking homes on the Pacific.

COURT HOUSE SQUARE, INDEPENDENCE, MISSOURI

From Charles A. Dana's "The United States Illustrated" (1855)

CHAPTER II

EIGHTEEN hundred and thirty-four was an important year in the annals of the Trail. It marked the building of the trading posts, Fort William (the predecessor of Fort Laramie), in the present Wyoming, and of Forts Hall and Boisé in what is now Idaho. It further marked the triumph of Astor's American Fur Company in the mountains, for though the great magnate retired in that year, what had been his organization achieved a monopoly of the field. At the rendezvous, in June, the Rocky Mountain Fur Company was dissolved; and though three of the partners, Fitzpatrick, Bridger and Milton G. Sublette, immediately formed a new organization, they came to an agreement with their powerful rival which made them its agents, and in the following year (1835) they became its employees. The year is further to be remembered as that in which the first missionaries, Jason and Daniel Lee, ventured to cross the continent and set up an establishment in Oregon.

This Oregon, so remote and for years regarded as so mysterious a land, had come to be better known in the East, and there had arisen a lively and much debated " Oregon question." It was on May 11,[6] 1792, that

Captain Robert Gray, of Boston, sailed across the bar
at the mouth of the long-sought River of the West. In
honor of his ship he named the stream " Columbia's
River." But for a decade or more men had spoken of
it as the Oregan or Oregon, and though the name Columbia was accepted by Vancouver, it made its way
slowly in the United States. To Jefferson, when in
1793, as Washington's Secretary of State, he gave instructions to André Michaux, it was the Oregon. He
had not then heard of Gray's discovery; but it was still
the Oregon (though with the alternative Columbia),
ten years later, when, as President, he gave instructions
to Meriwether Lewis. By another seven years, however,
the new name had generally supplanted the old. In the
articles of agreement between Astor and his partners of
the Astoria enterprise in 1810 the word Columbia is
used exclusively for the river; and as it became fixed for
the stream the word Oregon came to designate an unde-
fined region lying west of the Rocky Mountains and
north of California.

The derivation of the name still remains something
of a mystery. Much ingenuity and research have been
expended on the subject, and a half-dozen or more fanciful theories have been advanced. So far as known, the
word first appeared as Ouragon in a proposal drawn up
by Major Robert Rogers in August 1765, soliciting
royal patronage for an expedition to discover the northwest passage. It first appeared in print, both as Ouragon and as Ourigan, in Rogers' tragedy of *Ponteach, or
the Savages of America,* published in London in 1766.
It was again used, this time as Ourigan, in a second proposal by Rogers in February 1772. Rogers got the

word from the Indians.   Mr. T. C. Elliott, who has
made the latest and most thorough study of the subject,
suggests that it came from the Mohawks or some other
Iroquois who as trappers, hunters, or *voyageurs* had
been west of the upper Mississippi.   In 1778 it appeared
both as Oregon and Origan in Jonathan Carver's
Travels Through the Interior Parts of North America,
published in London.   Carver had made his journey
under the orders of Rogers and may have heard the word
before starting out.   What the Indians probably meant
by it was some unidentified river east of the Rockies;
what Carver meant by it was " the River of the West,
that falls into the Pacific Ocean at the Straits of Anian."
In early days, as it came to be spoken in the East, it
may have been usually stressed on the second syllable,
for Bryant so used it in the first printed version of
" Thanatopsis," though the modern accent was indicated in later versions.[7]

Spain, Great Britain, Russia, and France had set up
more or less exclusive claims to the region.   Gray's discovery, joined with his voyage, four years earlier, fifty
miles up the strait of Juan de Fuca, added another
contender.   The French claims, whatever they were,
passed to the United States with the Louisiana purchase
of 1803, and further ones were set up by the Lewis and
Clark expedition of 1804–06 and the establishment of
Astoria in 1811.   Then came the War of 1812, the
forced sale of Astoria to the British North West Company and the taking of formal possession of the whole
region by a British gunboat.   The peace of 1814 restored to the combatants the territory (except certain
islands in the Atlantic) which each had taken from the

other, and after three years of diplomatic fencing Great
Britain yielded possession of Astoria, which in the meantime had been rechristened Fort George. Astor would
have reoccupied his trading post had the Government
given him a small command of soldiers for its defense;
but though the matter was put before President Madison (probably in March 1816) by Albert Gallatin, nothing was done.

   In the same year (1818) that Astoria was restored to
the United States, a conference between representatives
of the two nations was held in London to settle the outstanding questions of the peace of 1814. Agreement was
easily reached that the western boundary between
Canada and the United States should run from the
northwest corner of the Lake of the Woods to the 49th
parallel and thence to the summit of the Rocky Mountains. But as to the continuance of the line through territory claimed by the two powers and by Spain and
Russia, the views of the two sets of commissioners were
far apart. The Americans proposed the 49th parallel,
and the Britons peremptorily rejected it. They had no
objection to the parallel as far as the Columbia River,
but beyond that they thought the river itself the proper
line, and they declined all proposals that did not give
them at least joint possession of the river's mouth. Since
no settlement was then possible, the commissioners did
the next best thing: they left the matter for others to
settle at some future time, and agreed that for a period
of ten years all territory claimed by either nation should
be open to the subjects of both. In the following
year (1819) Spain, by the treaty which ceded Florida,
relinquished to the United States all claims on the
Pacific coast north of the 42d parallel, the northern

boundary of the present California, Nevada, and a part of Utah.

The claimants were now reduced to three. For several years following the collapse of the Astoria venture, the American people paid little attention to the subject of Oregon. On December 19, 1820, the House of Representatives appointed a committee, headed by John Floyd of Virginia, to inquire into the situation of settlements in the Pacific Northwest and into the expediency of occupying the Columbia River. In January of the following year the committee made a report that dealt with the fur trade and the rich gleanings of the Hudson's Bay and the North West Companies and recommended the establishment of a military post at the mouth of the Columbia. But the proposal was regarded as trivial and fantastic, and the report was laid on the table.

Russia had made sweeping claims to the Northwest Coast, and the Russian American Fur Company had established a trading post at Bodega Bay, in the present Sonoma County, California. In 1821 Alexander I issued a ukase declaring exclusively Russian all the coast north of the 51st parallel and forbidding foreigners to enter it. Though a modification of earlier claims, it was formally protested by both Great Britain and America. Secretary John Quincy Adams denied the validity of all Russian claims south of latitude 55. In 1823 the three powers began joint negotiations. America proposed that Russia should make no settlements south of latitude 55, and Great Britain none below latitude 51, promising at the same time not to intrude above the latter parallel. But the Presidential message of December 1823, containing the afterward famous Monroe doctrine, brought up new issues, and no agreement was reached.

Nevertheless, in the following April (1824), Russia and the United States came to terms in a treaty by which, though granting for ten years access of ships of either country to interior waters, the former bound itself to prohibit its citizens from settling south of the line 54° 40', and the latter to prohibit its citizens from settling above the line. Russia thus surrendered her claims in so far as the United States was concerned, and in the following year made a like surrender to Great Britain.

Only two contenders were now left. The earlier American pronouncements regarding Oregon reveal less of desire for possession than of a determination to resist European colonization. Many Americans wished to see the Northwest an independent republic. Jefferson wrote to Astor in 1813 that he viewed Astoria " as the germ of a great, free, independent empire," and that " liberty and self-government spreading from that, as well as this side, will insure their complete establishment over the whole." But a number of factors, including the discussion of the Floyd report, gradually brought about a change of view. Adams, who in 1818 had considered the Oregon question too trivial for serious diplomatic discussion, in 1824 declared it of increasing importance and the territory as " a country daily assuming an aspect political, commercial and territorial of growing interest to the United States." In this year negotiations with Great Britain were reopened, but failed. President Monroe, in his last message to Congress, recommended the establishment of a military post at the mouth of the Columbia or at some place within the acknowledged limits of the United States, and in 1825 President Adams repeated the recommendation, but a bill embodying the proposal was tabled in the House of Representatives.

In the summer of that year General Ashley returned from the Wyoming country with his first opulent cargo of furs and also with new testimony as to the hold which the Hudson's Bay Company (now united with the North West Company) was maintaining over the whole Oregon country. More persons than ever before were thus led to think of Oregon and of the nation's material interest in its products. As the ten-year period of joint occupancy approached its end, fresh negotiations were made, this time Great Britain taking the initiative. The Americans again offered the 49th parallel, and again the Britons refused it. During these negotiations the whole question of Oregon was thoroughly discussed, but for about a year with no apparent headway toward a settlement. On August 6, 1827, a compromise was reached by which joint occupation was indefinitely extended, with the proviso that at any time after October 20, 1828, either party could, on giving a year's notice to the other, annul the convention.

In the meantime there had arisen a popular movement for the assertion of American rights to the region. Hall Jackson Kelley, a Boston schoolmaster, had become interested in Oregon as early as 1815. In 1824 he started an active campaign for its colonization and the Christianizing of its Indians. In December 1828, a bill was introduced in the House of Representatives providing for the organization of a territory over the entire country up to 54° 40', for the establishment and garrisoning of a military post and for granting lands to settlers. The bill, after a hot debate, was defeated; for the majority held that the country was of little importance, that it was too remote ever to become a State of the Union and that to organize it into a territory would contravene the agreement of joint occupancy.

Kelley, however, continued his work. In 1829 he published his *Geographical Sketches of Oregon,* made up from the journals of Lewis and Clark, from public documents and from personal interviews with men who had visited the region. In the same year he formed the American Society for Encouraging the Settlement of the Oregon Territory, and through its influence a new society was organized in New Orleans and another in Ohio. In 1831 he issued a general circular explaining the characteristics of the country and giving directions for reaching it. He planned an expedition to leave the East on the first of January 1832, but the date was later postponed for two months, and the plan changed to allow for two expeditions. The number of volunteers was small, and the plan was again changed to allow for the joining of the two.

It was here that Wyeth, whose first expedition was mentioned in the previous chapter, entered the scene. He had shown an interest in Kelley's plan, but when the start was again postponed, this time till June, he withdrew and began the organization of a joint stock company of fifty persons to leave St. Louis by May 1. Those who could be got together assembled on an island in Boston Harbor on March 1, where for ten days they " played at being frontiersmen." On the 10th they sailed for Baltimore. Thence they journeyed by rail to the Alleghenies, across the mountains on foot and by steamboat from Pittsburgh to Independence. There were twenty-seven of them when, with Sublette's trapping party, they set out from Independence for Oregon. Quarrels and defections on the way reduced the number to eleven. Wyeth, with ten of them, made the whole journey, and with only one of them returned in the following year. By the spring of 1834 he was back in Independence, with a new party, to repeat the journey.

The Wyeth plan is to be regarded as a business venture rather than as a colonization scheme. It was the missionaries who planted the first American colonies in Oregon. As early as 1820 the Presbyterian body styled the American Board of Commissioners for Foreign Missions had begun to receive reports concerning the Northwest Coast, and in 1829 the Prudential Committee sent the Rev. Jonathan S. Green, then in Hawaii, to inspect the region. Green visited several ports far up the coast, and though he made no landing in the Oregon country, recommended the planting of a mission somewhere near the Columbia. His report, however, brought no action.

The movement of the missionaries was a direct response to an Indian appeal for teachers. About the middle of September 1831, a delegation of four Indians from the remote Northwest pitched their large tepee on the banks of the Mississippi near the northerly limits of St. Louis. The Flatheads and the Nez Percés had heard, probably from men of the Hudson's Bay Company, that their own mode of worship was wrong, and that they could learn the right mode from the whites. The elders remembered General Clark, who had passed through their villages in the fall of 1805 and again in the spring of 1806, and they resolved to send messengers to him for information. According to Marcus Whitman, who is likeliest to have been accurate about this controverted and perplexing episode, the original delegation consisted of a chief and two principal men from each of the tribes and a young volunteer from the Nez Percés. The seven joined an eastbound fur expedition and reached old Council Bluffs, where two of the Flatheads and one of the Nez Percés turned back. The two chiefs, with one of the Flatheads and the young Nez Percé, came on to St. Louis.

All accounts agree that they visited Clark, and one account says that they appealed to him for a Bible and for teachers. A contemporary Catholic account says that they " came to see our church and appeared to be exceedingly well pleased with it," but that "unfortunately there was no one who understood their language." One of them died on October 31 and another on November 17, Catholic priests officiating at both funerals. In the spring the remaining two took passage on the *Yellowstone* for the first steamboat voyage ever made to the upper Missouri. George Catlin, the famous Indian painter, who was a passenger, became much interested in them and painted their portraits, which are now in the National Museum in Washington.[8] He gives their names as The Rabbit's Skin Leggins and No Horns on His Head. One of them, doubtless the latter, died near the mouth of the Yellowstone, and the former, the young Nez Percé, was the only one to return to his home.

William Walker, an educated Wyandot, came to St. Louis early in November, in connection with the project

PETER H. BURNETT (1807–1895) IN 1849
From Zoeth Skinner Eldredge's "History of California" (1915)

REV. JASON LEE (1803–1845)
Pioneer missionary to Oregon

of removing his tribesmen from the neighborhood of Sandusky, Ohio, to the present Kansas, and learned the story.   Fourteen months later, on January 19, 1833, he wrote an account of it, which was published on March 1 in the *Christian Advocate and Journal and Zion's Herald,* the leading publication of the Methodist Episcopal Church.   It was a highly dramatic and moving account, and though later censured for certain exaggerations and inaccuracies, it resulted in immediate action.[9]

The Methodist Missionary Society decided to establish a mission in the Flathead country, and on July 17 chose the Rev. Jason Lee as its head.   This pioneer missionary of the Far West, the son of a Revolutionary soldier, was born in 1803 at Stanstead, Quebec, then supposed to be within the boundaries of Vermont.   In his twenty-third year, to prepare for the ministry, he entered Wilbraham Academy, where he soon attracted the friendly interest of its president, the Rev. Wilbur Fisk.   After graduating, he served for a time during 1832–33 as a minister to the Wesleyan Methodists in Stanstead and vicinity.   A forceful and dominating personality he was to become, and a zealous promoter of the colonization of Oregon; but in the end he was to be dismissed from his post as one who had violated the spirit of the mission and sacrificed religion to material ends.   About his character there has been and will always be stiff dispute; for he has been portrayed both as a maligned saint and as an ambitious and a somewhat unscrupulous worldling.

Consulting with Wyeth, then in Boston preparing for his second expedition, Lee received permission to

ship his goods in a vessel which Wyeth was dispatching
for the Columbia. With his nephew, David Lee, and
two lay assistants, Cyrus Shepherd and P. L. Edwards,
he joined Wyeth's and Milton Sublette's companies,
which left Independence on April 28, 1834. At Laramie's fork of the Platte, which was reached June 1, they
saw the beginnings of Fort William, built by Robert
Campbell, of the firm of Sublette and Campbell, and
on the 19th they reached Green River. The rendezvous
that year was on the Green, about twelve miles above
the mouth of the Big Sandy. Here Wyeth endeavored
to deliver to Fitzpatrick a stock of goods contracted for
in the previous summer. But the Rocky Mountain Fur
Company was passing out; William L. Sublette, who
had arrived from St. Louis two days earlier, had sold
Fitzpatrick a stock of supplies, and Wyeth's goods
were refused. Wyeth, in resentment, passed on with
the missionaries westward, determined to establish a
trading post which would be a rival to the Fitzpatrick
interests. He followed the well-traveled path by Ham's
Fork to the Bear and the head of the Portneuf; and
on the Snake River, on July 14, he began the building of Fort Hall, named for the oldest member of his
company, Henry Hall, of Boston. Here Jason Lee
preached the first sermon ever delivered by a Protestant west of the Rocky Mountains. Leaving a
garrison, Wyeth went on with the missionaries
to Oregon, arriving at Fort Vancouver on September 16.

Whatever may have been the claims and the purposes
of the United States Government at the time, this territory was, in a sense, an alien land, and the missionaries
who entered it were intruders. The rulers of the coun-

try were the chiefs of the Hudson's Bay Company, backed by the British Government. With the War of 1812 and the capture of Astoria the North West Company had been left in sole possession; after that War, though Astoria was given back to the United States, President Madison neglected to support Astor in reoccupying his property; and with the union of the two British fur companies a more vigorous policy had been adopted for the control and exploitation of the region. Fort Nez Percés was expanded into Fort Walla Walla, and in 1824 a new post, Fort Vancouver, was erected on the Columbia, north of the mouth of the Willamette. Here for many years was the capital of the Pacific Northwest.

The vicegerent of the region was Dr. John McLoughlin, chief factor of the post. Trappers, missionaries, and emigrants found him, while unflinchingly loyal to the company's policy and interests, most generous and helpful to them in their need. Some of them he employed at good wages; to others he provided boats for their passage, or loaned money or equipment or gave seeds for planting. But he steadfastly discouraged American settlement north of the Columbia, and such was the weight of his influence that until 1844 no one attempted to disregard it. He had a position of infinite difficulty to maintain, and right nobly he maintained it. Yet he was to experience the ingratitude of Americans whom he had befriended and the suspicion of the company that employed him, and after more than twenty years of service was to be dismissed from his place. " The finest man I ever knew " — greater even than Whitman — was the testimony of the former trapper, F. X. Matthieu, who as a young man went to Oregon with Dr. White's party in 1842 and in his serene eighties gave his reminiscences for publication.[10]

For various reasons the missionaries decided to abandon the Flathead project, and on October 6 they settled on the Willamette, ten miles north of the present Salem. A cabin was put up, to which additions were later made and which became a home, mission, school, orphanage, and hospital. Ground was tilled, a small herd of cattle was brought in, later to be augmented by a large drove from California, and in a short time the little colony was securely established.

The Presbyterians were only a little less prompt than the Methodists in responding to the Indian call. The Rev. Samuel Parker, then in Middlefield, Mass., offered himself to the American Board in 1833. The offer was accepted in the following year, but he arrived in St. Louis too late to join the trapping expedition. He thereupon returned east, lecturing on Oregon and endeavoring to obtain assistants. In New York State he found five volunteers. Either at Rushville or at Wheeler he met Marcus Whitman, who had wished to be a minister but instead had become a physician, and who five months earlier had offered himself to the American Board. He also met Narcissa, the daughter of Judge Stephen Prentiss, of Angelica, who also wanted to go. Whitman was accepted by the Board and assigned as Parker's assistant. He reached St. Louis about April 1, 1835, and later, with Parker, joined the American Fur Company expedition, under Lucien Fontenelle. The route was by boat to old Council Bluffs (really Bellevue, for everything on the Nebraska side from the mouth of the Platte to beyond the present town of Fort

METHODIST MISSION AT THE DALLES
Drawn by Major Osborne Cross (1849)

Calhoun, in Washington County, was at the time known as Council Bluffs); then to the bend of the Platte and along its north bank to Fort William, where they crossed the Platte and struck the main Trail. Thence they journeyed on to the rendezvous near Bonneville's fort, in the Green Valley. Some two hundred whites and two thousand Indians were present, and there was sound of revelry both by day and night. Parker probably saw the famous gunfight between young Kit Carson and Bully Shunar, for in his *Journal of an Exploring Tour Beyond the Rocky Mountains* (1838) he gave an account of it and was thus the means of first introducing Carson to fame:

I will relate an occurrence which took place, near evening, as a specimen of frontier life. A hunter, who goes technically by the name of the great bully of the mountains, mounted his horse with a loaded rifle, and challenged any Frenchman, American, Spaniard, or Dutchman, to fight him in single combat. Kit Carson, an American, told him if he wished to die, he [Carson] would accept the challenge. Shunar defied him. C. mounted his horse, and with a loaded pistol, rushed into close contact, and both almost at the same instant fired. C's. ball entered S's. hand, came out at the wrist, and passed through the arm above the elbow. Shunar's ball passed over the head of Carson; and while he went for another pistol, Shunar begged that his life might be spared.

As the story breaks off abruptly, several modern writers have striven to repair the fault by retelling it in their own way. Unfortunately, there are too many discrepancies in the details. It may be that Shunar was killed outright, as some will have it, or that he died from his wound; and it may also be that a beautiful Arapaho maiden, the future wife of Carson, furnished the real *casus belli* between the combatants.   One writer has recently put forth, with highly decorative embellishments, what purports to be an account from Arapaho tradition — an account that would appear to have persisted in all its original purity among the tribesmen for ninety years.   But as the observant missionary who was on the ground at the time evidently knew nothing about any of these revelations, it will be well to view them with at least a moderate degree of caution.

Whitman performed a number of surgical operations, one of which was the cutting from Bridger's shoulder of a three-inch arrow-head which a bellicose Blackfoot had lodged there in a fight in the Three Forks region in October 1832.   It is good to know, from Parker's words, that "the Doctor pursued the operation with great self-possession and perseverance; and his patient manifested equal firmness."

Whitman and Parker, after conferences with the Flatheads and the Nez Percés at the rendezvous, agreed that the minister should proceed and look over the ground, while the physician should return and bring out a corps of helpers.   Parker went on to Pierre's Hole (now known as the Teton Basin) and by a northerly route reached Oregon, but after a year's sojourn sailed from the Columbia for the Sandwich Islands, whence he returned home.   Whitman, taking with him two Indian boys, reached his old home probably in November and spent the winter in preparing for his next journey. In February 1836, after a brief courtship, he married Narcissa Prentiss, and in March he obtained the consent of the Rev. Henry Harmon Spalding and his wife, then under appointment to the Osage Mission, and also of a

TROOPS GUARDING THE OVERLAND MAIL

From a photograph of an old drawing loaned by Professor LeRoy R. Hafen. Published in Root and Connelley's "The Overland Stage" and later, by permission, in Hafen's "The Overland Mail"

AN OVERLOADED CONCORD COACH

From an old Photograph

lay brother, William H. Gray, of Utica, to accompany him.

The Whitmans and the two Indian boys started in March, took the steamboat at Pittsburgh, were joined by the Spaldings at Cincinnati, and soon afterward arrived at St. Louis. Here they received permission to accompany the expedition of the American Fur Company, under Fitzpatrick, which was to ascend the river by steamboat to Bellevue. They went to Liberty, where Gray joined them. It was probably also here that they picked up the adventurous sixteen-year-old boy, Miles Goodyear, later to become a famous mountain man and the first white to plant crops in the Salt Lake Valley. By this time they had assembled two wagons, fourteen horses, six mules, and seventeen cattle.

Possibly by inadvertence, more probably by design, the boat did not stop for them. The determination of two women to cross the Rocky Mountains was an unheard-of thing. Catlin, making the unsubstantiated assertion that once before a woman had attempted the journey, with the result that her party was massacred and she was taken into captivity, never to be heard of again, had further declared that the missionaries' wives would certainly be captured. The hard-headed but kind-hearted Fitzpatrick doubtless considered the venture an act of extreme foolhardiness. Lee, at the end of his journey two years earlier, had written that the hardships and dangers were too great to warrant the risk and had sent for his women helpers to come by the Horn. Spalding, who at Fort Laramie joined with Sublette and Fitzpatrick in a plea to his wife that she return, afterward wrote to the Home Board: " Never send another woman over these mountains, if you have any regard for human life." At Cincinnati and at St. Louis the suggestion had been made that the civil authorities should prevent the women from going. But neither then, nor at any later time, amid many dangers and hardships, did either the radiant and well-poised Narcissa Whitman nor the frail, ill, and neurotic Eliza Spalding show the slightest hesitation. They had determined to reach their goal, come what may, and no dissuading plea nor argument could move them.[11]

When the party learned that it had been forsaken it hurried with its goods and cattle to the ferry opposite Fort Leavenworth, crossed the river and began a night-and-day chase to intercept the expedition on the Platte. It reached that river at the Oto Agency, near the present Greenwood, Nebraska, swam its cattle and floated its wagons across, only to learn that the expedition was several days ahead. The chase was continued, and the expedition was overtaken at the mouth of the Loup, the farthest point to which so small a party could safely travel. Once inside the safe fold of the fur expedition, the Whitman party received every courtesy and help. But whether or not any apologies were made by Fitzpatrick the record does not say.

Bonneville in 1832 had taken wagons across the Green. Whitman determined to take wagons to the Columbia. The fur expedition had seven, as well as a cart, and Whitman had two, one of which had been brought by Spalding, who helped construct it, from Holland Patent, New York. At Fort William (which had passed to the American Fur Company, to be renamed Fort John), the expedition abandoned its

STATUE OF MARCUS WHITMAN (1802–1847)

On a façade of the Witherspoon Building, Philadelphia

wagons, and Whitman was reluctantly persuaded to abandon one of his own. With the other, as well as with the company's cart, of which Fitzpatrick had put him in charge, he went forward.

At the rendezvous, on Green River, the missionaries joined the Hudson's Bay party of Thomas McKay and John McLeod. They followed the main course, then by Ham's Fork, of the Oregon Trail. Against baffling discouragements Whitman persisted in taking the wagon, which was frequently stalled until a way could be cleared for it, and perhaps as often upset. Most of the company wanted to abandon it. Even Mrs. Whitman joined the adverse chorus. Writing on July 18, at the junction of Smith's Fork and the Bear, on the present Idaho-Wyoming boundary, she says:

Husband has had a tedious time with the wagon to-day. It got stuck in the creek this morning when crossing, and he was obliged to wade considerably in getting it out. After that, in going between the mountains, on the side of one, so steep that it was difficult for horses to pass, the wagon was upset twice; did not wonder at this at all; it was a greater wonder that it was not turning somersaults continually. It is not very grateful to my feelings to see him wearing out with such excessive fatigue, as I am obliged to. He is not as fleshy as he was last winter. All the most difficult part of the way he has walked, in laborious attempts to take the wagon. Ma knows what my feelings are.

And again on the 28th, two or three days before reaching Fort Hall:

One of the axle-trees of the wagon broke to-day; was a little rejoiced; for we were in hopes they would leave it, and have no more trouble with it. Our rejoicing was in vain, for they are making a cart of the back wheels this afternoon, and lashing the fore wheels to it — intending to take it through in some shape or other.

They reached Fort Hall, still owned by Wyeth and in charge of his agent, Captain Thing, though in the following year (1837) it was to be bought by the Hudson's Bay Company. Here young Goodyear declared that either he or the cart would quit. Whitman decided for the cart, and Goodyear remained behind. Still escorted by McKay's and McLeod's party, the missionaries went on along the Trail, with frequent disasters to the cart, until they reached the Hudson's Bay post of Fort Boisé. Told that he could not possibly take the cart farther, Whitman at last yielded and left it behind. The remaining journey was made to Fort Walla Walla and then by boat and portage down the Columbia to Fort Vancouver, where the missionaries arrived September 12. Whitman soon returned to the Walla Walla region, establishing his mission among the Cayuses at Waiilatpu, "the place of rye grass," twenty-five miles up the river, where he was joined by Mrs. Whitman in December. The Spaldings settled among the Nez Percés at Lapwai, in the present Idaho.

So Whitman failed to bring either a wagon or a cart to the Columbia. In later years, if not from the first, his main thought was the Americanization of Oregon; he wished to see the country peopled from the States, and he knew that unless wagons could be drawn along the Trail there would be little settlement. He was to wait seven years to see them pass his door. Three years before that event, however, he was to welcome the arrival of three half-wagons, if one may so call them — the first

wheels to reach the Columbia.   After 1836 no vehicle
was taken as far as Fort Hall until 1840, when a wagon
was brought in by Joel P. Walker, brother of the noted
Joseph Reddeford Walker, and two wagons were
brought in by the missionary party of the Rev. Harvey
Clark and Messrs. Alvin T. Smith and P. B. Little-
john. Warned that they could go no farther on wheels,
these pioneers disposed of their wagons and proceeded
by pack-train.

The men who acquired the wagons had other opinions about the possibilities of the Trail. These men were
the trappers, Caleb Wilkins, Robert ("Doc") Newell,
later Speaker of the Oregon Assembly; Joseph L.
Meek, later special envoy of the Oregon Provisional
Government to Washington and first United States
Marshal of Oregon Territory, and a Hudson's Bay
Company factor, Frank Ermatinger. The fur trade
was vanishing; the trappers, one after one, were leaving
the mountains, and Newell and Meek decided to settle,
with their Indian families, on the Willamette. Meek
tells the story, and with his usual indulgence in fiction,
asserts that the wagons had been Whitman's. Elwood
Evans tells it in a much more likely version.[12] The
wagons could not have been Whitman's, for one of these
was back at Fort William, six hundred miles away, and
the other, reduced to a cart, two hundred miles ahead.
Newell and Meek hitched up and with their families
started for the Columbia; and with them went Wilkins,
Ermatinger and several other men about the fort. But
they found the roads so rough, the hills so steep and in
the comparatively level places such a forest of sage
brush, " higher than the mules' backs," that they finally

threw away the wagon beds and went on only with the
running gear. Whitman met them at his station and
applauded their act. When Newell expressed doubts
as to the merit of the performance, Whitman replied:

Oh, you will never regret it. You have broken the ice, and
when others see that wagons have passed, they, too, will pass,
and in a few years the valley will be full of our people.

They took their three *chasses* on to Fort Walla Walla
and there left them till the following year. Nothing
else on wheels appeared until the arrival of the Great
Emigration of 1843, when Whitman himself, returning
from a heroic mid-winter ride across the mountains to the
East, led the way.

By land and by sea more missionaries — women as
well as men — arrived in Oregon, and for a few years
the work was vigorously carried on. The Methodists
established new missions in the Clatsop country, near
the mouth of the Columbia; at the Dalles, at Oregon
City and at Nisqually, on Puget Sound. The Presbyterians established a mission among the Spokanes, in
eastern Washington, and a second one among the Nez
Percés, at Kamiah, sixty miles east of Lapwai. The
Catholics also established several missions, and they were
far more successful in engaging the interest of the na-
tives than either of the Protestant sects.

The Methodist missions had, however, by 1840 about
run their course. The Indians had proved intractable,
and the missionaries and their lay helpers had become
more interested in business ventures and in politics than
in the seemingly futile task of converting the heathen.
In 1844 Jason Lee was recalled. The Rev. George

WHITMAN'S MISSION AT WAIILATPU IN 1843

From Myron Eells' "Marcus Whitman, Pathfinder and Patriot" (1909)

Gary, who was sent out to succeed him, in the following year closed all the missions except the one at the Dalles, which in 1847 he turned over to the Presbyterians, thus ending the local missionary labors of his church. Whitman and his colleagues continued their work, through alternate seasons of encouragement and despair, till the massacre of November 29, 1847, a tragedy that closed eastern Oregon to the whites for a period of twelve years.

Though the missionaries failed in their appointed task, they planted the first American settlements in the Pacific Northwest. By the end of 1840 the Oregon country had an American population of at least one hundred men, women, and children, of whom probably about thirty belonged to the missions. Of the adults among them probably few had made the long journey to establish a permanent residence. Some of them were servants of the church, ready at its call to go wherever they were bidden. Others were men who had drifted in to look at the country, and finding what they sought had remained. A new ferment in the East was now to bring to the region another element of population — the seekers of permanent homes — and to start a wave of migration that in a few years would people all its fertile valleys.

CHAPTER III

THE FIRST CARAVANS

THE region adjoining the Mississippi River had been rapidly filling up. Illinois, from a mere 12,000 of population in 1810, had by 1840 reached the figure of 476,-189. The western sections of Kentucky and Tennessee had received large additions, bringing the total population of the former state to about three-quarters of a million and of the latter to more than 800,000. Even the wilderness of Wisconsin was being opened; within the present boundaries of the state probably 11,000 persons were settled by 1836, and four years later the number had grown to 30,000.

The Mississippi proved no bar to the onward movement. Missouri, its center, grew from slightly less than 20,000 population in 1810 to 140,000 in 1830 and to 383,000 in 1840; while Arkansas, which in 1810 could number only 1,062 inhabitants, now numbered 97,754. Iowa, the last of the three states to yield a foothold to the settler, was virtually closed until 1835. By the end of the following year more than 10,000 persons had found homes therein, and by 1840 more than 43,000. The wedge of settlement moved on along the line of the lower Missouri; towns sprang up as though at the wave of a magician's wand, and as the head was driven farther westward, the sides broadened out into the valleys.

But at the bend of the Missouri the tide of settlement stopped short. From the founding of Independence to the first settlements a few miles away in Kansas was a matter of twenty-seven years. Immediately beyond were the Indian reservations, a part of the great Indian Country set apart for all time by the Government as a home for its savage wards. From the Red River of the South along an approximately straight line to the mouth of the Kansas ran the boundary, upward along the Missouri River to the present southern boundary of Iowa, eastward almost to the Mississippi, and then by a series of loops and curves to the Green Bay of Wisconsin. An earlier line had run straight north from the Kansas' mouth, but by the Platte Purchase of 1836 the Government had taken over the triangular space between that line and the Missouri River and had given the Iowas and a part of the Sauks and the Foxes new lands across the river.

This Indian Country, theoretically closed to the white man, had been increasingly traveled by trappers, traders, and missionaries, but few of them had ever thought of it as available for the white man's use. Some of them even made little distinction between the nearby prairie — marvelously fertile, wooded along the streams and in spring and summer beautiful with flowers and herbage — and the remoter plains, unwooded, more arid, with a less fertile soil, and yet capable of supporting enormous herds of livestock. To most persons this vast and diverse region constituted the " Great American Desert." Lieutenant Zebulon Pike, after his journey of 1806–07, had written of it as a barrier " placed by Providence to keep the American people from a thin diffusion and ruin," and Major Stephen H. Long, after his exploration of 1820, reported it unfit for agriculture. Many others accepted the judgment as final. A traditional view had somehow become established, and though travelers saw the rich luxuriance of the prairie and the millions of buffalo finding sustenance in the grass of the plains, they did not care to stake their opinion against an accepted view. Among the people there was no clamor for the opening of these nearby lands.

The growing interest in Oregon was greatly stimulated by the panic of 1837. Its effects were more severe, and they lasted longer, in the Middle West than in the East. This Middle West, confident of a rapid growth, had indulged in a multitude of extravagant schemes of banking, town building, and railway construction. The depression brought a stoppage of industry, a shortage of money, and a bewildering drop in the prices of farm products. The migratory impulse of the settlers, checked for a time by the boundary of the Indian Country, was again awakened. To move on, in the hope of finding better times farther toward the setting sun, had been the popular answer to the recurring business depressions and to the individual frustrations of effort; and this new and continuing depression caused men who were yearning for new horizons to turn their gaze toward the remote Pacific.

California, and not Oregon, was the intended goal of the first emigrant train to set out from the Missouri River for the Pacific; and not until the vicinity of Fort Hall was reached did half the company decide for homes in the Northwest. The promoter of this pioneer movement was an upstate New Yorker, John Bidwell, later one of the most useful and distinguished citizens of California and a figure of national prominence. In 1839, at the age of twenty, he had drifted from Ohio into the newly opened Platte Purchase. In the neighborhood of Weston he taught school, and here also, enchanted with the country, he took up land. But in the summer of 1840 a gunman jumped his claim and held it by force of arms. Bidwell accordingly decided to move on. About this time he met " a Frenchman named Roubideaux," who told him such wonderful tales of California that he determined to go there. He thereupon called a meeting of neighbors and had the Frenchman repeat his statements. As a result, the Western Emigration Society was formed, and the names of about five hundred interested persons were soon enrolled. All pledged themselves to meet at Sapling Grove, near Independence, on the 9th of May, 1841, armed and equipped for the journey.

It would be well to know which one of the four famous brothers thus set in motion so epochal a migration, but the matter seems unsolvable. *Robidou* they spelled the name (though their descendants have tacked to it a terminal *x*), and they were known throughout the frontier. This one may have been Joseph, who then had a trading post in the Blacksnake Hills, where, in July, 1843, he founded the city of St. Joseph; or it may have been Louis, a few years later to become justice of the peace of the infant colony of San Bernardino; but we do not know that either of them had at that time seen California. Most likely it was Antoine, that indefatigable and adventurous trapper and trader who from Taos had penetrated to western Colorado and southern Utah as early as 1824 and who at this time may have been on a visit east.

Though the movement started with so vigorous an impulse, it came near to an early collapse. In February or March 1841, according to Bidwell, a letter on the Pacific country, copied from a New York newspaper, appeared in a newspaper of Liberty, Missouri. It was by Thomas J. Farnham, who with a small company known as the " Peoria party " had crossed the mountains in 1839 and who had returned in 1840, and it gave a depressing picture of the Coast. Bidwell's neighbors, one after one, backed out, and the young enthusiast, with a wagon but nothing to pull it, was left to carry on alone. But just at the moment of his greatest discouragement an invalid from Illinois, George Henshaw, rode up on a fine black horse and declared himself ready for the journey. Bidwell persuaded him to allow his horse to be traded for " a yoke of steers to pull the wagon and a sorry-looking, one-eyed mule for him to ride." They went to Weston to lay in supplies and were there joined by two persons who had again changed their minds and who fortunately were possessed of another wagon. The little party then moved south, crossed the river presumably at Independence and reached Sapling Grove, to find but one wagon ahead of them.

During the next five days other prospective emigrants came in until they had a company of sixty-nine men, women, and children. They organized temporarily and chose for captain John Bartleson, who lived in the neighborhood. A worse choice could hardly have been made, but as Bartleson had with him seven or eight husky men

JOHN BIDWELL (1819–1900) IN 1850

*From C. C. Royce's "John Bidwell, Pioneer
Statesman, Philanthropist" (1906)*

who would be useful, and as he had given an ultimatum that he would go as captain or not at all, there was nothing to do but elect him. It was an impecunious party: Bidwell doubted that there was so much as a hundred dollars among them. None of them knew where to go. Of the western country they were appallingly ignorant. They were certain that somewhere in California was the ranch of a "Doctor" John Marsh, a graduate of Harvard College, who four or five years earlier had journeyed there from Independence by way of Santa Fé, and who had written home advising others to follow, and they purposed to find that ranch. Bidwell had provided himself with maps, but they turned out to be worse than useless. They showed, for instance, Great Salt Lake — that Dead Sea of the Great Basin — as a narrow body of water three or four hundred miles long, with two large rivers flowing from it and with pomp of waters unwithstood making their way through the towering Sierras into the Pacific.

From a late recruit they learned that a party of Catholic missionaries, piloted by a mountain man, was on its way from St. Louis to the Flathead country and would reach their encampment in a few days. They waited, and in a short time it arrived. It was composed of Fathers P. J. de Smet, Nicolas Point and Gregory Mengarini, with five teamsters, two trappers and a pleasure traveler, piloted by Thomas Fitzpatrick. One of the trappers, then making his second journey to the mountains, was the afterward famous " Jim " Baker.

The combined company, the emigrant section of which was later to be known as the Bidwell-Bartleson party, started about May 12. There was another party that was to have united with this one; but arriving too late, it set out for Santa Fé, where it was joined by other emigrants under William Workman and John Rowland, all of whom finally reached California by the old Spanish Trail. All of the Bidwell-Bartleson party traveled by the Oregon Trail as far as Soda Springs, south of Fort Hall, and half of it traveled the Trail to the mouth of the Walla Walla.

On the 18th, at the Kansas crossing, the party effected a permanent organization, re-electing Bartleson as captain and accepting Fitzpatrick as guide. In this action it set a precedent, since ever afterward the Kansas crossing was the place for the making of new rules and the tightening up or re-forming of the companies that followed the Trail. In the four or five days from the starting place there had usually accumulated enough discord to compel a reshuffling of the cards and a new deal.

On the 19th, with Fitzpatrick in the lead, followed by the mounted missionaries, with their four mule-drawn carts and one small wagon, and the emigrants, with their eight wagons drawn by mules and horses, and their five wagons drawn by oxen, the party set forth. On the 23d it was overtaken by Joseph B. Chiles, with a wagon and five men, and on the 26th by an eccentric Methodist preacher, Joseph Williams, who so far had traveled unarmed and alone. It numbered, as nearly as one can make out from the several discordant accounts by members of the company, forty-seven men and twenty-two women and children, who with Father de Smet's party of twelve made a total of eighty-one.

The pilgrims crossed the Little (Red) Vermillion and the Big (Black) Vermillion and the Big Blue — names to become famous through the journals of the

pioneers and the travelers. Following the general line
of the Little Blue, on June 1 they reached the Platte.
Near this river they had an Indian scare, which came to
nothing. They witnessed a buffalo stampede, in which
all might have perished but for Fitzpatrick forcing the
men to the front to build fires and to discharge a cease-
less rain of rifle balls on the advancing herd, thus com-
pelling it to drift to one side of their camp. They had
their share of the terrible storms which all the diarists
record; and once a huge waterspout, laden with the
muddy liquid of the Platte, swirled by them, though
missing them by a comfortable margin. They had in
many places to make their own road, cutting down the
steep banks of streambeds, filling gulches and removing
stones.

On June 22 they reached the trading post by this
time generally known as Fort Laramie, and on July 5
Independence Rock. The buffalo at this time had
begun to disappear forever from the region west of
the North Platte. Bidwell, in his *Recollections,* avers
that none were seen on the Sweetwater, but had he consulted his *Journal* or that of Preacher Williams, he
would have seen that a number were killed and that
several days were spent in curing meat. On July 18
the pilgrims crossed South Pass and on the 23d reached
Green River. The annual rendezvous, the great mid-
summer fair of the mountains, had been held for the last
time in 1840. But some of the emigrants refused to
believe that such a thing as the abandonment of these
gatherings could have happened, and therefore one of
the party, John Gray, was sent out to find if any trappers were in the neighborhood. He came upon Henry
Fraeb, former partner in the Rocky Mountain Fur

Company, with a party of twenty men; and on Green River, near the mouth of the Big Sandy, the emigrants and the trappers spent two days together.

The trappers wanted whiskey, and some of the emigrants, particularly Bartleson, had a stock to sell. That is (according to Bidwell), they had alcohol that had been watered down to one-third or one-fourth of its strength, and of this the trappers bought generously. Bidwell says nothing of the incident in his journal; but in his *Century* article, published thirty-nine years later, he writes:

Years afterwards we heard of the fate of that party; they were attacked by Indians the very first night after they left us and several of them killed, including the captain of the trapping party, whose name was Frapp. The whisky was probably the cause.

Bidwell had in the meantime become a Prohibitionist — he was the Prohibition candidate for President in 1892 — and it is to be feared that in relating this story he allowed his zeal to affect his judgment. It happens that the purchase of the whiskey took place at the Green River crossing on July 23–24. The battle in which Fraeb and four of his men lost their lives occurred on August 21–22, and the place was on the Colorado line, at least 125 miles away. It was, moreover, one of the most heroic contests in the annals of the frontier, the large attacking party of Sioux and Cheyennes being badly worsted by a small company of trappers. If any of that small stock of whiskey remained (which is more than doubtful), it seems not to have dampened the courage or lessened the fighting abilities of those who shared it.

From Green River the company went southwest to Ham's Fork, a tributary of Black's Fork, followed it to its headwaters and then crossed over to the Bear, reaching Soda Springs on August 10. Here the De Smet party, with Fitzpatrick, left them, to journey to the Flatheads, in the Idaho-Montana country. The emigrants, now reduced to sixty-four, divided. The way to Oregon was known, that to California was a trackless wild. Thirty-two set out for Oregon, and not being able to sell their wagons at Fort Hall abandoned them, packed their belongings on horses and mules, and went on to Whitman's mission and to the Columbia.[13] The other thirty-two, including the wife and infant daughter of Benjamin Kelsey, first American woman and child to reach California by the overland route direct from the States, started south.[14] They descended the Bear River almost to Great Salt Lake and then turned westward. They found little game; over much of the route there was neither grass nor water, and both emigrants and their stock endured great privations. On September 16, probably somewhere in the neighborhood of where the Southern Pacific railway crosses the western boundary of Utah, the wagons were abandoned.

There was no trail. Trappers at Fort Hall had warned some of the members of the party not to go too far north, where they would lose themselves in a region of deep canyons and towering peaks, nor to go too far south, where they would find no water. They did, however, push too far to the south, but on the 23d they reached the South Fork of the Humboldt River, which they followed northwestward to the main stream.

Down the Humboldt they went to what later became
known as Carson Sink. Missing the luxuriant Truckee
meadows, near the present Reno — where they would
have found an Indian trail to a pass — they moved on
southward to the vicinity of Walker Lake, from where
they began the ascent of the Sierras. After further
great hardships they arrived on the headwaters of the
Stanislaus River, down which they proceeded to the
San Joaquin Valley, which they crossed, and on November 4 reached the base of Mount Diablo, east of the
present Oakland, where they found Dr. Marsh's ranch.

The emigration to Oregon in 1841 was insignificant
in numbers and of no particular effect on the history of
the Pacific Northwest. That of 1842 really begins the
epic of the settlement of Oregon and the acquisition of
the whole region by the United States. The promoter
of this emigration was Dr. Elijah White, who had been
a member of the missionary enterprise on the Willamette, but had disagreed with Lee and had returned
east. Early in 1842 President Tyler appointed him
Indian sub-agent for Oregon, and he at once set about
forming an expedition. The emigrants assembled at
Elm Grove, about twenty miles southwest of Independence. Here, on May 14, they organized and elected
a "scientific corps," composed of C. Lancaster (who
shortly afterward left the expedition), Lansford W.
Hastings and Amos L. Lovejoy (later to accompany
Whitman on his famous ride), "to keep a faithful and
true record of everything useful to government or future engagements." James Coates was selected as pilot,
and White was elected captain for a term of one month.

They started on May 16, with sixteen or eighteen

covered wagons and a company of about 107 persons.[15]
It was a party of divergent wills, and it had a stormy
time. Two days after starting it had its first controversy. There were evidently too many dogs in the
party, and at a meeting it was resolved to kill all of them.
They would all go mad on the plains, it was argued, and
even if they didn't they would be sure, by their barking
and growling, to acquaint any prowling Indians with
the fact that here was a party to be plundered. The
counter argument that their barking would also apprize
the emigrants of the presence of Indians did not, apparently, carry sufficient weight, and a motion was
passed that all the dogs be shot. Medorem Crawford, in
his journal, and Miss A. J. Allen, the author of the
book of White's travels, say that the dogs — a total of
twenty-two — were killed. Hastings, however, in his
A New History of Oregon and California, says that
the motion produced a great deal of ill feeling; that
after a few were killed one owner after another declared
that any man attempting to shoot his dog would himself
be shot, and that as a consequence the execution stopped
then and there.

On June 15, at the end of White's term as captain, a
contest was held between Hastings and Stephen H. L.
Meek, brother of Joseph, and the former was elected.
He was, according to Bidwell, an energetic and ambitious man, and he seems to have had something of what
we should now call a Napoleonic complex. After his
arrival on the Coast and his subsequent removal to California, he is said to have formed the plan of overturning
the California government and establishing an independent republic, with himself as president. His as-

sumption of the leadership was a little more than White could stand, and on the next day, with a small following, he separated from the party.

Nothing of further consequence happened until the emigrants reached Fort Laramie on the 28th. So far they had suffered no loss of life or property. But the Sioux and the Cheyennes were on the warpath, still smarting over their repulse by Fraeb's party the previous August, and they threatened vengeance. Frémont, then on his first expedition to the Rockies, reached the fort about a week later, and tells the story as follows:

The emigrants to Oregon and Mr. Bridger's party met here, a few days before our arrival. Division and misunderstandings had grown up among them; they were already somewhat disheartened by the fatigue of their long and wearisome journey, and the feet of their cattle had become so much worn as to be scarcely able to travel. In this situation, they were not likely to find encouragement in the hostile attitude of the Indians, and the new and unexpected difficulties which sprang up before them. They were told that the country was entirely swept of grass, and that few or no buffalo were to be found on their line of route; and, with their weakened animals, it would be impossible for them to transport their heavy wagons over the mountain.

Under these circumstances, they disposed of their wagons and cattle at the forts, selling them at the prices they had paid in the States, and taking in exchange coffee and sugar at one dollar a pound, and miserable, worn-out horses, which died before they reached the mountains. Mr. Boudeau [Bordeaux, in charge at Fort Laramie, during the absence of Papin] informed me that he had purchased thirty, and the lower fort eighty head of fine cattle, some of them of the Durham breed.

Mr. Fitzpatrick, whose name and high reputation are familiar to all who interest themselves in the history of this country, had reached Laramie in company with Mr. Bridger;

FORT LARAMIE IN 1842

From Frémont's Report

and the emigrants were fortunate enough to obtain his services to guide them as far as the British post of Fort Hall, about two hundred and fifty miles beyond the South Pass of the mountains. They had started for this post on the 4th of July and, immediately after their departure, a war party of three hundred and fifty braves set out upon their trail. As their principal chief or partisan had lost some relations in the recent fight, and had sworn to kill the first whites on his path, it was supposed that their intention was to attack the party, should a favorable opportunity offer; or, if they were foiled in their principal object by the vigilance of Mr. Fitzpatrick, content themselves with stealing horses and cutting off stragglers. These had been gone but a few days previous to our arrival. . .

I subsequently learned that the party led by Mr. Fitzpatrick were overtaken by their pursuers near Rock Independence, in the valley of the Sweet Water; but his skill and resolution saved them from surprise, and, small as his force was, they did not venture to attack him openly. Here they lost one of their party by an accident, and, continuing up the valley, they came suddenly upon the large village. From these they met with a doubtful reception. Long residence and familiar acquaintance had given to Mr. Fitzpatrick great personal influence among them, and a portion of them were disposed to let him pass quietly; but by far the greater number were inclined to hostile measures; and the chiefs spent the whole of one night, during which they kept the little party in the midst of them, in council, debating the question of attacking them the next day; but the influence of " the Broken Hand," as they called Mr. Fitzpatrick, (one of his hands having been shattered by the bursting of a gun,) at length prevailed, and obtained for them an unmolested passage; but they sternly assured him that this path was no longer open, and that any party of whites which should hereafter be found upon it would meet with certain destruction. From all that I have been able to learn, I have no doubt that the emigrants owe their lives to Mr. Fitzpatrick.

It is a somewhat overwrought account, faulty in a number of particulars. Neither Crawford nor Miss

Allen mentions the sale of any wagons, though Crawford says that some of them were transformed into carts. Hastings, whose statements are often undependable, says that " several of our party disposed of their oxen and wagons," but he has many subsequent references to the wagons of the expedition. Some of the cattle were disposed of in the belief that they could not go farther because of sore feet, but those that were kept went all the way through. As for the Indian episode, it seems to have been much less thrilling than Frémont reports it.

The emigrants left Fort Laramie, according to Crawford, on July 3. The two parties, now sensible of their danger, traveled together. About a mile out they met Bridger and Fitzpatrick with a party coming in from the west, and White employed Fitzpatrick as a guide. On July 15 Hastings was again elected captain. They forded the North Platte at the usual place and on July 13 reached Independence Rock. The Indian episode is told by Hastings in a turgid and grandiloquent way, and one is made to feel that the whole party escaped massacre solely by his own valorous and defiant bearing. Crawford, however, dismisses it in a few words. White, in a letter of August 15 from Fort Hall, says that when the company moved on from Independence Rock Hastings and Lovejoy remained behind to inscribe their names. A band of several hundred Sioux suddenly appeared and seized and stripped them, making demonstrations as though to kill Lovejoy. Here they remained with their prisoners for some two hours, when they held a general consultation and then advanced toward the company. Seeing their approach, the company drew their wagons into a circle, stowed the women and children safely away and made ready for battle. Fitzpatrick went forward alone and motioned the Indians to stop, which they did, thereupon releasing the two prisoners, who at once rejoined their comrades. The savages, evidently expecting a generous reward for their liberality, asked for largess, but they got little, and the episode was closed.

The emigrants crossed South Pass, and at the Little Sandy they had another split. As usual, the accounts vary so much that the truth of the matter is not discoverable. Hastings says that a part of the company decided to leave their wagons; that Fitzpatrick remained behind with them while they made pack saddles, and that he, after selecting Meek as pilot, moved forward with the wagon train. White says that it was the wagonless party that hurried ahead. At any rate they all reached Fort Hall about the same time, August 15, and here Fitzpatrick left them. The wagons were abandoned, the chief factor of the Hudson's Bay Company generously buying a few of them, though professing that they were not needed. Hastings was again elected captain, and the company went on, with a Hudson's Bay Company clerk named McDonald as guide. White, with his immediate following, again detached himself from the company and went ahead, arriving at Whitman's mission about September 11, with the others trailing along some three or four days later. From here they reached the Columbia, which they descended to the Willamette.

Matters had not gone smoothly with the Presbyterian missionaries, and unfavorable tales had been circulated back east. To Whitman, White had brought letters, one of which was a staggering ukase from the Prudential Committee of the Board at Boston. It ordered the discontinuance of the missions among the Cayuses and the Nez Percés, the discharge of Spalding, another missionary (the Rev. Asa Bowen Smith) and two lay helpers and the transfer of Whitman to the Spokanes. But in the meantime Smith and the two lay helpers had withdrawn, and a degree of harmony had been restored. Under the changed circumstances the missionaries were determined to carry on. A conference held at Whitman's place on September 26–28 formally resolved to continue all the missions and to petition the Board for a rescinding of its order. To his colleagues Whitman announced his intention of immediately starting east and of making a personal protest to the Board. He had another motive for going, which most of his subsequent words and acts show to have been the dominant one. As the conference had determined to continue the stations, and as the petition was expected to bring a favorable response from the Board, the missionary cause alone could hardly have prompted him to undertake so desperate a journey. He had learned from the emigrants that a larger party would set out from Independence in the following spring; and it seems probable that he judged, rightly or wrongly, that there existed at the time some special danger to the cause of the Americanization of Oregon. " It was to open a practical route and safe passage," he wrote to the Board four and a half years later, " and secure a favorable report of the journey from the emigrants, which in connection with other objects, caused me to leave my family, and brave

the toils and dangers of the journey, notwithstanding
the unusual severity of the winter and the great depth
of snow." How much of his main purpose was known
to his colleagues cannot be said; but after some dissent
they approved his decision to make the journey.

With a companion, Lovejoy, who had just arrived
from the East, he set out on horseback, October 3. In
eleven days the men arrived at Fort Hall. Having
encountered severe weather and now hearing a report
of Indian disturbances on the Trail to the east, they
resolved on a southerly course. A guide was employed,
and they set out for one of Antoine Robidou's posts,
Fort Uinta, in the northeastern part of the present
Utah. From there, with a new guide, they started for
the other post, Fort Uncompahgre, on the upper Grand
(now Colorado), and though delayed by heavy snows
reached it in safety. They then set out for Taos, New
Mexico. In this almost impassable mountain region,
blocked with drifts, they ran into a terrible snowstorm,
and the guide lost his way. Leaving Lovejoy with the
packs and the extra animals, Whitman made his way
back with the guide to Fort Uncompahgre, obtained
a new pilot and in seven days rejoined his companion.
Suffering greatly from hunger and cold, they fought
their way through deep gorges, across icy streams and
over towering heights, and in thirty more days reached
Taos. From there they proceeded to Bent's Fort.
Parting with Lovejoy, Whitman hurried forward and
overtook an eastbound trading party with which he
continued on to the settlements.

Whitman arrived in St. Louis about the end of
February 1843. He went on to Washington, where he

talked with Tyler's Secretary of War, James M. Porter, in behalf of a proposal that the Government establish garrisoned posts along the Trail as a protection
against Indians. He must have argued to some effect,
since he was asked by the Secretary to draft a bill embodying his views. Doubtless he also talked Oregon, a
subject with which his mind and heart were full, to
other Government officials. He went on to New York,
where he met Horace Greeley, with whom he had a long
interview, which the great editor reported in his happiest
vein. Next he went to Boston, where he reported to his
Board, and then to his old home in upper New York.
Early in May he was back in Independence, ready to
accompany the emigration.

A number of writers have sought, with misdirected
energy, to discredit Whitman's share in the Americanization of Oregon, and some of them have even
denied that the missionary had a political motive in his
heroic ride. Among the extremists in this sorry crusade
the late Principal William I. Marshall easily takes the
lead. With a fire and fury that suggests a personal
antipathy to Whitman he wrote many letters, a booklet,
a pamphlet or two, and a ponderous two-volume work
on the subject. The late Professor Edward Gaylord
Bourne, in a different manner but with a hardly less
violent distortion of the evidence, also took a prominent
part in the controversy. It is to be conceded that the
anti-Whitmanites have rendered a service to history by
exploding a number of absurd myths that had grown
about the Whitman legend. Had they stopped at that
point, their contribution would have been an unmixed
blessing. They have, however, in the fervor of their

contention, served to muddle the evidence till the wayfarer and looker-on can hardly distinguish what is true from what is false. Yet out of it all the figure of Whitman emerges in a more splendid light. We shall see more of him later on and come to realize the greatness of the man. In this particular matter of the purpose of his ride we have, against the speculations of his detractors, the word of his companion, Lovejoy, and his own repeated testimony. He was a man of rugged honesty, open and forthright in speech, not given to vainglory or boastfulness. It matters little that his wife, less politically minded than he, says nothing of a political motive. Nor does it matter that he may have been wrong in suspecting at the time some special danger to the cause he had so deeply at heart. Others also, even at a later day, had this feeling. In the St. Louis *Weekly Reveille* of October 21, 1844, appeared a letter quoted from the *Platte Argus* and written by a resident of Multnomah City, Oregon, which said:

Uncle Sam had better be doing something for this country, for if not, within three years *it will be too late.* You laugh, but if you live you will see it.

Even could all of them be proved wrong, the proof would be irrelevant. A misreading of current events has prompted heroic actions from before Agamemnon's time. The true share of Whitman in the Americanization of Oregon can never be determined, though the controversy last till doomsday. It is enough to know that he had the cause at heart, and that to the furthering of the cause he gave his most devoted service.

CHAPTER IV

THE GREAT EMIGRATION

IN far-away Oregon the little group of colonists had set up a government. A constable and a magistrate, provided by the Methodist missionaries, had been the first civil officers; and with these to keep the peace the community waited for some action by Congress. In March 1838, a meeting of missionaries and settlers in the Willamette Valley drew up a petition, to which were affixed thirty-six signatures, asking the Government to extend its jurisdiction over the country. When Lee, in May, left on a visit to the East, he took with him this petition and sent it to Caleb Cushing, chairman of the House Committee on Foreign Affairs. During the winter session bills were introduced in both houses, but no action was taken.

In May 1840, Lee returned by way of the Horn, with fifty-two men, women, and children; and the increase of the colony brought a further realization of the need of civil control. As Congress would do nothing but debate the matter, a movement began to organize a government at home. The death, in the following winter, of Ewing Young, the famous trapper and trader, who had come into the territory with Hall Kelley in 1834,[16] brought matters to a head. Young left considerable property; it was necessary to administer his estate, and

68

to do so required the action of a probate judge. On February 17–18, 1841, at the Salem mission, a general meeting elected a judge and took initial measures toward organizing a government. But the Canadian settlers were either indifferent or hostile; Lieutenant Charles Wilkes, of the Navy, who was then on a tour of the country, gave assurance of speedy action at Washington, and so the movement lapsed.

The arrival of the emigration of 1842, doubling the American element of the population and bringing the news that Congress was still debating the problem, brought about a revival. On May 2, 1843, at Champoeg, a meeting was held to organize a government. Nearly half of those who attended, former employees and present partisans of the Hudson's Bay Company, protested and withdrew. The remainder went on with the organization. They chose, instead of a governor, a " legislative committee " of nine, and they further chose a judge, a clerk, a sheriff, a treasurer, four magistrates, four constables, and a major and three captains. The meeting then adjourned, and the legislative committee set itself to the drawing up of a scheme of community organization. On July 5, at a second general meeting, the committee submitted its report, which in effect was a constitution. It was promptly adopted, and the government at once began functioning. The experiment was a bold one; the government had the support of only a fraction of the population, and it might easily find itself thwarted by the powerful British interests surrounding it. But already the emigration that was to give it the backing of numbers and determination had passed Fort Laramie on its westward way.

This emigration of 1843 is known as the Great Emigration, because of its size, till then unprecedented; because of the outstanding ability of many of its members, who immediately took rank as the leaders of the infant colony, and because of its decisive influence in bringing the vexed " Oregon question " to an end. Its numbers have been put at the precise total of 875, but from various accounts the figure seems too low. According to Whitman, in his letter to Secretary Porter, it comprehended " no less than 200 families, consisting of 1,000 persons of both sexes," and they took with them more than 120 wagons, as well as " 694 oxen and 773 loose cattle." The number of animals seems to have been much greater than Whitman states. The missionary had wanted sheep. " A great many cattle are going," he wrote from Westport, May 28, to his brother-in-law, J. G. Prentiss, " but no sheep, from a mistake of what I said when passing [on his eastward journey, in February]. . . Sheep and cattle, but especially sheep, are indispensable for Oregon."

There is plenty of first-hand documentary material on this emigration; but though the larger facts regarding it are rendered clear enough, the details of date and incident are sadly discrepant. The covered wagons began assembling about Independence early in May. On the 18th a meeting was held, and two committees were appointed, one of which was to confer with Whitman. The missionary apparently declined appointment as guide, and the choice went to Captain John Gantt, noted as an army man, trapper, trader, Indian fighter, and onetime companion of Kit Carson. For the modest recompense of one dollar a head — counting men,

women, and children — Gantt agreed to lead them as
far as Fort Hall. Soon the wagons began trekking
toward the announced rendezvous, Elm Grove, then
marked by only one or two trees, which at once were cut
down for fuel; and on the 22d the advance set out for
the Kansas. On the 26th the river was crossed by an
improvised ferry, and several days later an organization
meeting was held, at which Peter H. Burnett (later to
become the first Governor of California) was elected
captain and James W. Nesmith (later to become a
Senator from Oregon), orderly sergeant.

Within a few days the company broke into two factions. The emigrants who had cattle naturally enough
demanded that guard duty should be obligatory upon all
the men of the company. Those without cattle admitted
the necessity of a reasonable degree of standing guard,
but the great herds of the company required more frequent service than they were willing to give, and they
accordingly rebelled. Burnett found that he could do
nothing in the matter and therefore resigned. A new
election was held. The men without cattle elected
William Martin, and the others General M. M. Mc-
Carver. The General, however, declined to serve, and
Jesse Applegate was chosen in his place. The lighter
column moved ahead, and the other, ever after to be
known as the cow column, took the rear.

The two parties kept within supporting distance.
Later, for practical reasons, they divided into four sections. They found the Trail in excellent condition except for a few days before the crossing of the Big Blue,
when heavy rains forced them to seek higher grounds.
The dissensions that delayed the progress of the forward

wagons enabled the late starters to overtake them, and among them was a California party of eighteen persons, led by Joseph B. Chiles, which kept in contact with the main company all the way to the vicinity of Fort Hall. Chiles had gone out with the Bidwell-Bartleson party in 1841, had returned the following year and was now, with three wagons, taking out a load of machinery for a mill. In his party were the two daughters of George C. Yount, a former wandering trapper who had left his home and family in Missouri back in 1825 and was now a prosperous rancher in the Napa Valley.

Whitman had stayed on behind at Westport, or at the Shawnee Mission, evidently to hurry on the late arrivals. In his letter of May 28 he wrote that though some of the wagons had been gone a week, others were just setting out. The night of June 4 he spent with Frémont, just starting on his second expedition. He probably followed the emigration the next day, since he overtook it, as Waldo remembered, at the crossing of the Big Blue, though according to Applegate, on the Platte. By this time all were traveling in co-operation.

Its earlier dissensions healed, the company settled down to the business of getting to Oregon with the least delay. It became a good-natured, cheerful, and orderly company. The rules made for conduct were enforced, and a court of elders tried and sentenced the occasional delinquents. Gantt, as the pilot, was assisted throughout by Whitman, who often, in addition to caring for the ill, took the lead in guidance. " The Doctor," wrote Nesmith, " spent much time in hunting out the best route for the wagons, and would plunge into streams in search of practicable fords, regardless of the depth or temperature of water; and sometimes, after the fatigue of a hard day's march, would spend much of the night in going from one party to another to minister to the sick." In that classic of the literature of the emigration era, " A Day with the Cow Column of 1843," written by the Hon. Jesse Applegate thirty-three years later, one gets an unforgettable picture of the life of the expedition and of the labors of Gantt and Whitman in carrying it along. Whitman's " great experience and indomitable energy," says Applegate, " were of priceless value to the migrating column. His constant advice, which we knew was based upon a knowledge of the road before us, was, ' Travel, *travel*, TRAVEL; nothing else will take you to the end of your journey; nothing is wise that does not help you along; nothing is good for you that causes a moment's delay.' . . . it is no disparagement to others to say that to no other individual are the emigrants of 1843 so much indebted for the successful conclusion of their journey as to Dr. Marcus Whitman."

At two miles an hour the ox-drawn wagons lumbered along. On a good day, with nothing to retard them, they made twenty miles. But there were some days when they made but five or ten miles, and other days when the company rested and no miles were scored. How did these people spend the terribly tedious time? Applegate gives the picture of a good marching day somewhere along the Platte:

It is four o'clock A. M.; the sentinels on duty have discharged their rifles — the signal that the hours of sleep are over — and every wagon and tent is pouring forth its night tenants, and slow-kindling smokes begin largely to rise and float away in the morning air. Sixty men start from the corral, spreading as they make through the vast herd of cattle and horses that make a semicircle around the encampment, the most distant perhaps two miles away.

The herders pass to the extreme verge and carefully examine for trails beyond, to see that none of the animals have strayed or been stolen during the night. This morning no trails led beyond the outside animals in sight, and by 5 o'clock the herders begin to contract the great, moving circle, and the well-trained animals move slowly towards camp, clipping here and there a thistle or a tempting bunch of grass on the way. In about an hour five thousand animals are close up to the encampment, and the teamsters are busy selecting their teams and driving them inside the corral to be yoked. The corral is a circle one hundred yards deep, formed with wagons connected strongly with each other; the wagon in the rear being connected with the wagon in front by its tongue and ox chains. It is a strong barrier that the most vicious ox cannot break, and in case of an attack of the Sioux would be no contemptible intrenchment.

From 6 to 7 o'clock is a busy time; breakfast is to be eaten, the tents struck, the wagons loaded and the teams yoked and brought up in readiness to be attached to their respective wagons. All know when, at 7 o'clock, the signal to march sounds, that those not ready to take their proper places in the line of march must fall into the dusty rear for the day.

There are sixty wagons. They have been divided into fifteen divisions or platoons of four wagons each, and each platoon is entitled to lead in its turn. The leading platoon today will be the rear one tomorrow, and will bring up the rear unless some teamster, through indolence or negligence, has lost his place in the line, and is condemned to that uncomfortable post. It is within ten minutes of seven; the corral but now a strong barricade is everywhere broken, the teams being attached to the wagons. The women and children have taken their places in them. The pilot (a borderer who has passed his life on the verge of civilization and has been chosen to the post of leader from his knowledge of the savage and his experience in travel through roadless wastes), stands ready, in the midst of his pioneers and aids, to mount and lead the way. Ten or fifteen young men, not today on duty, form another cluster. They are ready to start on a buffalo hunt, are well mounted and well armed, as they need be, for the unfriendly Sioux have driven the buffalo out of the Platte, and the hunters must ride fifteen or twenty miles to reach them. The cow drivers are hastening, as they get ready, to the rear of their charge, to collect and prepare them for the day's march.

It is on the stroke of seven; the rush to and fro, the cracking of whips, the loud command to oxen, and what seemed to be the inextricable confusion of the last ten minutes has ceased. Fortunately every one has been found and every teamster is at his post. The clear notes of a trumpet sound in the front; the pilot and his guards mount their horses; the leading divisions of the wagons move out of the encampment, and take up the line of march; the rest fall into their places with the precision of clock work, until the spot so lately full of life sinks back into that solitude that seems to reign over the broad plain and rushing river as the caravan draws its lazy length towards the distant El Dorado.

The long march of the day is over; the corral has been formed by placing the wagons in a closely locked circle; outside of it the animals have been picketed or hobbled, and inside the fires have been lighted and the suppers cooked and eaten. Applegate continues:

It is not yet 8 o'clock when the first watch is to be set; the evening meal is just over, and the corral now free from the intrusion of cattle or horses, groups of children are scattered over it. The larger are taking a game of romps; " the wee toddling things " are being taught that great achievement that distinguishes man from the lower animals. Before a tent near the river a violin makes lively music, and some youths and maidens have improvised a dance upon the green; in another quarter a flute gives its mellow and melancholy notes to the still night air, which, as they float away over the quiet river, seem a lament for the past rather than a hope for the future. It has been a prosperous day; more than twenty miles have been accomplished of the great journey. The encampment is a good one; one of the causes that threatened much future delay [a childbirth case] has just been removed by the skill and energy of that "good angel" of the emigrants, Doctor Whitman, and it has lifted a load from the hearts of the elders. Many of these are assembled around the good doctor at the tent of the pilot (which is his home for the time being), and are giving grave attention to his wise and energetic counsel. The care-worn pilot sits aloof, quietly smoking his pipe, for he knows the brave doctor is "strengthening his hands."

But time passes; the watch is set for the night; the council of old men has been broken up, and each has returned to his own quarter; the flute has whispered its last lament to the deepening night; the violin is silent, and the dancers have dispersed; enamored youth have whispered a tender "good night" in the ear of blushing maidens, or stolen a kiss from the lips of some future bride — for Cupid here, as elsewhere, has been busy bringing together congenial hearts, and among these simple people he alone is consulted in forming the marriage tie. Even the doctor and the pilot have finished their confidential interview and have separated for the night. All is hushed and repose from the fatigues of the day, save the vigilant guard and the wakeful leader, who still has cares upon his mind that forbid sleep. He hears the 10 o'clock relief taking post and the "all well" report of the returned guard; the night deepens, yet he seeks not the needed repose. . . the last care of the day being removed, and the last duty performed, he too seeks the rest that will enable him to go through the same routine tomorrow.[17]

They found the Laramie River so high and swift that it could not be forded. It was decided to connect the wagon beds for a ferry boat and to draw them across by rope. " No one," wrote William Waldo, " was willing to risk himself in swimming the river and carrying the line but Dr. Whitman, which he did successfully." They found the North Platte at the crossing also in flood, and here again Whitman took the lead, repeatedly swimming his horse through the raging current to find the best ford and finally ordering the wagons chained in a long line and conducting them safely to the farther shore.

On Independence Rock they left the inscription: " The Oregon Company arrived July 26, 1843." Along the Sweetwater and through South Pass and across the Green they went, and on to Ham's Fork. Here they parted from the old Trail and took a southerly detour. Bridger had just established his trading post and blacksmith shop on Black's Fork, and here it was understood repairs could be made and some supplies obtained. To Fort Bridger they went and were thus the first emigrants to travel the route which ever afterward was a section of the main Oregon Trail.

They went on to Bear River, to Soda Springs, and to Fort Hall. Here the Chiles party separated from the others. At Fort Laramie that restless wanderer, Joseph Reddeford Walker, who had led the Bonneville expedition to California in 1833, had been picked up as a guide. Leaving him in charge of the wagons, most of the men and the two women, Chiles and several companions went north to Fort Boisé and striking across the little known wastes of southern Oregon found their way into northern California. Walker led the remainder of the party across to the Humboldt and on to Carson Sink and thence far to the south of Walker Lake, whence it ascended the intermediate ranges to Owen's Lake. The wagons with the machinery were abandoned, and keeping to the south, the party crossed the main range at Walker's Pass and safely reached the lowlands. About the first of the year Yount was joined by his two daughters. The wagons of this party were the first that entered California from the Oregon Trail, the arrival antedating that of the Townsend-Murphy-Stephens party by a year.[18]

The Oregon company encountered its crisis at Fort Hall. Thus far it had come by wagons, and so on, to the end, it had meant to continue. But at the fort the emigrants were told by Captain Grant, the chief factor, and by others, that they could not take their wagons farther. This warning statement, though new to these emigrants, was one familiar to every American who had hitherto brought wagons to Fort Hall. It had been made to Whitman when in 1836 he came by with his cart; in 1840 it had caused the Rev. Harvey Clark and his companions to abandon their wagons; again, in the following year, it had been successfully used with the Oregon-bound section of the Bidwell-Bartleson party, and in 1842 with the members of the White-Hastings party. As good British subjects and loyal employees of the Hudson's Bay Company, the factor and his men were not encouraging settlers — and particularly settlers from the States — to invade the Oregon country. They wanted to retain it as a fur preserve. They repeated their warnings in 1844 and again in 1845, after long wagon trains had successfully made the journey. General Joel Palmer, of the emigration of the latter year, says that

the two crossings of Snake River and the crossing of the
Columbia and other smaller streams were represented by those
in charge of this fort as being attended with great danger; it
was also said that no company heretofore attempting the passage of those streams succeeded but with the loss of men from
the violence and rapidity of the currents. In addition to the
above, it was asserted that three or four tribes of Indians in
the middle regions had combined for the purpose of preventing
our passage through their country. In case we escaped destruction at the hands of the savages, we were told that a more
fearful enemy, famine, would attend our march, as the distance
was so great that winter would overtake us before making the
Cascade Mountains. On the other hand, as an inducement to
pursue the California route, we were informed of the shortness
of the route, when compared with that to Oregon, as also of
the many other superior advantages it possessed.

The members of the emigration of 1843 heard with
dismay the warnings of the men at the fort. Whitman
for a time was absent from the camp, and it was during
this absence that a mood approaching despair seized
upon the emigrants. On his return he quickly brought
about a feeling of reassurance. He had promised them
that they and their wagons would be taken through to
the Columbia, and he now repeated the promise.

They again set forth, Whitman and a companion in
a light wagon at the front to make a track. Eager to
get home at the earliest moment, he tried, as he afterward wrote, " to leave the party at various points, but
found that I [he] could not do so without subjecting
the emigrants to considerable risk." At the Grande
Ronde, east of the Blue Mountains, he received word
that Spalding and his wife were both dangerously ill.
Leaving the emigrants in charge of one of his converts,
a Cayuse chief, Istikus (a name accented on the second

syllable, and usually spelled Stikkus), he hurried ahead. Istikus, wrote Nesmith, "was a faithful old fellow, perfectly familiar with all the trails and topography of the country from Fort Hall to the Dalles, and although not speaking a word of English, and no one of our party a word of Cayuse, he succeeded by pantomime in taking us over the roughest wagon road I ever saw." They reached the vicinity of Whitman's mission on the 10th of October, went down the Walla Walla to the Columbia and down the Columbia to the Dalles, whence by boats and batteaux they reached the Willamette.

Two other emigrations, one of them much larger, were to follow before Great Britain, in 1846, yielded her claims to most of the region south of the 49th parallel. This one of 1843 clinched the argument for the United States. It has been said that "Oregon was taken at Fort Hall." It might, of course, have otherwise been taken, but the matter is problematical. Whitman's unwavering determination that the emigrants should reach the Columbia with their wagons was a weighty factor in solving the question that opened with the Louisiana purchase.

Fort Boisé

Drawn by Major Osborne Cross (1849)

Fort Walla Walla

*From Myron Eells' "Marcus Whitman, Pathfinder
and Patriot" (1909)*

CHAPTER V

THE flow of migration had now become continuous, even if irregular. For the next five years it was to reach its greatest height in 1847 and its lowest ebb in the year following. Widely fluctuating in numbers, this emigration distributed itself somewhat capriciously between California and Oregon. That of 1841 divided equally, but virtually all that of the two following years went to the northern country. Not all of these pioneers were content with their goals; some of them, indeed, found no resting place for years. From Oregon they would start southward, and on the road mayhap would meet a party from California; news and views would be exchanged, the blessings or disadvantages of one country would be weighed against those reported of the other, and sometimes a section of each party would turn back to the country it had abandoned.

The emigration of 1844 consisted of four parties, independently organized. There was another party — a small one of health and pleasure seekers, led by William L. Sublette — which went beyond the mountains, but it does not count with the emigration. In this year for the first time starts were made from places other than Independence. General Cornelius Gilliam's company, which was made up of several small groups,

crossed the Missouri at various places between Fort
Leavenworth and Capler's Ferry, north of the newly
established St. Joseph, and may possibly have broken
the first wagon road to the junction with the Oregon
Trail at the present Marysville, Kansas. According to
John Minto, its chief chronicler, it consisted of about
eight hundred persons, of whom 235 were capable of
bearing arms. Two hundred and sixteen of the men,
with their families, went to Oregon, seventeen to California, and two died on the way. A small company, led
by John Thorp, started from near Bellevue and followed the north bank of the Platte to Fort Laramie,
where it joined the main Trail. Another company of
about forty men, with a large proportion of women
and children, in twenty-seven wagons, under the lead
of Elisha Stephens, an old mountain man, started from
Independence and traveled off and on with the larger
trains until it reached Cassia Creek, beyond Fort Hall,
where thirteen wagons turned off for California. Like
the Chiles-Walker party of the previous year, it took
its wagons into the Sierras, and also, like its predecessor,
was compelled to leave them there. It had the distinction of supporting a disproportionate number of leaders
to followers. It is generally known as the Stephens-
Townsend-Murphy party, though Clyman speaks of
the California section of it as " Mr. Hitchcock's party."

In some respects the most important of these parties
was that which left Independence on May 14. It consisted of from five hundred to seven hundred persons,
according to Clyman, one of its members, and it was
piloted by the famous mountain man, Major Moses
(" Black ") Harris. It started without any organization, but on the 25th, before reaching the Kansas, it

elected Colonel Nathaniel Ford its captain, and it is usually known as Ford's company. This was the year of the great flood in eastern Kansas and Nebraska. Torrential rains, day after day, caused all the streams to overflow their banks, and the usually firm turf of the prairie became so soggy that the wagon wheels sank in it almost to the hubs. All the caravans were greatly delayed; Ford's company, though it passed Gilliam's beyond the South Platte crossing, did not reach Fort Laramie until the seventy-eighth day after its start. Minto says that the Ford, Gilliam, and Thorp parties never united. It is evident, however, that all four of the parties (including Sublette's) which went by the south bank of the Platte were in frequent contact; that after reaching Fort Laramie Thorp's party also traveled within reach, and that Harris acted as a general guide for the whole emigration.

Most of these pilgrims went to Oregon. There is, in the records of this movement, a curious discrepancy for which no one has offered a satisfactory solution. Accepting the estimates of the chroniclers of the various parties, one finds that considerably more than a thousand persons left the Missouri. But the numbers of those said to have started can not be reconciled with the numbers admitted to have arrived. There were no serious Indian troubles, and there was no epidemic; none of the emigrants was lost, none turned back, and none settled on the way. Yet the Oregon histories acknowledge an emigration for the year of only from 475 to seven hundred, and the California histories one of less than two hundred. Obviously the figures at both ends of the line need considerable revision.

The emigrants had heard of a nearer way to reach the

Willamette. At the Grande Ronde, about the 1st of October, they turned aside from the road to Whitman's mission, crossed the Blue Mountains in a northwestward direction, and striking the head of the Umatilla followed it to the Columbia, whence they went on to the Dalles. Those of the party who descended the Columbia by water reached their destination safely, but those who sought to take their wagons through the Cascade Mountains were compelled, after suffering greatly from cold and hunger, to return and complete their journey by water. With this year the route by Whitman's mission ceased to be the main terminal of the Oregon Trail. It continued to be used, but in a lessening degree, until the massacre of November 29, 1847, when it was closed. By this time most of the Oregon travel was reaching its destination by way of northern California.

The year 1845 saw the largest of the first five emigrations. Though fewer than two hundred persons went to California, Oregon received more than three thousand. From Fort Boisé some traveled the route of the previous year, but a large party, assured by Stephen Meek that he could guide them to the Willamette by a nearer and easier way, followed him to the headwaters of the Malheur, where he became hopelessly lost. Messengers reached the Dalles, where supplies and guidance were obtained; and the emigrants, after suffering terrible hardships, were brought there, whence gradually they were taken down the Columbia. The difficulties of the attempted land route from the Dalles around the north shoulder of Mount Hood now prompted an effort to find a way to the south of the mountain. During the fall S. K. Barlow explored such a route, known afterward as the Barlow road, which in spite of its difficulties was used for a time, but ultimately abandoned for the more southern routes.

One section of the rather colorless emigration of 1845 will always hold a certain interest, since it furnished the setting for one of the most valuable first-hand documents of the pioneer era. It was the section led by General Joel Palmer, who two years later published his *Journal of Travels Over the Rocky Mountains.*[19] Palmer was an Indiana farmer, who had been elected to the Legislature, but who preferred seeing Oregon to serving out his official term. Arriving at Independence too late to join the regular wagon train, he hurried forward and overtook it at the Kansas crossing. It was a train of 145 wagons, which subsequently was divided into sections, and over one of these, consisting of thirty-seven wagons, Palmer was made commander. At Fort Hall he declined to follow the guidance of Meek into the unknown wilderness and went on with the other wagons to the Grande Ronde, and by the route of 1844 to the Dalles. Here he joined Barlow in the measurably successful effort to cut a new road to the Willamette. During the winter he made a careful examination of the settled part of the country; in the spring of 1846 he visited Whitman and Spalding, and he then returned east. In 1847, taking his family with him and leading a company known as Palmer's party, he again went to Oregon. For nearly twenty years he served the territory and state in various capacities, afterward retiring to private life and dying in 1881. The admirable record of his experiences and reflections that he gave to the world shows him to have been a keen observer and a close inquirer after the truth and to have been blessed with an uncommon degree of the quality somewhat loosely called common sense.

Emigration in 1846 dwindled to less than half the figure for the previous year, and it yielded a somewhat larger share than usual to California. At least 1,350 persons went to Oregon and perhaps three hundred to California. The Oregon party in the main traveled from Fort Hall by a new route explored by Jesse Applegate and others just before their arrival. This route, after striking the Humboldt, ran westward from the bend (in the present Pershing County) and then northwestward to the head of Pit River, to the Klamath Lakes, and on to the Willamette.

The emigrants who started for the disputed territory of Oregon were eventually to learn that while on their way the treaty had been signed which made it a part of the United States. Negotiations for a settlement had been going rather badly for several years, and the Presidential campaign of 1844, with the jingoistic cry of the Democrats, " Fifty-four forty or fight! " did not help matters. A further strain was brought about by the somewhat defiant language of Polk's inaugural address. Conferences were resumed in the summer of 1845, but the tension was too extreme for a settlement. Secretary Buchanan offered the compromise of the 49th parallel, but it was rejected, as it had repeatedly been rejected from the earliest negotiations. In his first message to Congress, in December, Polk took strong ground and recommended giving a twelve-months' notice of the abrogation of the treaty and the extension of our laws to American citizens in the country. Great Britain, in return, proposed arbitration, but this was refused.

Thus for a time the matter rested. But a conciliatory resolution was passed by Congress on April 23, 1846, and it brought an immediate and friendly response from Great Britain. Negotiations were reopened, Great Britain accepted the 49th parallel to the Gulf of Georgia and proposed a continuation of the boundary through the strait of Juan de Fuca, leaving Vancouver Island in her possession. Polk sent the proposal to the Senate on June 10, and two days later that body formally advised the President that it be accepted. On June 15 the treaty was signed, and on June 17 it was formally ratified by the Senate.

Perhaps five hundred persons entered California by way of the Trail in 1846. Those who made the start expecting to enter Mexican territory were to find themselves, on their arrival, still living under the Stars and Stripes. A revolution had taken place, and following that, a conquest. Frémont, on his third expedition, crossing Truckee Pass with a part of his command, had arrived at Fort Sutter on the previous December 9. Reuniting his command farther south, he had been ordered from the country by General Castro, had proceeded northward to Upper Klamath Lake, from whence, after meeting Lieutenant Gillespie, who had followed him, he had returned to Fort Sutter. The American settlers, now augmented to a number that could put eight hundred armed men in the field, had become restless and had, with Frémont's aid, committed an overt act of war in capturing the village of Sonoma. Here, on June 15, they raised the Bear Flag and proclaimed California an independent republic. Commodore Sloat, though knowing that war had been declared, hesitantly sailed into the harbor of Monterey; but on learning there of the operations on land, on July 7 took possession of the country in the name of the United States Government. When the emigrants began to arrive, the almost bloodless conquest was accomplished; but though there was to be further fighting, and though peace was not finally reached until after the second capture of Los Angeles and the treaty of Cahuenga (January 13, 1847), California, with the raising of the Bear Flag, had virtually passed from Mexico to the Union.

The outstanding tragedy of the Trail for that year was the fate of the Donner party in the Sierras. The party originated in a group formed at Springfield, Illinois, by George and Jacob Donner and James Frazier Reed, with their families and some friends, and it reached Independence in May. Here it was joined by Patrick Breen and his family and others. It left Independence with the general emigration, though keeping together as a distinct group. At Fort Laramie it met James Clyman's pack-train returning from California. Clyman and Reed had served with Abraham Lincoln in Jacob Early's company in the Black Hawk War (1832) and were well acquainted. Clyman spoke of the new route by which he had just come in company with L. W. Hastings through the Nevada-Utah deserts and around the south end of Great Salt Lake — a route which was already becoming known as Hastings' Cut-off. For the most part it was the route first taken by Fitzpatrick's detachment of Frémont's party in 1845. Hastings had traveled it but once, when with Clyman's party, and had adopted it as his own and begun to advertise it to the emigrants. Clyman advised Reed strongly against it and urged him to follow the Fort Hall route.

On the 19th of July the Donners reached the Little Sandy River, just west of South Pass. Here they camped with four other parties, most of the members of which were bound for Oregon. A meeting was held to discuss a missive entitled "An Open Letter," written by Hastings and delivered by a special messenger on horseback. It was addressed "to all California emigrants now on the road," and urged them, on account of the war with Mexico and the probable resistance of the Californians to further American immigration, to concentrate their numbers and also to take the new route. Assurance was given that they would save nearly two hundred miles as compared with the Fort Hall route, and also that Hastings would remain at Fort Bridger to give further information and to conduct the emigrants on their way.

After a general deliberation a party was formed to take the new route. It included most of the original Springfield company, and was joined by a number of others. George Donner was elected its captain, and it thereupon became definitely known as the Donner party. "All the companies broke camp and left the Little Sandy on the 20th," writes Eliza P. Donner Houghton. "The Oregon division, with a section for California, took the right-hand trail [Greenwood's or Sublette's Cut-off] for Fort Hall; and the Donner party the left-hand trail [the main Oregon Trail] to Fort Bridger."

The Donners reached Fort Bridger on July 25. Here they were informed that Hastings had gone forward as pilot to a large emigrant train but had left instructions that all later arrivals should follow him. Edwin Bryant, later the author of *What I Saw in California,* had left

Fort Bridger with a small pack-train only five days before the arrival of the Donners. J. R. Walker, whom he met there, just in from the trail, had spoken discouragingly of the Hastings Cut-off, and though Bryant's party had resolved to take it because they were unimpeded by wagons, Bryant wrote letters to his friends among the emigrants expected at the fort, advising them to go by way of Fort Hall. On the day of his departure he wrote in his diary: " There is no trail, and we are guided in our course and route by the direction in which Salt Lake is known to lie." The Donners, however, resolved to follow, and on the 28th they started. " The trail from the fort was all that could be desired," writes Mrs. Donner Houghton, " and on the 3d of August we reached the crossing of the Weber River."

They soon found, however, that for wagons the trail was an exceedingly difficult one. They were compelled to stop from time to time to remove obstructions and to improve the roadbed. The diarists among the Mormon Pioneers, who followed the route in the following year, express amazement at the evidences of the amount of work done. Finally, after great delays, a detour was made over the mountains, and the company reached the Great Salt Lake Valley. They then followed the Cut-off to the Humboldt River, whence they kept to the regular trail to the Truckee meadows. The season was late, but in spite of the fact they stopped for a few days to rest their cattle. On October 23, nearly three months after leaving Fort Bridger, they started forward. When they reached Truckee Lake (since called Donner Lake) snow was falling. Several attempts to proceed were blocked by increasing snowfall, and by the middle of November they realized their peril. One of their number, Charles T. Stanton, had some time before been sent forward to return with provisions. Sutter had liberally provided him, and he had returned while yet the party was slowly traveling through Nevada, but the provisions soon became exhausted. A council decided upon killing the mules and cattle for food, abandoning the equipment and making the remainder of the way on foot, but the increasing snowfall made progress impossible. The emigrants found a cabin which the Stephens-Murphy-Townsend party had built two years before, and they hastily added a number of rough structures for habitation. Breen's diary, which runs from November 20 to March 1, tells the frightful story. There were divided counsels and bitter quarrels. The food supply disappeared until nothing but hides were left. In mid-December a volunteer party of fifteen men and women, with six days' rations, started forward to seek relief, but became snowbound. At their camp four of the members died and were eaten, and later four others died, but the remainder reached the settlements. At different dates a total of four rescue parties was sent out to bring in the survivors at the main camp. Here many others were found to have died, and here also cannibalism had been practised. Of the original eighty-one of the party there were but forty-five survivors.[20]

Wagons crowded the Trail in 1847. The acquisition of the new territories acted as a spur to emigration, and thousands of home-seekers set out for the coast. At least 4,500 of these went to Oregon and perhaps one thousand to California. Though the northern California route to Oregon had now become the favorite

one, some of the emigrants still made the journey by
Whitman's mission. The last of these had passed by
hardly a month before the occurrence of the atrocious
massacre of November 29, in which Whitman, his wife
and twelve others were slain by the Cayuse Indians.
The local government raised a force of volunteers who
pursued the Indians, defeated them in battle and drove
them across the Snake. It also sent Joe Meek in a
breakneck race across the continent to inform the President and Congress of the tragedy and to plead for Federal help. Congress at last awoke to its duty, and on
August 14, 1848, the last day of the session, passed the
bill organizing the Territory of Oregon. General Joseph Lane was appointed Governor and Meek United
States Marshal. On March 2 of the following year they
were to arrive on the Willamette and set up the new government.

The year 1847 also marked the beginning of the Mormon hegira to the Great Basin. Driven out of Nauvoo,
Illinois, the Mormons had crossed the Mississippi and
gradually concentrated about the village of Kanesville
(the present Council Bluffs). The winter of 1846–47
found most of them settled in what has ever since been
known by them as Winter Quarters, on the west side of
the Missouri from Kanesville. They were ill prepared
for the winter and suffered greatly. Under their new
leader, Brigham Young, they were planning to found
a community in the Far West. Some of them had
read Frémont's reports, and had become convinced that
the valley of the Great Salt Lake was their destined
Canaan. In later times the boast was made that they
were led to this spot by divine guidance. The matter of

divine guidance can not, of course, be settled by any available tests. But the questions asked by Young and his companions of mountain men like Bridger and Harris, as well as the bee line they made for the goal, would indicate that their sole interest was in the Great Salt Lake country. On April 16 an advance party, known in Mormon history as the Pioneers, headed by Young, left the camp at Elkhorn River, about fifteen miles west of Winter Quarters, traveling along the north bank of the Platte. It was composed of 143 men and boys, three women and two children, and it had seventy-two wagons and a considerable collection of animals, including horses, mules, oxen, cows, dogs, and chickens.

Ever afterward this route, though followed by tens of thousands of other emigrants, has been known, not improperly, as the Mormon Trail. But the Mormon contention that the Pioneers broke this trail is quite unsupported by the facts. On their second day out they met wagons, and again on the following day. On the 19th Clayton writes that "the roads are very good" and on the 21st "the roads being good and very level." The Mormons chose, however, at various places to make their own trail. On the 30th Clayton writes: "We had thus far followed the Indian Trail, which now was so overgrown with grass and so little used that it was hardly discernible." They were traveling a natural highway, though till then infrequently used.

On June 1, at a distance of 543 miles from Winter Quarters, they reached a point opposite old Fort Platte, near the mouth of the Laramie and about two miles from Fort Laramie. They ferried across the river and for the remainder of the journey, as far as Fort Bridger, they traveled by the main line of the Oregon Trail. Though in frequent contact with other emigrants, there were no collisions. At the North Platte crossing, near the present Casper, Wyoming, they did a highly lucrative business with the Gentiles. The river, usually fordable, was now in flood, and a small party bound for Oregon was speculating vainly about how to get across when an advance party of Mormons arrived. The Mormons had a large skiff, made of sole leather, and capable of carrying from 1,500 to 1,800 pounds. A deal was soon arranged, by which the goods were to be ferried in the skiff and the empty wagons floated across. For $1.50 a wagon-load the Mormons transported the goods, taking their pay in bacon, meal, and flour, the last at $2.50 a hundredweight, though, as the Mormon diarist cheerfully admits, flour was really worth at least $10 a hundredweight at that point. The Gentiles were entirely satisfied with the trade, and the Mormons were elated. " It looked as much of a miracle to me," wrote Apostle Wilford Woodruff, " to see our flour and meal bags replenished in the Black Hills, as it did to have the children of Israel fed with manna in the wilderness." As the elders and their party went on, they left a small detachment to carry on the ferrying business.

At Pacific Springs, just west of South Pass, on June 26, they met Major Harris, and two days later, at the Big Sandy, they met Bridger. Of both men they asked innumerable questions about the region and especially about the Great Salt Lake Valley. At Fort Bridger, which they reached on July 7, they left the Oregon Trail and started southwest by the Hastings Cut-off. The

advance party, led by Orson Pratt, found the trail in
places overgrown with grass and in other places too
rough for travel.   Several detours were made, and some
time was spent in improving the bad spots for the wagon
train behind them.   The advance party arrived at the
site of the present Salt Lake City on July 22, and two
days later came the main party headed by Young.   Behind the Pioneers, and leaving the Elkhorn River about
July 1, came a caravan of two thousand of the saints,
with 566 wagons and large herds of livestock.   At the
Green River it broke up into smaller parties, which began arriving at the new settlement about the middle of
September.   Eastward also the Mormons used the Trail
this year.   From the newly founded Salt Lake City a
party of seventy-one men started on the return to
Winter Quarters on August 16–17, and Young, with a
larger party (108 men), on August 26.   A colony had
been planted; some 2,800 residents had been settled
there, and the leaders, with their escort, were returning
to the base to make new preparations and to bring out
a new emigration in the spring.[21]

The travel season of 1848 found the Trail almost
monopolized by the Mormons.   From Winter Quarters
the leaders, with a large company, started on their return to Salt Lake City; and from time to time others
set out to follow.   But of non-Mormon emigrants there
were few.   The Oregon chronicles acknowledge an addition for the year of seven hundred souls, but we know
very little about them.   Perhaps half as many went to
California.   The energetic Chiles had again come east,
and in the spring of this year led out a party of forty-
eight wagons.   Clyman also, who seemed never to be

at rest, but who was soon, at the age of fifty-nine, to
marry and settle down, started westward over the Trail.
He was with the Lambert Mecombs party of eighteen
wagons, and it was a daughter of Mecombs that was to
be his bride.   There was also Pierre B. Cornwall's party
of twenty-five wagons, that of James T. Walker of
ten wagons, and two small pack-train parties.   Emigration to the Coast had dwindled away, and beyond the
range of the Mormon travel the Trail was quiet.   This
lull was, however, in the following spring to be broken
by a rush of travel never before seen on any trail in any
country of the globe.

CHAPTER VI

WITH THE WAGONS TO THE PACIFIC

THE history of the Trail divides naturally at the close of 1848. Before that were the pioneers — missionaries and home-seekers — in the main a homogeneous folk, orderly and industrious, the founders of an empire. After that, beginning with the gold rush of the following spring, new elements crowded the Trail. There were still, and would long continue to be, home-seekers in vast numbers; but there came also adventurers, restless wanderers, gamblers, gunmen, thieves, loose women and all the misfits of a maladjusted world. It will thus be well, at this point, before continuing the narrative, to look back upon the Trail for a glimpse of the life that thronged it in the early days; and afterward to trace it in detail, as far as possible, in terms of its natural features as well as of the towns and settlements that now mark its course.

Each spring, at the earliest sign of sprouting grass, the wagons began moving toward Independence or the later established towns north of the bend of the Missouri. The first emigrants started the long journey with little preparation and less means. In their eagerness to get away they utilized anything at hand. Those of a later time learned better. Stories came to them of the tragedies of the Trail — of suffering and hunger, of broken-down wagons, of the death of livestock — and they saw the necessity of taking every precaution against possible disaster. Back on the farms and in the little villages they had made such provision as they could; but at the jumping-off place they found that there was much more to do. After a time guide-books began to be printed; but for several years even the most prudent had to depend upon letters of those who had arrived at the goal or upon oral advice from those who had returned.

Captain R. B. Marcy's *The Prairie Traveler,* the best of the guide-books, did not appear until 1859. It gave the ripened knowledge of an army man and an explorer who had traveled widely through the West and who had passed through many harrowing experiences. Though written for the emigrants of more than a decade later than the time so far treated here, the advice given was, in the main, as applicable to the earlier travelers as to the later ones. First, there was the matter of wagons. They should be simple, strong and light, and of well-seasoned timber. To avoid shrinking of wheels and loosening of tires in the hot and dry regions farther to the west, Osage orange should be used; but if it was not obtainable white oak would make a fair substitute. The wagon-tongue must be a jointed or " falling " one, since a rigid tongue would be sure to be broken when the wheels were bumping in and out of short and abrupt holes. The bolts or coupling pins attaching the bed to the running gear must be removable so that the wagon could, when necessary, be transformed into a cart, or in crossing flooded streams be used for a boat; and since nuts tended to loosen and twist off, all bolts other than the coupling bolts must be riveted.

Men were still discussing, in 1859, as they had done a decade and more earlier, the relative value of mules and oxen. Under certain conditions Marcy preferred mules. They were more expensive, it was true; six mules would cost $600, while eight oxen could be had for only $200. But with good roads and plenty of grain the mules traveled faster and better endured the heat. Even without grain they were preferable for distances up to one thousand miles. For the longer journeys, over rough, sandy or muddy roads, young oxen were preferable. They held out better against the prolonged strain; they made, in the long run, equally good time with the mules; they were less likely to be stampeded by Indians, and they were always available for beef. It was well also to have at least a few cows along. Their milk made a valuable addition to the menu, and they could, in emergencies, be used in harness.

The carrying of grain was something that rarely occurred to the earlier emigrant, for he expected to find grass all the way to the Pacific. But with the increase of migration the first trains each spring had all the advantage; the later ones found little or no grass, and so the carrying of grain and the purchasing of further supplies on the way came to be a common practice. In the forties there was hardly a farm, except on the Indian reservations, west of the Missouri. By May 1859, eastern Kansas and Nebraska had seen nearly five years of colonization and farm cultivation. One could travel, says Marcy, for 150 miles from the Missouri through settled country where grain could be obtained at low prices.

The growing uncertainty of finding game compelled greater provision of foodstuffs. Various schedules of the needed quantities were made. Marcy recommended, on the basis of an assumed 110 days' journey from the Missouri River to the Pacific Ocean, an allowance for each adult of 150 pounds of flour (or its equivalent in hard bread), twenty-five pounds of bacon or pork, supplemented by beef driven on the hoof; fifteen pounds of coffee and twenty-five of sugar, with a proper supply of such seasoning as salt and pepper and of auxiliaries such as saleratus or yeast powder. Butter could be taken (and also incidentally kept sweet and with little impairment of flavor) by boiling it, removing the scum and soldering up the refined product in tin cannisters.

There were other recommended travel foods, not so widely known. One of these was pemmican, a preparation which the trappers had learned from the Indians, and the emigrants from the trappers. It was buffalo meat, dried and powdered, placed in a hide bag and covered with melted grease. It kept well, was highly nutritious and when mixed with a little flour and boiled, palatable. Obviously, however, at the time of the migrations, little buffalo meat was obtainable in the settlements, and the use of beef as a substitute does not appear to have been common. Whatever pemmican the emigrants carried they must have prepared in their halts after reaching Grand Island, the beginning of the buffalo country; but it is not certain that it was extensively used among them.

There was also *penole,* which Marcy calls "cold flour" — a preparation originating in the Spanish Southwest. It was parched corn pounded fine and mixed with sugar (or molasses) and cinnamon. Combined with water and vigorously stirred, it made an economic as well as a wholesome food, for a half bushel was enough to subsist a man for thirty days. Lieutenant G. Douglas Brewerton, in his vivid narrative, " A Ride with Kit Carson," published in *Harper's Magazine* for August 1853, speaks highly of *penole* as a travel ration:

[It] is almost invaluable to the travelers in the wilderness of the far west; as it requires no fire to cook it, being prepared at a moment's warning by simply mixing it with cold water. It has the further advantage of occupying but little space in proportion to its weight; but when prepared for use, it swells so as nearly to double in quantity. A very small proportion is therefore sufficient to satisfy the cravings of hunger.

There was also *atole,* another corn product, to be cooked into a mush. But these two preparations, though in common use among the trappers and doubtless often recommended to the emigrants, seem to have been regarded by the latter as too foreign and to have been generally ignored.

It is uncertain how early dessicated vegetables came into general use. The vegetables were pressed until the juice was drawn off and then dried in an oven until the resulting lump was almost as hard as a rock. "A small piece of this," says Marcy, " about half the size of a man's hand, when boiled, swells up so as to fill a vegetable dish, and is sufficient for four men." It was regarded as an excellent anti-scorbutic, and if guarded from dampness would keep for years.

The wiser emigrants soon learned to protect their food from deterioration. They packed their bacon in strong sacks, one hundred pounds to the sack. To prevent the fat melting away under the great heat of the plains, they put it in boxes and surrounded it with bran. Flour they put in stout sacks of double canvas and sugar in sacks of India rubber. They learned also to equip themselves with the many utensils and accessories needed in traversing the long journey. Extra parts for the wagon and harness were taken, and also gutta percha or painted canvas sheets for protection against the dampness of the ground; axes, hatchets, and spades; trusty firearms, a medicine chest, large needles, awls, coarse linen thread, beeswax, and buttons. Such of the emigrants, moreover, as had become acquainted with the new-fangled fire-lighters known as matches laid in a store and incidentally put them in bottles and kept them tightly corked. Doubtless in every company there were men who looked with some contempt on all this meticulous care in preparation: but they were to learn at the end that the far-sighted and the prudent came through the arduous journey with the least loss and discomfort.

Everything arranged, and a temporary organization effected, the wagons started on their way. The first experience of the pilgrims was usually with the petulance of man and the next with the turbulence of nature. Many sorts and conditions of men had gathered at the starting points, and no sooner had they assembled than a contrariety of views and purposes began to manifest itself. Some were for this and some for that; wrangling took the place of reason, and only through a gradual realization that some kind of organization must be formed and maintained could agreements be reached. Often no more could be done by the time the wagons began to move than to agree that the first organization should be temporary and that on the north bank of the

Kansas, or at some other point four or five days toward the west, another council should be held for a more definite regulation of the march.

Hastings, who captained for most of the way the emigration of 1842, gives a convincing picture of the start in his *Oregon and California*. On many matters of fact undependable, he is here an expert witness, since he was himself given to most of the faults that he attributed to others. Ambitious and designing, he soon undermined the authority of Dr. Elijah White, the first captain, and at the end of a month succeeded him in the post and held it to the end. Most of the diarists record these wrangles and mutinies in the parties they accompanied, and it was a rare thing that any party went all the way to the end as it was originally formed.

Nature was often in a rampageous mood. Virtually all the diarists mention as a new experience the frightful thunderstorms of the prairie region. Whether or not weather conditions have changed since then cannot be said. Local pride will probably aver that the diarists somewhat overdid their descriptions of the storms, and that anyhow the heavens that hang above the prairie country have grown more kindly with the progress of settlement. But the emigrants and the pleasure travelers were certain that here they experienced storms of an unmatched violence — with deafening thunder, flooding rains and sometimes terrific winds. Parkman, the record of whose summer jaunt in 1846 is known to most readers, is particularly impressed with them. Of one of them, near Westport, he writes:

Such sharp and incessant flashes of lightning, such stunning and continuous thunder, I had never known before. The woods were completely obscured by the diagonal sheets of rain that fell with a heavy roar, and rose in spray from the ground; and the streams rose so rapidly that we could hardly ford them.

And again, a week or more later, on the St. Joseph Trail, which he had reached from Fort Leavenworth:

Toward sunset, however, the storm ceased as suddenly as it began. . . But all our hopes were delusive. Scarcely had night set in, when the tumult broke forth anew. The thunder here is not like the tame thunder of the Atlantic coast. Bursting with a terrific crash directly above our heads, it roared over the boundless waste of the prairie, seeming to roll around the whole circle of the firmament with a peculiar and awful reverberation. The lightning flashed all night, playing with its livid glare upon the neighboring trees, revealing the vast expanse of the plain, and then leaving us shut in as by a palpable wall of darkness.

Edwin Bryant, who went out in 1846, tells of more than one frightful storm. Rufus B. Sage, who went to the mountains in 1841, describes his first storm as the worst he had ever seen; but a few days later he experienced another that was still worse, and a week later a yet more terrific one. Tempestuous winds sometimes ripped the covers from the wagons, scattered the tents and filled the air with camp equipage. As in other cases, the prudent fared best. One chronicler tells of the care with which his party, seeing an approaching storm, secured their tents and wagon covers and thus escaped serious damage. Moving forward the next day, they overtook another party whose members had taken no precautions and whose camp presented the appearance of indescribable wreck.

The wild animals of the plains were always a source

of thrilling interest, and among these the buffalo easily took first rank.   The enormous herds, the danger from stampedes, the excitement of the chase, are commented upon in many pages.   At the numbers of these animals the emigrants were amazed.   Bidwell, of the 1841 emigration, wrote of them:

I have seen the plain black with them for several days' journey as far as the eye could reach.   They seemed to be coming northward continually from the distant plains to the Platte to get water, and would plunge in and swim across by thousands — so numerous were they that they changed not only the color of the water, but its taste, until it was unfit to drink; but we had to use it.[22]

And Hastings, writing of the following year, has this:

No adequate conception can be formed of the immensity of the numerous herds, which here abound.   The entire plains and prairie are densely covered, and completely blackened with them, as far as the most acute vision extends.

The danger from a stampede of these animals was a real and terrible one, which had often to be guarded against, and many are the instances recorded.   William M. Case, an emigrant of 1844, tells of such an experience along the Platte:

As the two divisions were moving along deliberately, at ox-speed, in the usual parallel columns, the drivers were startled by a low sound to the north as of distant thunder.   There was no appearance of a storm, however, in that or any other direction, and the noise grew louder and louder, and was steady and uninterrupted.   It soon became clear that there was a herd of buffaloes approaching and on the run.   Scouring anxiously the line of hills rimming the edge of the valley, the dark brown outline of the herd was at length descried, and was distinctly made out with a telescope, as buffaloes in violent motion and making directly for the train. The front of the line was perhaps half a mile long and the animals were several columns deep, and coming like a tornado. They had probably been stampeded by hunters and would now stop at nothing. The only apparent chance of safety was to drive ahead and get out of the range of the herd. The oxen were consequently urged into a run and the train itself had the appearance of a stampede. Neither were they too quick; for the flying herds of the buffaloes passed but a few yards to the rear of the last wagons, and were going at such a rate that to be struck by them would have been like the shock of rolling boulders of a ton's weight.[23]

Trappers or emigrants so threatened had little time to get out of the way. In such cases they found safety only by firing the grass and concentrating their rifle volleys on the head and flank of the charging herd until the flames and the pile of dead bodies compelled it to shift its course. There is at least one recorded instance when by such means a stampeding herd was forced to divide, leaving the party islanded in the center while the two columns thundered by.

Exceptional was the man or youth who did not eagerly join in the chase for buffalo. In the well-regulated parties the privilege was usually given only to the experienced hunters under regulations which promised the best results in killing game. But in other companies the first contact with a buffalo herd was a signal for a general sortie by every male capable of riding a horse and firing a gun. It was soon found that the untrained hunters on untrained horses could accomplish nothing. The horses would become frightened; in the presence of the buffalo they would bound, snort, and plunge, and in spite of the vigorous use of the spur keep a circumspect distance. When the herd passed they might sometimes be forced into the presence of the bodies the trained hunters had slain, but again they took fright, and in spite of rein and spur usually galloped back to the wagons. Only by repeated experience, if at all, could such horses be trained for the task.

With the trappers and the early emigrants, as well as with the Indians, the flesh of the buffalo was the main staple of food. " I relish it well," wrote Mrs. Whitman in a letter of June 27, 1836, " and it agrees with me. My health is excellent. So long as I have buffalo meat, I do not wish anything else." Bidwell adds his testimony: " There is no better beef in the world than that of the buffalo." So does Burnett. " Perhaps the flesh of no animal," he writes, " is more delicious than that of a young buffalo cow, in good order. You may eat as much as you please, and it will not oppress you." It must have been appetizing food, according to Burnett, who believed himself " not more of a gourmandizer than others on the road." On the Sweetwater Captain Gantt made him a present of some choice pieces of the meat, and Mrs. Burnett cooked him six large slices. Starting in to eat three of them, he ate all. Two hours later he had supper, when he ate until he grew ashamed, although he left the meal hungry. Then he visited Gantt in his tent and was persuaded to try some buffalo tongue. He again ate until shame stopped him, and when he went to bed he was still hungry.[24]

Not always, however, was buffalo meat obtainable. The buffalo moved constantly, and often an emigrant party missed them for much of the way. The earlier emigrants, who made little provision for the journey, were often forced, when supplies failed, to make use of anything that would sustain life. Horses, mules, and oxen were sacrificed, even at the risk of the safety of the expedition. Along the Snake River salmon could sometimes be obtained from the Indians, and there were other food commodities obtainable from the savages somewhat less choice. Bidwell tells the story of a kind of meal sold by the California Indians to Frémont's men in 1845. " It was rich, spicy and pleasant to the taste," he writes; and the demand grew until the Indians became careless in its manufacture, and the consumers began to discover in it the legs, wings and heads of grasshoppers. It was simply grasshopper meal.[25] Of his own experience on the journey of 1841 he writes:

We saw many Indians on the Humboldt, especially toward the Sink. There were many tule marshes. The tule is a rush, large, but here not very tall. It was generally completely covered with honeydew, and this in turn was wholly covered with a pediculous-looking insect which fed upon it. The Indians gathered quantities of the honey and pressed it into balls about the size of one's fist, having the appearance of wet bran. At first we greatly relished this Indian food, but when we saw what it was made of — that the insects pressed into the mass were the main ingredient — we lost our appetites and bought no more of it.

Horseflesh was a staple, and continued to be used by some of the settlers even after they had made their homes. The Whitmans served it regularly at their Waiilatpu home for nearly five years. " I do not prefer it to other meat," wrote Mrs. Whitman, " but can eat it very well when we have nothing else." In 1838 they received a part of the meat of the first cow beefed east of the Cascades. The creature was old, toothless, quite useless to its owner (the factor at Fort Walla Walla) and was accordingly made into meat. Not until October 1841 was horse-meat banished from the Whitman table.[26]

In time of privation men learned to use substitutes for most of the things they had deemed indispensable. Captain Marcy and his men, on their terrible journey from Fort Bridger across the Colorado mountains to Fort Massachusetts, in the winter of 1857–58, ran out of tobacco, coffee, and salt. For tobacco they used the inner bark of the red willow, known generally as *kinnickinick*. It was not so bad, considering the fact that most Indians and some whites invariably used it, even in prosperous times, to mix with their tobacco in the compound known to Parkman as *shongsasha*. But the dried leaves of the horse mint must have proved a poor substitute for coffee, and hardly less so the salt-and-pepper substitute. "By burning the outside of our mule steaks," writes Marcy, "and sprinkling a little gunpowder upon them it did not require a very extensive stretch of the imagination to fancy the presence of both salt and pepper."[27]

The old saying of trapper days that there was "no law west of Leavenworth" had no application to these moving communities. They had courts and judges and officers to execute verdicts. Infractions of the common welfare were punished, and from the sentence the culprit had no appeal. Many of the journals relate incidents of punishment for offenses. The venerable Ezra Meeker, in his *Kate Mulhall,* which, though mainly

reminiscence, is naively labelled fiction, tells of the fate
that overtook an offender who must have been the
" champion mean man " of the emigration of 1852. He
owned a team and wagon, and had joined with a neighboring family of husband, wife, and three small children
for the journey. Somewhere on the Platte, while traveling apart from the wagon train, this man became
abusive and then pitched out all the family's personal belongings and drove ahead with the common stock of
provisions. The bewildered and helpless family were
found near the roadside a few hours afterward by other
emigrants, some of whom immediately started in pursuit.
The culprit, traveling ahead by night, was overtaken by
three armed men who " soon convinced him that resistance was useless and submission to arrest the only safe
course."

The " unwritten law " of the plains [says Meeker] was a
tacit consent that all grievances, misdemeanors or accusations
of crime must be laid before a jury of elderly men; and no one
should take the law into his own hands — in a word, no mob
violence. Squire Mulhall soon succeeded in bringing together
several of the older pioneers, who resolved to take immediate
action; swift and adequate justice was administered, and the
incident was almost immediately closed. This code of action
prevailed all along the line; no one was punished without a
hearing, but there were no delays on technicalities, or any
appeals.[28]

Applegate, in his " A Day with the Cow Column in
1843," also tells of the work of such a court:

Today an extra session of the council is being held, to settle
a dispute that does not admit of delay, between a proprietor
and a young man who has undertaken to do a man's service

on the journey for bed and board. Many such engagements exist, and much interest is taken in the manner in which this high court, from which there is no appeal, will define the rights of each party in such engagements. The council was a high court in the most exalted sense. It was a senate composed of the ablest and most respected fathers of the emigration. It exercised both legislative and judicial powers, and its laws and decisions proved it equal and worthy of the high trust reposed in it. Its sessions were usually held on days when the caravan was not moving. It first took the state of the little commonwealth into consideration; revised or repealed rules defective or obsolete, and enacted such others as the exigencies seemed to require. The common weal being cared for, it next resolved itself into a court to hear and settle private disputes and grievances. The offender and the aggrieved appeared before it; witnesses were examined, and the parties were heard by themselves and sometimes by counsel. The judges being thus made fully acquainted with the case, and being in no way influenced or cramped by technicalities, decided all cases according to their merits. There was but little use for lawyers before this court, for no plea was entertained which was calculated to hinder or defeat the ends of justice. Many of these judges have since won honors in higher spheres. They have aided to establish on the broad basis of right and universal liberty two pillars of our great Republic in the Occident. Some of the young men who appeared before them as advocates have themselves sat upon the highest judicial tribunals, commanded armies, been governors of states and taken high position in the senate of the nation.

The day's routine of camping, marching, and guarding was a heritage from the trapping companies, expanded to meet new conditions. What had then been found serviceable was handed on by guides like Fitzpatrick and Gantt to the emigrants. Applegate, in a passage given in a previous chapter, has pictured this routine as it was followed in 1843. Mrs. Whitman, writing in 1836, gives briefly a similar picture:

In the morning as soon as the day breaks the first that we hear is the words, " Arise, Arise! " Then the mules set up such a noise as you never heard, which puts the whole camp in motion. We encamp in a large ring, baggage and men, tents and wagons on the outside, and all the animals, except the cows, which are fastened to pickets, within the circle. This arrangement is to accommodate the guard, who stand regularly every night and day, also when we are in motion, to protect our animals from the approach of Indians, who would steal them. As I said, the mules' noise brings every man on his feet to loose them and turn them out to feed. . . While the horses are feeding, we get breakfast in a hurry and eat it. By this time the words, " Catch up! Catch up! " ring through the camp for moving. We are ready to start usually at six, travel till eleven, encamp, rest and feed, start again about two, travel until six or before, if we come to a good tavern [i.e., any spot under the skies where wood, water, and grass were obtainable], then encamp for the night.[29]

Every traveling party with carts or wagons invariably, on arriving at camp, formed a corral. Even on the march, at the first sign of an Indian menace, the corral would be hurriedly made. The wagons were parked in a circle (occasionally a square) and often chained to one another. Inside this haven men, women, and children were secure. Such a formation, guarded by even fifty well-armed men, was proof against assault by almost any number of Indians likely to be met. For the savage, though willing enough to fight and plunder, had no stomach for attacking a fortified position. It has been well said of him that though brave he did not like to get hurt. He wanted all the odds of position,

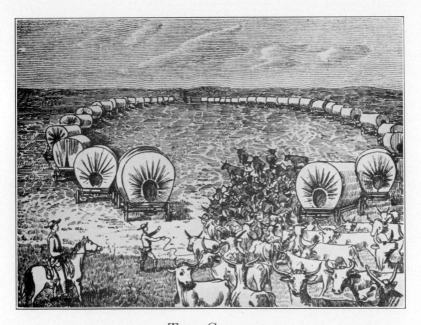

THE CORRAL

From T. S. Kenderdine's "A California Tramp" (1888)

EMIGRANT TRAIN CROSSING NEBRASKA

*From Henry Howe's "Historical Collections
of the Great West"* (1859)

numbers, and whatever else there might be. Stragglers might be cut off, plundered, beaten or killed; and horses, mules, and cattle stampeded or craftily stolen, but every person or thing circled by the corral was safe. To the invariable observance of this precaution was largely due the small proportion of losses borne by the pilgrims from savage attacks during the emigration era.

The trials and discomforts of the journey fell hardest on the women. Yet the testimony of all the diarists is that most of them bore their part heroically, as befitted pioneers. Clyman, a poor speller and grammarian but a good reporter, in camp with Ford's party of 1844 on the Wakarusa, tells of " me[n] women and children dripping in mud and water over Shoe mouth deep " and adds:

I Thought I never saw more determined resolution even amongst men than most of the female part of our company exhibited.

And a few days later, near the Kansas crossing, he writes:

. . . and here let me say there was one young Lady which showed herself worthy of the bravest undaunted poieneer of [the] west for after having kneaded her dough she watched and nursed the fire and held an umblella over the fire and her skillit with the greatest composure for near 2 hours and baked bread enough to give us a verry plentifull supper. . .

The housewife's art was practised under many and depressing difficulties. In the rainy belt, between Independence and the Platte, cooking had often to be suspended entirely. Water was everywhere; and blessed was that family whose thoughtful head had provided a

wagon cover of double thickness and of specially prepared canvas. Otherwise the frail fabric let in the rain,
to the thorough drenching of every person and thing
in the wagon bed. Under such circumstances to keep her
youthful charges dry was a duty that taxed all the re-
sources of the careful mother. To keep them clean and
garbed in freshly laundered clothes was a harder task.
During the rainy spells there could be little laundering
and no drying, and when the higher and more arid altitudes were reached, the whirling dust clouds often deposited more dirt on the garments hung up to be sunned
than had just been washed from them. The earlier
parties made small provision for washing clothes. Mrs.
Whitman, at Fort Boisé, six months out from her New
York home, tells of her third washing day:

> Last night I put my clothes in water, and this morning fin-
> ished washing before breakfast; this is the third time I have
> washed since I left home, once at Fort William [on the Laramie]
> and once at Rendezvous [on the Green].

The two trapper parties with which she traveled may
be presumed not to have concerned themselves overmuch
with the matter of clean clothes. The emigrant parties
of a later time, however, were more considerate, and
clothes-washing day was frequently, if not regularly,
observed.

There was courting on the way, and many were the
unions formed from acquaintanceships here first made.
Young John Minto, penniless but strong and active
and with a mind and heart open for adventure and romance, started for Oregon in the spring of 1844. He
crossed the Missouri at Capler's ferry, where Gilliam's

company was preparing for the start, and among the tents and wagons sought a job. He heard of a thrifty farmer named Wilson Morrison, on the east side of the river, who was selling out to make the journey and might need a lad. Recrossing the river, he found Morrison, and on the promise of bed, board, and transportation engaged to tend stock and make himself generally useful. He had just seated himself to begin a petty task when something caused him to look up, and he saw a young girl coming from the house. Instantly he thought: " There, Johnny Minto, there goes your wife that is to be." She was, as he soon learned, his employer's younger daughter. For some reason he seems to have resolved not to reveal his secret until the journey was done. But the keen-eyed and jolly-hearted mother must soon have divined it. One day, in camp on the prairie, she offered him, holding it carefully by the stem, a sprig of foliage, telling him that if ever he had treated badly any girl back home it would betray his conduct by wilting. The gulled youth, eager for such a test, grasped at the teasing bait; it was a sprig of the sensitive plant, and of course the leaves shrivelled; and he stood there, abashed and speechless, until the rippling laughter of the mother assured him that all had been done in a spirit of play. It is pleasant to record that in this case the course of true love ran with perfect smoothness and that the girl became his bride.[30]

There were marriages (but no divorces) on the journey. Even the first emigrant party of sixty-nine persons had two. There were births also, and many a Pacific genealogy contains the name of a " covered-wagon baby." From the incident given by Applegate

one learns that more than one expectant mother started
with the emigration of 1843:

But a little incident [he writes] breaks the monotony of the
march. An emigrant's wife, whose state of health has caused
Doctor Whitman to travel near the wagon for the day, is now
taken with violent illness. The Doctor has had the wagon
driven out of line, a tent pitched and a fire kindled. . . There
are anxious watchers for the absent wagon, for there are many
matrons who may be afflicted like its inmate before the journey
is over; and they fear the strange and startling practice of this
Oregon doctor will be dangerous. But as the sun goes down
the absent wagon rolls into camp, the bright speaking face
and cheery look of the doctor, who rides in advance, declare
without words that all is well, and both mother and child are
comfortable.[31]

Of deaths there were many thousands. The cholera
years of 1849, 1850, and 1852 took a frightful toll. Exceptional circumstances, such as the attempt to break
new trails when near the end of the journey, often resulted in tragedy. The Oregon-bound party of 1845
led by Stephen Meek to the headwaters of the Malheur;
the Donner party of 1846; the Oregon party of the same
year by the new Applegate trail, as well as many parties
in later years, suffered many losses.

But on the main Trail, apart from the epidemic years,
the record of deaths is astonishingly small. The stupid
practice of leaving loaded and cocked rifles in the wagons
sometimes resulted in mortal accidents, but relatively
few deaths came from natural causes. Despite all the
discomforts of the journey, it was to many a reinvigor-
ating experience. Probably most of those who undertook it were of sound stock, more or less inured to hard-

ship. But there were also invalids and semi-invalids among them. The change of scene and the pure, dry air of the higher altitudes wrought marvelous changes in the condition of the ailing and brought many of them to journey's end restored to sound health.

With sturdy, mature men the journey served only to toughen the fibers. With boys and young men it was an unending delight. Wherever youth speaks in the authentic records of the diaries and reminiscences it expresses itself in exuberant happiness. The strange scenes of a new world, the spice of danger, and the sense of freedom brought forth a bubbling exhilaration of spirits. When, in addition, the youth owned a rifle and a pony and was permitted to join in the chase, his joy was seraphic. Says Minto:

I once was placed near two young men during [religious] exercises one Sunday, when the late Rev. E. E. Parrish prayed God " to remove the wild beasts and savage men from our pathway." One of the boys whispered to his comrade, he " hoped God would not hear all that prayer," for he was " bound to kill a buffalo, and he would like to see a grizzly bear."

With Minto a thrilling sport was to help in " swimming the cattle." When the streams were normal it was mere pastime, but at high floods there was all the danger craved by passionate and confident youth. At the Big Blue the emigrants found a raging torrent, with a number of large whirlpools. They must, nevertheless, cross and pursue their way. The practice was first to determine the proper landing place on the opposite bank and then to start four or five guides, each on the downstream side of an ox, to lead the way. With one hand the guide held on to the withers of his charge and with the other cuffed the animal into keeping a straight line despite the force of the current.

Minto and his ox plunged in, but before the youth could get to the beast's head, a whirlpool sucked them both under. No sooner did the boy come to the surface than he was swept away to the next whirlpool and again carried down. Under the water he felt something touch his side, and reaching for it found it to be the back of his ox. Holding on as he came to the surface, he saw that the animal was now successfully breasting the current, and after being thrice given up for lost he got safely to shore.

Bidwell, still in spirit a boy, though he had just passed his twenty-second birthday, tells how the urge of adventure prompted him and a comrade named James John to a lark of foolhardy recklessness. On a day of intense heat the wagon train was passing through a savage wilderness down the Bear River toward Great Salt Lake. The boys, somewhat apart from the train, saw snow on a distant mountain, and by a common impulse, indifferent to danger and inconsiderate of the paralyzing effect their absence would have upon their companions, resolved to reach it. He writes:

Without losing time to get our guns or coats or to give notice at the camp, we started direct for the snow, with the impression that we could go and return by sundown. But there intervened a range of low mountains, a certain peak of which seemed almost to touch the snow. Both of us were fleet of foot and made haste, but we only gained the summit of the peak about sundown. The distance must have been twelve or fifteen miles. A valley intervened and the snow lay on a higher mountain beyond. I proposed to camp. But Jimmy gave me a disdainful look, as much as to say, " You are afraid to go," and quickened his gait into a run down the mountain toward the snow. I called to him to stop, but he would not even look back. A firm resolve seized me — to overtake him, but not again to ask him to return. We crossed the valley in the night, saw many Indian campfires, and gained a sharp ridge leading up to the snow. This was first brushy and then rough and rocky. The brush had no paths except those made by wild animals; the rocks were sharp, and soon cut through our moccasins and made our feet bleed. But up and up we went until long after midnight, and until a cloud covered the mountain. We were above the timber line, excepting a few stunted fir trees, under one of which we crawled to wait for day, for it was too dark to see.

Day soon dawned, but we were almost frozen. Our fir-tree nest had been the lair of grizzly bears that had wallowed there and shed quantities of shaggy hair. The snow was still beyond, and we had lost both sight and direction. But in an hour or two we reached it. It was nearly as hard as ice. Filling a large handkerchief, without taking time to admire the scenery, we started toward the camp by a new route, for our feet were too sore to go by way of the rocky ridge by which we had come. But the new way led into trouble. There were thickets so dense as to exclude the sun, and roaring little streams in deep, dark chasms; we had to crawl through paths which looked untrodden except by grizzlies; in one place a large bear had passed evidently only a few minutes before, crossing the deep gorge, plunging through the wild, dashing water, and wetting the steep bank as he went up. We carried our drawn butcher knives in our hands, for they were our only weapons. At last we emerged into the valley. Apparently numerous Indians had left that very morning, as shown by the tracks of lodge-poles drawn on the ground. Making haste, we soon gained the hills, and at about 2 p. m. sighted our wagons, already two or three miles on the march. When our friends saw us they stopped, and all who could ran to welcome us. They had given us up for lost, supposing that we had been killed by the hostile Blackfeet, who, as Captain Fitzpatrick had warned us, sometimes roamed through that region. The company had barricaded the camp at night as best they could, and every man had spent a sleepless night on guard. Next morning they passed several hours in scouring the country. Their first questions were: " Where have you been? " " Where have you been? " I was able to answer triumphantly, " We have been up to the snow! " and to demonstrate the fact by showing all the snow I had left, which was now reduced to a ball about the size of my fist.[32]

Others of a maturer age sometimes found in the journey much of the delight experienced by adventurous youth. Among these was Hugh Cosgrove, the head of a family, who journeyed to Oregon in 1847. Fortune may have smiled upon him all the way across, for if he experienced discomforts he did not in after years remember them. He was a prudent and far-sighted man, who made every possible provision for the journey. His wagons were strong and light, his wagon covers the best obtainable, his oxen young and tough, his stock of provisions was ample for every probable emergency. And so, forty-three years afterward, he could look upon the journey as a glorious adventure:

He now recalls the journey [writes H. S. Lyman] that followed as one of the pleasantest incidents of his life. It was a long picnic, the changing scenes of the journey, the animals of the prairie, the Indians, the traders and trappers of the mountain country; the progress of the season, which was exceptionally mild, just about sufficed to keep up the interest, and formed a sort of mental culture that the world has rarely offered. Almost all migration has been carried on in circumstances of danger and distress, but this was, although daring in the extreme, a summer jaunt.[33]

CHAPTER VII

WHERE THE TRAIL RAN

AS the years pass, a keener interest attaches to the determination of the exact line of the Trail. There is a growing sense of the historic importance of this highway; associations are formed to set up markers along its course; towns and cities proclaim with pride their location on or near it; and from time to time Congress is pestered to designate as a part of the Oregon Trail some stretch of roadway which may or may not deserve to carry the name.

More than twenty-five years ago Hiram M. Chittenden, in *The American Fur Trade of the Far West,* roughly traced the Trail. Within the last few years the work has been done in minute detail by Professor Archer Butler Hulbert in four volumes of the series known as the *Crown Collection of Maps.* Among students of the subject there are, however, inevitable disagreements as to particulars. The testimony upon which any labor of this kind is mainly based — that of the diarists who traveled the Trail — is often vague or conflicting and therefore subject to various interpretations. Moreover, the Trail underwent a number of modifications. Though some of them were but temporary, others marked a definite shift of the line; while at the east it developed new starting points and at the west many new radials to the goal. The tracing here given, though it includes mention of all the important detours, feeders, and terminal lines, is of the original Trail, with Independence as the starting point and Fort Walla Walla as the end.

Leaving Independence, the wagons followed the Santa Fé Trail. They passed through Westport, eight miles out, and about a mile farther crossed the state boundary into the Indian Country. Close by was the Shawnee Mission, established near the present Turner, by the Rev. Thomas Johnson, a Methodist, in 1830, and moved to this location in 1838. Here, though it continued to be known as the Shawnee Mission, it took the formal name of the Shawnee Indian Manual Labor School. Boys were taught to become farmers, blacksmiths, brickmasons, and carpenters and girls to become spinners, weavers, cooks, and seamstresses. The Shawnees, who in their earlier home had been one of the bravest, the best disciplined and the most resolute of the tribes that opposed the white man's invasion of the West, had been humbled, and in their new home readily accepted the white man's way. Intelligent, industrious and self-reliant, they soon transformed the virgin prairie into a region of cultivated farms that produced rich harvests. One who wants to know the story of this episode will find it vividly presented in the pamphlet, *The Old Shawnee Mission* (1928), written for the Shawnee Mission Memorial Foundation by Mrs. Edith Connelley Ross.

The Indian Country was unsettled. In the early forties, except for an agency building with the Kaws and another with the Potawatomies on the Kansas, there

MAIN BUILDING OF THE SHAWNEE MISSION, NEAR WESTPORT, MISSOURI

From a photograph supplied by William E. Connelley

was not a white habitation from the Shawnee Mission to
Fort Laramie. The wagons passed the site of Olathe,
and at a distance of thirty-three miles from Independence came to Elm Grove (also known as Round Grove
or Caravan Grove), a favorite camping place. Doubtless it once had some trees. Wislizenus, in 1839, said
that there then remained but " a venerable elm tree that
must have seen many ages "; and this, with another
which he must have overlooked, was cut down for fuel by
the emigrants of 1843.

Over the site of Gardner the wagons rolled, and a few
miles farther on — forty-one miles from Independence
— they came to the junction of the Oregon and Santa
Fé Trails and the military road running north to Fort
Leavenworth. Here, in the early days, some well-
disposed person had set up a sign with the words, " Road
to Oregon." " Surely," says Chittenden, " so unostentatious a sign never before nor since announced so long
a journey."

Turning northwestward they forded Captain's Creek,
then went westward across the Little Wakarusa, till
they reached the present Sibleyville, when another
northward turn brought them to the Wakarusa, fifty-
three miles on their journey. Northwestward again,
they passed south of the site of Lawrence. The low rich
bottoms of the Wakarusa and the high, rolling prairie of
the present Douglas County are often mentioned in the
journals. Paralleling the Kansas River, they went on
to Big Springs, near the boundary between Douglas
and Shawnee Counties, where the Trail divided. The
emigrants who meant to take an upper ford of the Kansas here turned to the left and by a wide curve reached

the river at the point where later was founded a village called Uniontown, which long ago disappeared. The others kept on westward for a time, and then turning toward the river reached it at the site of Topeka.

The location of the main ford of the Kansas is disputed. Chittenden places it at Topeka, and so also, though giving the alternative crossing of Uniontown, does Professor Hulbert. Mr. William E. Connelley, whose word on any matter of frontier history no one will lightly dispute, puts it at Uniontown. The Kansas had, in fact, many crossing places. Bonneville's party, as well as that of Sublette, Campbell and Wyeth, in 1832, made the passage near the present Williamstown, a few miles west of Lawrence. The journals and reminiscences of the trappers and emigrants indicate that though many thousands crossed at Topeka, other thousands, especially when the river was high, kept moving up its south bank until they found what they deemed a safer ford. The upper fords would seem to have been more generally used in the earlier days; but after 1844, when a ferry was established at the Topeka site by two half-breeds named Papin, this lower crossing seems to have become the favored one. The boats were crude, and in times of high water the overflow of the bottom land rendered approach to them difficult, while the raging current made the crossing hazardous. Not infrequently the passage of the river was attended with disaster.

Crossing at Topeka — that is, at Pappan's Ferry, as the name was usually spelled — the emigrants would halt and gather for a talk. They were eighty-one miles on the way, and they had much to consider before going farther. The north bank of the Kansas was usually, as has been said, a resting and reorganizing place. By this time there would always be an accumulation of grievances and resentments that needed to be allayed. New regulations would be made, new officers elected or old ones confirmed in their posts. Here, as a rule, the emigrants made their first acquaintance with the Kansas or Kaw Indians. Nearly all the diarists set down highly unfavorable opinions of these savages. Clyman, in 1844, speaks of them as " a misrable poor dirty Lazy Looking Tribe and disgusting in the extreme." They were, he said, too lazy to work and too cowardly to hunt buffalo for fear their enemies might attack them. Sneak thieves and beggars, they were generally called, and Sage has given a picture of one of their chiefs importunately begging for whiskey.

With ranks re-formed and all the pressing problems at least temporarily solved, the trains would move forward westwardly along the river. A few miles from the crossing, near the present Mencken, a trail came in from Fort Leavenworth, which in time became a section of the military road to Fort Riley. On went the wagons through the present Rossville, where they were joined by those that had crossed at Uniontown; and then to St. Mary's, where in 1847 the Catholics established a mission. Here the Trail left the river, and running northwestwardly reached the Little (or Red) Vermillion, 119 miles from Independence, at the present Louisville, whence in later times, after Fort Riley was built, the Leavenworth trail ran off to the southwest.

Another forty-one miles brought the emigrants to the Big (or Black) Vermillion at the present Bigelow.

Here was a well-timbered valley, and some one was always sure to tell them that it was the last place in which to lay in a stock of hickory for axe-handles; but Palmer, of the 1845 emigration, says that there were two other supply places farther along.

As the Trail approached the crossing of the Big Blue it divided into many branches. Chittenden says that the main ford was near the mouth of the Little Blue, but the journals indicate that it was farther north, in the neighborhood of the present Marysville, 174 miles from the start. Here, in 1851, three years before the country was opened, a settlement was started which became, in the stage-coach era, a place of importance. Near this ford came in the main trail from Fort Leavenworth and St. Joseph (and in later years Atchison). The Big Blue crossing was always a resting place for a day or two. Sometimes there were fresh dissensions to be healed, always there were repairs to be made, and generally, there were stocks of clothing to be laundered.

All travel so far had been in the prairie region, " the fairest country in America," as Mr. Connelley has called it.[34] Many of the journals dwell upon its charm. Of one expanse of it Bryant, in 1846, wrote in rapture:

As we approached what is called the Blue Prairie, the road became much drier and less difficult. The vast prairie itself soon opened before us in all its grandeur and beauty. I had never before beheld extensive scenery of this kind. The many descriptions of the prairies of the west had forestalled in some measure the first impressions produced by the magnificent landscape that lay spread out before me as far as the eye could reach, bounded alone by the blue wall of the sky. No description, however, which I have read of these scenes, or which can be written, can convey more than a faint impression to the imagination of their effects upon the eye. The view of the illimitable succession of green undulations and flowery slopes, of every gentle and graceful configuration, stretching away and away, until they fade from the sight in the dim distance, creates a wild and scarcely controllable ecstasy of admiration. I felt, I doubt not, some of the emotions natural to the aboriginal inhabitants of these boundless and picturesque plains, when roving with unrestrained freedom over them; and careless alike of the past and the future, luxuriating in the blooming wilderness of sweets which the Great Spirit had created for their enjoyment, and placed at their disposal.

The trail entered Nebraska at the extreme southwestern corner of Gage County, following, at some distance, the general course of the Little Blue. It passed north of Fairbury, in Jefferson County, and north of Hebron, in Thayer County — a few miles beyond reaching the banks of the river, to which it kept close. It passed Oak, in Nuckolls County, Springranch in Clay County, and between Muriel and Leroy, in Adams County. The valley of the Little Blue was the favorite range of the Pawnees, who, if they happened to be near, seldom failed to exact toll of the passing trains. "Vicious savages and skilful and daring thieves," says one chronicler. The unlucky traveler who fell into their hands was always plundered, and sometimes beaten or killed.

In the neighborhood of Leroy the Trail left the Little Blue, and crossing the low sand dunes to the north ran to the Platte, 316 miles from Independence. "About twenty miles above the head of Grand Island," say Chittenden and others of this point of intersection, but the place was anywhere the emigrants chose. Bryant's party reached the river eight miles below the head of Grand Island, or nearly thirty miles to the east. Here came in another feeder from the east — the Old Fort Kearney (or Nebraska City) road, which from the Missouri River ran northwestward to the Platte near the present Linwood, and then followed its south bank. Across the Platte, though not joining the Oregon Trail until Fort Laramie was reached, was an old route that with the year 1847 became known as the Mormon Trail. On the south side, near the head of Grand Island, in April 1848 a military post was established, the first of its kind along the Trail. Shortly afterward it became the new Fort Kearney, its misspelled name given in honor of the famous General Stephen Watts Kearny, who died on October 31 of that year.

The Platte was from early days the subject of praise because of its beauty in certain sections, and of derisive jests because of its imputed worthlessness. De Smet, who quotes Irving's statement that it was " the most magnificent and most useless of rivers," gives the other side:

Abstraction made of its defects, nothing can be more pleasing than the perspective which it presents to the eye. . . [Its] islands . . have the appearance of a labyrinth of groves floating on the waters. Their extraordinary position gives an air of youth and beauty to the whole scene. If to this be added the undulations of the river, the waving of the verdure, the alternations of light and shade, the succession of these islands varying in form and beauty, and the purity of the atmosphere, some idea may be formed of the pleasing sensations which the traveler experiences on beholding a scene that seems to have started into existence fresh from the hands of the creator.

The travelers found it in dry seasons a mere trickle of water among sandy shoals, and in rainy spells a roar-

ing current of muddy liquid. It abounded in quick-
sands, and therefore was difficult to ford. The trappers,
though often attempting to use it in bringing their furs
to market, found it unnavigable, even for light-draft
flatboats or for bullboats. Root, in *The Overland Stage,*
repeats the story of the stage-drivers that it never over-
flowed, since its flood waters carried so much mud that
it made new banks as it rose. In the Kansas constitu-
tional convention, held at Wyandotte in July, 1859, a
delegate asserted that it could not be forded since it had
a quicksand bed, that it could not be bridged because one
could not find a bottom for piers, and that it could not
be ferried for want of water.

Along the south bank of this river of paradoxes the
wagons headed westward. Here the prairie ceased, and
the plains began. Between the upper reaches of the
Little Blue and the Platte the timber had gradually
thinned out until nothing was found but a few cotton-
woods and willows. Though Grand Island was wooded,
the banks of the Platte farther westward were usually
bare.

These immense plains [writes Sage of the years 1841–44]
are generally clad with a short, curly grass, (the buffalo
grass,) very fine and nutritious, and well adapted to the sustenance of the countless herds of buffalo and other wild animals
that feed upon it. Their soil is generally of a thin vegetable
mould, upon a substratum of indurated sand and gravel.

In many places it is quite sterile, producing little other than
sand-burrs and a specimen of thin, coarse grass, that sadly
fail to conceal its forbidding surface; in others, it is but little
better than a desert waste of sand-hills, or white sun-baked
clay, so hard and impervious that neither herb nor grass can
take root to grow upon it; and in others, it presents a light

superfice, both rich and productive, beclad with all that can beautify and adorn a wilderness of verdure.

The treeless, monotonous scenery, the increasing altitude (to which many could only slowly accustom themselves) and the heat told heavily upon the spirits of the emigrants and brought on fits of despondency. But it was the buffalo country, and the hunters, especially in the earlier days, kept the larders full. Occasionally a willow-grown island provided wood, but usually the fuel was buffalo chips, which at every camping place the men would gather in sacks and bring in to the campfires.

A hundred miles beyond Fort Kearney they came to Cottonwood Springs, near the spot where Fort McPherson was built in 1863, and a few miles beyond to the forks of the Platte. The earlier fords on the South Platte were at various places. Palmer's party, in 1845, crossed about five or six miles above the forks, and Bryant's party, in 1846, thirty-four miles above. What came to be known as the Lower California Crossing is a few miles west of Brule, Keith County, about sixty-three miles from the forks. Thirty-five miles farther on, and just west of the mouth of Lodge Pole Creek, was the Upper California Crossing, increasingly used in the later years. From the lower crossing the trains reached the North Platte opposite the present town of Cormick, at Ash Hollow. The name was derived from a few scattering ash trees in the dry ravine, and it was made memorable by being given to the battle fought between Harney's men and the Brulé Sioux, some miles to the north, in 1855. In this section dust and sand covered everything, says Bryant, and the general aspect was that of aridity and desolation. But as the wagons dragged along on the tedious journey the face of the country began to change; and in the distance, where the Platte cuts through the Highlands into the plains, loomed that strange conformation of landscape about which nearly all of the diarists have something to say. There were Court House Rock, Chimney Rock, and Scott's Bluffs. The tall spire of Chimney Rock, which could be seen forty miles away, is often described. Some of the travelers estimated it to be three hundred feet high. To Palmer, the matter-of-fact agriculturist, it had the " unpoetical appearance of a haystack with a pole running far above its top." Court House Rock also brought out many tributes. To Bryant it appeared from three hundred to five hundred feet high and about a mile in circumference:

Its walls so nearly resemble masonry, and its shape an architectural design, that if seen in an inhabited country, it would be supposed some collossal edifice, deserted and partially in ruins.

Sir Richard Burton, who saw it fourteen years later, refused, however, to be impressed. Under date of August 13, 1860, he writes that it " resembled anything more than a court house," and that it really looked like an irregular pyramid. To Chimney Rock, though its spire had lost by erosion much of its height, he felt more kindly disposed. Scott's Bluffs, which was the Court House Rock on a grander scale, was almost invariably mentioned. Frémont thought that Chimney Rock, consisting of " marl and earthy limestone," was rapidly eroding and would lose much of its height. Indeed, most of the diarists predicted the disintegration of these nat-

ural monuments. But the photographs taken in November 1904, and published in J. Sterling Morton's
Illustrated History of Nebraska, show them much as
they must have appeared to the emigrants; and a recent
letter to the author says that it is doubtful that in the
twenty-four years following they have suffered any no-
ticeable change.[35]

Court House Rock is near the present city of Bridge-
port. Here the trail from the Upper California Crossing, by what was known as the Ridge Route, rejoined
the parent trail. Some ten or twelve miles on is Chimney Rock, twenty miles farther the present town of
Gering, and just beyond are Scott's Bluffs, now one of
the national monuments. From Broadwater, in Mor-
rill County, Nebraska, to beyond Fort Laramie, the
face of the country has undergone a great transformation, and where all was drouth and desolation are now
prosperous farms and thriving villages. Irrigation from
waters stored by the Pathfinder Dam, at the mouth
of the Sweetwater, now serves a region on both sides
of the North Platte approximately one hundred
miles long and at its greatest breadth twenty-five miles
wide.

Keeping on from Gering, the emigrants passed the
mouth of Horse Creek (630 miles), where in 1851 was
held the greatest Indian council in the history of the
West. Thirty miles farther they came to a small trading post, known as Fort Bernard, and seven miles
farther, after fording Laramie River, they came to Fort
Laramie (667 miles), where they halted for a rest.
Here the Mormon Trail united with the Oregon Trail;
and from here, first traveled about 1863, ran northwest-

CHIMNEY ROCK

*From Frederick Piercy's "Route from Liverpool
to Great Salt Lake Valley" (1855)*

DISTANT VIEW OF DEVIL'S GATE

Drawn by Major Osborne Cross (1849)

ward another noted highway, the Bozeman Trail, or Montana Road.

With good luck and a resolute captain to keep the trains moving to the best advantage, the journey from Independence to Fort Laramie might be made in forty days. Lee and Frost, in their *Ten Years in Oregon* (1844), estimate a time of thirty-one days of actual travel at twenty miles a day; but the estimate understates the distance and overstates the rate of travel. Few trains, if any, made so good an average for any considerable distance. Ford's company of 1844, compelled repeatedly to halt because of the continual rains, soggy grounds and flooded streams, used up seventy-eight days on the journey. Between Grand Island and Fort Laramie some of the trains might be delayed by occasional brushes with the Indians, for bands of Oglala and Brulé Sioux, Cheyennes and Arapahos crossed and recrossed the Trail. In the main, however, until the sixties, the stealing of stock and the occasional plundering of a straggler or of a small train marked the limit of savage depredations on this part of the Trail.

The original post at this point, as has already been noted, was built in June 1834, by Robert Campbell. In honor of his partner, William L. Sublette, he named it Fort William. A year later it was sold to Fitzpatrick, Milton G. Sublette, and Bridger; but as these men had reached an understanding with their powerful rival, the American Fur Company, it thus became virtually a company post, and in the following year (1836) the transfer was formally made. It was afterward, in honor of John B. Sarpy, renamed Fort John. To the trappers, missionaries, and travelers, however, it came to be known as Fort Laramie. Mrs. Whitman, in 1836, uses the name once, though in two other instances calling the post Fort William. Just when, if ever, the company accepted the name for the original structure cannot be said.

Fort William was erected on the east (north) bank of the Laramie, about three-quarters of a mile from the junction with the Platte. Later (possibly in 1841), the company built another and larger fort on the same side of the river, about a mile upstream, and thereupon abandoned, leased or sold the first building. It was the new post that became the famous Fort Laramie, so named by the owners. Possibly its proper name for a time was Fort John, but the question cannot at present be settled. The comments of the diarists on these two forts, their names, appearance, construction, and even location, are amazingly contradictory. The presence nearby of two posts on the Platte — Fort Platte above, and Fort Bernard below, the mouth of the Laramie — adds to the confusion. Both Chittenden and Thwaites sought, with no great success, to unravel the tangle, and doubtless others have since essayed the task. Though Palmer, in a note probably written in the winter of 1846–47, says that Fort John had been demolished, the Mormon diarists of 1847 still use the name and in such a way as to leave in doubt which fort they mean.

The real Fort Laramie was bought by the Government on June 26, 1849, after having been occupied by a garrison a month or so earlier during the negotiations. It continued as a military post until 1890, when it was abandoned. No other fort west of the Mississippi has such a background of stirring and colorful history.

Leaving Fort Laramie, the caravans paralleled, though often at several miles' distance, the arc-like course of the Platte. At thirteen miles they reached Big Spring (called also Warm Spring, because its water was not icy cold), and passing the present Wendover came to the noted camp on Horseshoe Creek, where there was plenty of timber and usually good pasturage. This is the foothill country, and the going was rough; the hills were steep, and the ground was covered with large stones and boulders. But the scenery was beautiful, the sky usually clear, the sunshine warm; and many of the diarists record their impressions of delight. Timber was more plentiful, but grass grew scarcer as they proceeded. From the camp at Horseshoe Creek, south of the present Glendo, a route ran to the river, traveling the Lower Platte Canyon for some eight miles and rejoining the main route in the vicinity of La Bonte. The emigrants crossed La Bonte Creek (733 miles) and Wagon Hound Creek (sometimes spelled *Mound*), three miles farther, and came to Deer Creek (769 miles), always during the life of the Trail a favored camping place because of its plentiful supply of water, wood, and grass. A few miles beyond they crossed Muddy Creek, which in 1849 marked the westward range of the cholera epidemic.

A little above the present Casper (794 miles) was the crossing to the north side of the Platte, though in the later years the road ran downstream to a crossing near the mouth of Poison Spider Creek. The Casper crossing was usually fordable, but at times of high water required a ferry. In the early sixties it was spanned by a bridge. Crossing the river, the Trail veered off south-

west. The picturesque Red Buttes — two high bluffs
to the left — were passed. The river here flows through
a deep canyon, the " Fiery Narrows " of Robert Stuart's journal, and the place where Frémont was wrecked
in 1842. Most of the diarists speak of the sterile and
barren country on both sides of the Trail. An occasional
spring was found, but the waters were sometimes
strongly impregnated with alkali. One delightful
camping place is almost always mentioned — Willow
Creek Spring, with pure, cold water, good, plentiful
grass and a willow grove.

The Trail rounded Independence Rock (838 miles),
one of the most famous natural phenomena on the Trail.
It is a solitary pile of gray granite, standing in an open
plain, says Palmer, one-eighth of a mile long, six or
eight rods wide and sixty or seventy feet above the plain,
with the beautiful Sweetwater running along its south
side, leaving a strip of some twenty or thirty feet of
grassy plain for a roadway. Father de Smet called it,
from the number of inscribed names that it bore, the
" Great Register of the Desert." The matter of the
numerous stories that have arisen in regard to its naming has already been mentioned, in a note to the first
chapter. As to the naming of the Sweetwater also there
have been many conjectures. Chittenden suggests a
French origin. Perhaps Granville Stuart's statement
(*Forty Years on the Frontier*) that it was named for
"its beautiful clear cold waters having a sweetish taste,
caused by the alkali held in solution . . . not enough,
however, to cause any apparent injurious effects," may
be the true one.

Up the Sweetwater, the lower course of which is now a

INDEPENDENCE ROCK

Drawn by Major Osborne Cross (1849)

part of the great Pathfinder Reservoir, ran the Trail to the Devil's Gate (843 miles), rounding it to the south. "This remarkable feature," writes Chittenden,

is a rift in a granite ridge through which the river flows. It is about four hundred feet deep, with sides nearly vertical, and less than three hundred feet apart at the top. It is one of the most notable features of its kind in the world. The traveler who takes the trouble to leave the road for a mile or so and walk out to the summit of the Devil's Gate is rewarded with a prospect such as no other point on the Trail affords. Beneath him is the tremendous chasm through the solid granite at the bottom of which courses the gentle Sweetwater. To the westward a magnificent valley spreads out before him as far as he can see, some ten or fifteen miles wide, a paradise in those days for buffalo and other game. Through the beautiful valley the serpentine course of the stream is plainly visible from the silver sheen of its surface or from the ribbon of foliage which grows along its banks. Below the Gate a similar valley lies spread out for many miles even to the mouth of the river. All over this region huge protuberances arise composed of detached masses of granite, the most interesting of which is Independence Rock. Lifting the eye above the surrounding plains it rests upon a cordon of mountains which completely encircles the beholder. To the northeast the Rattlesnake Hills, to the east the Caspar range through which the North Platte flows; to the southeast the Seminole and Ferris ranges; to the south and southwest the Green mountains; and finally to the west Crooks' Peak, which closes the horizon in that direction.

Past the Soda Lakes ran the Trail, and at the eastern approach to South Pass, near the present village of Rongis, it came to the marshy stretch known variously as Ice Slough and Ice Springs. Orson Pratt (1847), Major Osborne Cross, William Kelly, and A. Delano (all in 1849) and Granville Stuart (1852) say that at this point, in midsummer, there was a deposit of ice which a little digging would bring to the surface.

> Somewhere in this vicinity [writes Stuart] was a grassy swamp, where we dug down about eighteen inches and came to a bed of solid clear ice. We dug up enough to put into water-kegs and enjoyed the luxury of ice-water all that hot day, while we traveled through the famous " South pass ["] of the Rocky mountains.

Delano, anticipating the skepticism of his readers, explains at some length that the thick growth of high grass, protecting the ice from the sun, accounted for the apparent miracle. Randall H. Hewitt, who crossed the plains in 1862, asserted that the story was " a cold-blooded romance," written with the intent to deceive. He was, however, mistaken. The testimony is from credible witnesses and cannot be refuted. There were doubtless many years in which the ice melted before the emigrants came along, and one of these was evidently the year in which Hewitt made the journey. Two residents of the district write the author that they have no doubt the emigrants sometimes found ice there, and one of them suggests the explanation given by Delano.[36]

From Ice Springs the emigrants came to the site of the Burnt Ranch station of a later day, about forty-five miles farther on. From here a cut-off to the Snake was constructed by the Government in 1857–59. This was the Fort Kearney, South Pass, and Honey Lake Wagon Road, but better known as the Lander Road, for the efficient and energetic Colonel Frederick W. Lander, at first its chief engineer and afterward its superintendent. It was opened in time for the emigration of 1859, and Lander, in his report for that year, says that nine thousand emigrants had already made use of it. This trail ascended the Sweetwater to near its head, crossed the range by a gap considerably higher than South Pass, entered the Green Valley, crossed the Green at the mouth of its East Fork and then struck across to the Snake, which it reached in the vicinity of Fort Hall. From there it followed the Oregon Trail to the mouth of Raft River, which it ascended to the point known as City of Rocks, on one of the California trails. Though projected partly to give the emigrants a passage remote from the Mormons, the ending of the trouble between the Government and the church early in 1858 enabled Lander to draw upon President Young for large numbers of workmen, and the road was constructed mainly by Mormon labor. It seems not to have been generally traveled after the first few years, for the emigrants preferred the better established routes; but a considerable part of it is still used as a stock trail.

From Burnt Ranch it was but a short distance to South Pass, which Chittenden puts at 947 miles from the start, and Frémont at 962. Most of the early diarists express their astonishment at the almost imperceptible grade and the broad valley, twenty miles wide, by which they crossed the divide. They had expected to find a steep ascent through a narrow gap. So gradual was the slope, both eastern and western, that only careful measurement could tell them when the summit was reached. South Pass was at once the approximate half-way post of the journey and also the entrance to what was then known as Oregon. "Here, then, we hailed Oregon!" enthusiastically wrote Palmer in his journal.

Past Pacific Springs (952 miles), the Trail ran to the Little Sandy (969 miles). From here various short cuts to the Green and the Bear had their start. Most noted of them was Sublette's (also called Greenwood's) Cut-off, which saved some fifty-three miles to the Bear River, but as the fifty miles from the Big Sandy to the Green was without water the route was generally avoided. The main Trail kept down the general course of the Big Sandy until it approached the Green, when it broke into a number of branches. To judge from the diarists, the Green crossing was anywhere from the mouth of the Big Sandy to fifteen miles above it.

The emigrants found the Green a "beautiful clear stream about 100 yards wide, with a rapid current over a gravelly bottom," as Palmer described it, and Clyman also in almost identical words. From the Green (1014 miles), which was sometimes fordable, but oftener had to be crossed by ferrying or floating the wagon beds, the earlier Trail ran southwest to the vicinity of the present Opal, passed up Ham's Fork to Kemmerer, and ran westward to Bear River at the present Cokeville. But after the establishment (1843) of Fort Bridger it ran southward to the vicinity of the present Granger, and then by a wide southwesterly curve to the fort (1070 miles). Bridger's establishment was "a shabby concern," writes Palmer, " built of poles and daubed with mud "; and Bryant, in the following year, says that " the buildings are two or three unstable log-cabins, rudely constructed, and bearing but a faint resemblance to habitable houses." Moreover, as the diaries reveal, Bridger was seldom there; his partner, Colonel Louis Vasquez, was quite as frequently absent, and at times, even in the height of the emigrant season, the place was totally deserted. The Mormon Pioneers of 1847, who had met Bridger going east, at the Big Sandy, reached the " fort " only to find the blacksmith shop destroyed by fire and apparently nothing being done to restore it. Though the post had been built to furnish the emigrants with supplies and to repair their wagons, the wandering impulses of the two owners kept them moving about when they were most needed at home.

Somewhere in this neighborhood, though apparently not on the future Trail, a lone settler, doubtless the first in all the mid-region of the Far West, put up a cabin about the year 1834, and with his Indian wife made it his permanent home. He was John Robertson, in later days familiarly called " Uncle Jack Robinson," a highly respected trapper who journeyed and toiled with Bridger, Carson, and all the noted figures of the time. In her *Uinta County, Its Place in History,* Elizabeth Arnold Stone has thrown new light on his character and career. Through all the vicissitudes of that little theater of stirring action he kept his home in the neighborhood. Robertson was to see Bridger build his trading post and later to see him ousted by the Mormons; to see two Mormon colonies planted nearby; to see a United States army march in and put Bridger again in possession, only to lease from him the property and establish on it a military post; and through a long period of years to see the annual tide of migration flowing past Bridger's post to the West. He died about 1882, at the age of eighty.

Until February 1848 Fort Bridger was in Mexican territory, and in later days, if not before, Bridger and Vasquez claimed a Mexican grant of land. Also in Mexican territory was all that stretch of the Trail (including the Bridger section) from a point about three-fourths of the way down the Big Sandy to a point south of Cokeville, near the present Idaho boundary. It was below the 42d parallel, then the southern limit of the western part of the United States. Travelers, however, noticed no difference, for there were no Mexican settlements; they encountered no troops nor officials, and doubtless few of them were even aware that they were traversing a foreign land.

At Fort Bridger, beginning with 1846, was another parting of the trails. The Hastings Cut-off, or Salt Lake route, ran southwest — by way of the present Spring Valley, Knight, and Evanston, to Utah and California. The Oregon Trail ran northwest to the site of Carter and to Cumberland. From here it passed over the northern end of the Bear River Divide, descended Bridger Creek to the Bear, and the Bear to near the mouth of Smith's Fork, at Cokeville, where the Sublette Cut-off came in. From here it continued to follow the Bear, past Border, past Montpelier and on to Soda Springs (1206 miles).

Of this famous resting place and junction point, with its many springs, most of the diarists make favorable mention.

It was a bright and lovely place [wrote Bidwell]. The abundance of soda water, including the intermittent gushing so-called Steamboat Spring; the beautiful fir and cedar covered hills; the huge pile of red or brown sinter, the result of foun-

OUTER VIEW OF FORT HALL

Drawn by Major Osborne Cross (1849)

INNER VIEW OF FORT HALL

Drawn by Major Osborne Cross (1849)

tains once active but then dry — all these, together with the
river — lent a charm to its wild beauty and made the spot a
notable one.

Here the earliest California emigrant route — the one
taken by Bidwell's company — parted from the Oregon
Trail and ran southwest and south, following the general course of the Bear almost to Great Salt Lake,
where it turned west and southwest to the South Fork of
the Humboldt River. A later California route also
began at Soda Springs, but reached the Humboldt by
a more westerly course. What became for a time the
most favored route to the Golden Gate, however, followed the Oregon Trail to the junction of the Raft
River and the Snake.

The Oregon Trail ran northwest to Fort Hall (1288
miles). This was a general refitting and re-forming
place, and it was also a place where men changed their
minds as to their destination. Many of those who had
all along thought they were going to Oregon now decided in favor of California, and many of the California-
bound here decided that they preferred Oregon. Here
also the Oregon-bound emigrants of 1841 and 1842 left
their wagons because they were told that no vehicle could
be taken farther.

Fort Hall was erected, as has already been noted, in
July 1834, by Wyeth, while on his way to Oregon with
the missionaries Jason and Daniel Lee. It was built
in resentment over the ill treatment that he had just received from Fitzpatrick, Sublette, and Bridger, and
in the hope of dividing their trade. It had hardly been
built, however, when the owner found that he would have
to contend with another rival — the Hudson's Bay Com-

pany — which established the post of Fort Boisé, at first
on the Boisé River, about ten miles from its mouth, and
later moved it downstream to the Snake. Fort Hall
could hardly have been a profitable venture for Wyeth,
and in 1836, after his return east, he opened negotiations in London with the Hudson's Bay Company for
its sale. The matter was referred to the local factors of
the company; in 1837 the fort was bought, and it continued to be a Hudson's Bay property until the company abandoned the region. Mr. Miles Cannon [37] says
that in 1838 it was rebuilt, possibly on a different location.

The original fort was erected on the south side of the
Snake in the valley of the Portneuf. Mr. Cannon says
that the spot was six miles above the mouth of the Portneuf, Chittenden says nine miles, and Major Osborne
Cross, who visited it in 1849, about fifteen miles.
Others have given various approximations of the distance. It would seem either that the fort or the river
had the habit of frequently shifting its position, or that
travelers were somewhat careless in their statements.
But the conflict of testimony on the matter of the location of the fort is no greater than that regarding its
general history, and few matters connected with the
early frontier offer so perplexing a tangle. It is generally assumed that the Government bought and for a
time garrisoned the fort, but there is no official record
that it did so. [38]

In 1849 the Government sent Colonel W. W. Loring,
with the regiment of Mounted Riflemen, to march from
Fort Leavenworth to Oregon City, leaving detachments
at Forts Kearney and Laramie, and to establish a post

near Fort Hall. Major Cross, acting quartermaster of the expedition, who made a detailed report of the march,[39] says that in August a camp was established about three miles above the trading post and that two companies were left there. Documents in the Adjutant General's office show that the establishment was at first called Camp Loring and later Cantonment Loring. How long it was occupied does not appear in any available record. But in May 1870, the Government established a Fort Hall, often known as "New Fort Hall," about twenty-five miles northeast of the old trading post, and on October 12 of that year set aside the Fort Hall Indian Reservation for the Bannocks and some of the Shoshones, on territory including the new fort.[40]

In the Indian wars of 1855–56, according to Mr. Cannon, Fort Walla Walla was destroyed and Forts Hall and Boisé were abandoned and their stores moved to the Flathead country at Missoula. Some years later the Hudson's Bay Company filed a bill of staggering proportions against the United States Government for damages growing out of the company's abandonment of the Northwest country. On its own account it demanded $3,822,036.67, and on that of its auxiliary organization, the Puget's Sound Agricultural Company, $1,168,000. More than $81,000 of this amount was for the loss of Fort Walla Walla, $24,000 for that of Fort Hall and $17,000 for that of Fort Boisé. Hearings were held at various places in the Northwest by the Joint Claims Commission of the two nations in 1866–67. The voluminous *Papers* of the Commission reveal a mass of testimony from American pioneers to the

effect that the land and buildings of Fort Hall could
not have been worth more than from $2,000 to $5,000.
Argument also was made that no recompense whatever
was due, since the company had lost its possessory rights
throughout the region by the termination of its license
in 1859. At Washington, on September 10, 1869, the
long contest was brought to a close by the award of the
two Commissioners, which gave $450,000 to the main
company and $200,000 to its auxiliary. The bottoms
in the vicinity of the historic trading post are now wholly
submerged by the waters of the Snake, backed up from
the great dam at American Falls.

From Fort Hall the Oregon Trail ran southwest
along the south side of the Snake to near the mouth of
Raft River, where the town of Yale now stands, and
where a California trail branched off southwestward
to the Thousand Springs country of Nevada and the
headwaters of the Humboldt. The Oregon Trail kept
on along the Snake to the present Glenn's Ferry, where
it crossed, ran northwestward to the Boisé at about where
the city of that name now stands, and followed the river
to Fort Boisé, near its junction with the Snake. Here
the Snake was forded, and the Trail ran northwestward
to Vale and then north to the Snake at Old's Ferry and
Huntington, though a branch kept to the east side of
the river, rejoining the main line at Huntington. The
Trail ascended the Powder River to the present Baker
City, and then ran northward through a rugged country
and descended into the beautiful Grande Ronde Valley.
From here the original Trail ran in a northerly course
to Whitman's mission, near the present Walla Walla,
thence downstream to the fort, and later on to the Dalles.

Its course is indicated by Frémont in the map accompanying the combined report of his first two expeditions, printed by both the Senate and the House as a public document.[41] Of this long-forgotten stretch of the original Trail, and especially of the course taken by the Whitman party in reaching the Walla Walla, President Stephen B. L. Penrose, of Whitman College, writes the author as follows:

The Grand Ronde Valley where the town of La Grande now stands was in 1836 a marsh. Vast swamps filled the lower levels of the valley, and all trails necessarily avoided the lower land. The wagon trail in later years skirted the south side of the valley on the higher ground and climbed up over the Blue Mountains past what is now Meacham and down Cabbage Hill, at first going north to Athena, Weston, and Walla Walla, but later continuing down the Umatilla past Pendleton.

I can find no evidence whatsoever to warrant the belief that the Whitman party in 1836 thus skirted the south side of the valley. I infer rather that they took the north side of the valley to the neighborhood of what is now Somerville or Elgin and came over the Blue Mountains past what is now called the Toll Gate to descend into the Walla Walla Valley by means of the long hill which descends to the level at Milton. My reason for this inference is the description of the descent which Mrs. Whitman gives in her diary. She speaks, as I recollect, of the steep and shaly character of the hill. It is the only one of the several hills down which a wagon road has since been made which warrants such a description. The loose and slippery rock upon the Milton hill is still a striking feature of it.

There is apparently no person living who can give reliable information on this point. It is possible, I think, to determine that the wagon train of '43 came down Cabbage Hill, but concerning the route taken by the party in 1836, history is dependent solely, I believe, upon Mrs. Whitman's diary. The pioneers and historical students to whom I have submitted the question agree that her description corresponds only with the Milton hill.

The emigration of 1844 and a large part of that of 1845 went northwestward from the Grande Ronde to the present Pendleton, following for a time the Umatilla, crossing it and descending the Columbia to the Methodist Mission at the Dalles. Later emigrations, as a rule, took the Humboldt route and entered Oregon from northern California.

DESCENT AFTER LEAVING THE BLUE MOUNTAINS

Drawn by Major Osborne Cross (1849)

CHAPTER VIII

THE GOLD RUSH

THE early Californians knew that here and there gold could be washed from the gravelly streambeds along the coast. Horsemen and ranchmen, mainly concerned with their vineyards, fields, and herds and the marketing of wine, hides, and tallow, they thought little of the hidden wealth about them. Of the vast interior, thinly peopled by a low type of savages, they knew nothing, and cared not at all. The incoming Americans heard rumors of the finding of gold, and some of them searched for it, but with no success. It is an amazing thing that in many of the gulches afterward found so marvelously rich in the precious metal, experienced men had prospected for it in vain. Yet the dream of untold wealth to flow from a chance discovery persisted in the minds of many men. One of these was Sutter, who, though lord of a great and rich domain, wanted to cap his fortune with a mass of gold. To a Dr. Sandels, an able mineralogist, one day in 1843 he said: "Doctor, can you not find me a gold mine?" The Doctor replied: "Captain Sutter, your best mine is in the soil. Leave to governments to provide the currency."

It was, however, this man — Captain John Augustus Sutter — whose name was forever to be closely linked with the great discovery. He was born in 1803, in Kandern, Grand Duchy of Baden, of Swiss parents, and he always spoke of himself as a Swiss. At the age of twenty he graduated from the military college at Berne, and for some years during the reign of Charles X he served in the French army. In the summer of 1834 he landed in New York. He went west, where for a time he wandered about as a trader, at one time making the journey to Santa Fé, and later buying and operating a farm near St. Charles, at the mouth of the Missouri. In 1838 he sold his farm and started for Oregon, probably in the missionary party of the Rev. Cushing Eells. He wanted above all to get to California, about which he had heard wonderful tales; but finding the overland way impossible at that season, sailed from Fort Vancouver for Honolulu.

From here, after arranging for a party of Kanaka workmen to meet him in San Francisco Bay, he set sail for California. At Monterey he found Governor Alvarado friendly and generous. He had a grandiose scheme of establishing himself in the wilderness and building up a powerful colony. The Governor made him a Mexican citizen and gave him a tract of eleven square leagues of land wherever he chose to settle; and he began at once to make preparations for his establishment. From San Francisco Bay, with several launches and a company of workmen, he set sail for the little known Sacramento River. Near the mouth of the American River he landed on August 12, 1839, and after a further voyage as far as the Feather River returned and began his settlement. He put up habitations for his men and a tannery, gristmill, and winery; he drained the lowlands, sowed grain, and set out vines.

Before winter came he brought in five hundred cattle and seventy-five horses. With other accessions of laborers — Kanakas and local Indians — he swiftly extended his operations until he had put into use a large part of his grant, which later was increased by Alvarado's successor, Micheltorena, to thirty-three square leagues. In 1841 he began the erection of a large fort and he also purchased the Russian trading post of Fort Ross, eight or ten miles north of the Russian River, moving what he wanted of its effects to the Sacramento.

Over this baronial realm, with the title of Guardian of the Northern Frontier, he held undisputed sway. Many Americans became his employees, many others settled within or about his domain, and his fort became the rendezvous and capital of the American element of the population. Frémont, whom he had twice succored when in distress, treated him with some arrogance and a touch of ingratitude during the troublous time of 1846; but the transfer of his allegiance from Mexico to the United States was made gracefully and willingly. His prosperity increased, and though shorn of his official rank, he was still the most powerful figure in northern California. He was to lose everything through the accidental discovery on his own grounds of the precious metal for which he had longed.[42]

In the winter of 1847–48, much in need of lumber, he decided to build a sawmill. He had in his employ a man named James W. Marshall, a wheelwright and jack-of-all-trades. Marshall had crossed the plains to Oregon in Gilliam's company (1844), and had subsequently gone to California, served throughout the campaign of 1846–47 as a private and had then hired out to Sutter as a carpenter and general artisan. Bidwell, who knew him well, says that " almost everyone pronounced him half-crazy or hare-brained." He had, however, great confidence in his own ability to do anything as a mechanic. To Sutter he proposed that the sawmill be built at a point since called Coloma, about forty-five miles east of Sacramento, and that the sawn lumber be hauled for several miles and then rafted down the canyons of the American River. The proposal was, says Bidwell, a crazy idea worthy alike of the eccentric Marshall and the credulous Sutter. The mill was built, and it was a good one, but the gravelly bar below the old-fashioned flutter wheel backed up the water and stopped the wheel. Marshall employed a number of Indians to deepen the tail-race, and on the morning of January 24, 1848, looking into the clear, shallow water to see how the deepening process was going on, he saw a bit of glittering rock. He picked it out, and took it to Sutter. Tests proved it to be gold.[43]

According to Bidwell there was, for several months, no excitement. Gold in paying quantities was not believed to be present in the vicinity, and as other gold discoveries had from time to time been announced, the people were skeptical. The news was printed in the San Francisco *Californian* of March 15, but the rival paper, the *Star,* ridiculed the story and continued to do so as late as May 29.

At Sacramento Sam Brannan, one of the most picturesque characters of the Coast, kept a store. He was a Mormon who had arrived with his fellow-religionists on the little ship *Brooklyn,* from New York, on July 31, 1846. Doubtless he was one of the first to learn of the

FORT SUTTER

From Joseph W. Revere's " A Tour of Duty in California" (1849)

event at Sutter's mill, and as some of the employees of
the mill were discharged members of the Mormon Battalion, who brought their gold to trade with him, he
early knew the marvelous richness of the placers. On
the last day in which the *Star* was enabled to ridicule the
story of the discovery, Brannan arrived in San Francisco and rushed hatless through the old Plaza, "crying
out with his bull-throated bellow: ' Gold! Gold! Gold
from the American River!'" [44]

Bidwell claims the distinction of an earlier announce-
ment, but it fell upon heedless ears. The news now began to travel to all the world. The Oregonians were
perhaps the first outsiders to hear of it, and by the fall
probably two-thirds of all the men on the Willamette
capable of bearing arms had started for the placers.
Honolulu heard of it, for much of the quarter of a million dollars' worth of nuggets brought down to San
Francisco in June and July was taken there. Outgoing
ships carried the news to Mexico and the South American countries. A party of Mormons, formerly of the
Mormon Battalion, journeying to Salt Lake City in
the summer, gave the news to the arriving emigrants
and to the Mormon colony. One of these men, Henry
W. Bigler, had been employed on Marshall's mill-race
at the time of the discovery, and it is only from an entry
in his diary that the exact date is known. By New
Year's day, 1849, six thousand miners, many of them
from Mexico, are said to have been at work.

On August 19, 1848, what is believed to have been the
first information published in the East appeared in the
New York *Herald*. It is a simple sentence, buried in
a two-column front-page letter sent from San Fran-

cisco, on April 1, by a member of the 1st regiment of
New York Volunteers.

I am credibly informed [he writes] that a quantity of gold,
worth in value $30, was picked up lately in the bed of a stream
of the Sacramento.

Thomas O. Larkin, at Monterey, had sent the news
on June 1 to Washington, where it arrived in September; and Governor Mason, who with young William
Tecumseh Sherman had visited the placers, on August
17 sent further news, along with a tea caddy containing
about 230 ounces of the precious stuff.

So far, however, the East had received the news with
calmness or indifference. On October 6 the *California,*
the first mail steamship for the Pacific, set out from
New York harbor to round Cape Horn. Not a single
passenger made the voyage. Nearly two months later,
December 1, the second ship, the *Falcon,* started from
New York for the mouth of the Chagres with mail to
be picked up by the *California* at Panama. Though it
carried passengers, not a half-dozen among them had
apparently heard the news, and of the few informed
ones " not one had any faith in it. " [45]

Governor Mason's dispatch, with the famous tea
caddy, arrived in Washington about the end of November. The Secretary of War refused to divulge the contents of the dispatch, but from the Secretary of the
Navy and other sources the news was obtained, and the
public began to get interested. In the New York
Herald of December 3 is a Washington letter dated
two days earlier which says:

The California gold mania is again in the ascendant, and bids
fair to depopulate this side of the continent altogether. The

accounts of the immense riches to be acquired in the new El Dorado, instead of abating, are every day arriving in a more authentic shape, till even the most incredulous are compelled to believe.

On December 5 President Polk's annual message confirmed the news, and instantly the country became feverish with excitement. When, a week later, the *Falcon* reached New Orleans, the levees were found to be "black and clamorous with gold-seekers," and the ship left the port jammed to her utmost capacity. On December 28 the Chagres was reached, and the three hundred passengers immediately started across the Isthmus to board the *California*.

The *California,* greatly delayed, had reached Callao, Peru, on December 29, and here her officers and crew saw the first effects of the news. Her accommodations for a little more than a hundred passengers were at once filled. On January 30, 1849, she arrived at Panama, where more than a thousand crazed gold-seekers demanded passage. Three hundred, some of whom are said to have paid $1,000 or more for the passage, were taken on, and the vessel resumed her voyage, so crowded that it was difficult to move about her decks. In addition to running out of fuel, she encountered two tempests, four fires, and a mutiny; but somehow the little vessel forced her way along until February 28, when she arrived at San Francisco, where her crew (except the engineer) deserted to a man. Under such dramatic circumstances was the United States mail service introduced to the Pacific Coast.

Men who had the money for their passage started at once by steamer for the Isthmus of Panama. Those who lacked the means hurried, with the first signs of the breaking of winter, to the Missouri River crossings. Parties of horsemen with pack-trains took the lead. Parties with wagons and livestock, often accompanied by their wives and children, organized in companies and followed as soon as the grass began to sprout. From the south many went by the difficult and then little known routes across Texas, New Mexico, and Arizona, and even from Independence hundreds took the Santa Fé Trail, hoping to find some continuation of the route by which to complete the journey.

A new route, the Cherokee Trail, was first opened this year. It began at Fort Smith, Arkansas, crossed the Neosho River at Fort Gibson, in the present Oklahoma, ran north of west to the Verdigris, thence following its east bank for eighty miles; it then crossed the river and ran northwest to the Arkansas near old Fort Mann (in the vicinity of the present Dodge City), whence it followed the " Pike's Peak division " of the Santa Fé Trail along the Arkansas to Pueblo, then ran due north along the foothills to the head of Cherry Creek, which it followed to the South Platte, thence reaching the site of the onetime town of Latham, Colorado. Its further course was into Wyoming, past the present city of Laramie, whence it rounded the Medicine Bow range to the north, and passing westward through Bridger Pass, joined the Oregon, California, and Salt Lake Trails at Fort Bridger.

The Wyoming and northern Colorado section of this route had been traveled in part by Ashley's company in the winter of 1824–25; and doubtless other trappers had from time to time passed along some part of it.

Bridger knew it in detail, and two years later (1851) he was to use it in guiding Captain Howard Stansbury eastward to Fort Laramie. But it was first continuously traveled, so far as known, from Latham to Fort Bridger in the early spring of 1849 by a party of California-bound Cherokees, under a Captain Evans of Arkansas, and from this circumstance it received its name. It was to retain the name for at least thirteen years, and that part of it from Latham to Fort Bridger was to become a thoroughfare as frequently traveled as the Oregon Trail. When the first parties of horsemen and the first wagon trains, in their hope of saving a few miles of travel, or avoiding the Sioux and Cheyennes, began to push past Julesburg (the Upper California Crossing of the South Platte), they familiarized a way that became increasingly used. In 1862, when Ben Holladay, because of Indian attacks along the Upper Platte and the Sweetwater, transferred his overland stages to this route, it began to be known as the Overland Trail.

All of these routes had their thousands of travelers. But the great bulk of the gold rush was by the Oregon Trail. The number that gathered for the journey was amazing. In April 20,000 persons were camped along the Missouri. By May 18, said the St. Joseph *Adventure,* 2,850 wagons had crossed the river at St. Joseph, and 1,500 more elsewhere. The great caravans, spreading out along the Trail, gave the appearance of an occupied country. " The rich meadows of the Nebraska or Platte," wrote Bayard Taylor, " were settled for the time, and a single traveler could have journeyed for 1,000 miles, as certain of his lodging and regular meals as if he were riding through the old agricultural districts of the middle states."

It was in a holiday mood that they started. Many of the wagons, says H. H. Bancroft, were bright with streamers and flaring inscriptions, such as " Ho, for the diggings! " Some of the emigrants, keyed up by the double hope of finding gold and selling goods, carried stocks of merchandize. Many of them, too confident of their ability to get to California somehow, failed to make needed provision. The sober-minded emigrants of the years before had learned prudence from the tales of disaster that had come to them across the mountains, but the gold-seekers of 1849 threw caution to the winds.

For all this lightness of mood, most of the caravans started in the midst of an appalling epidemic. The cholera, in its progress west, had reached Independence, and one of its first victims was the trapper and guide, Major Moses Harris, who died on May 6, probably just as he was about to set out on another journey. Among the later arrivals on the Missouri its ravages were terrible. It followed the emigrants along the Trail to a hundred miles beyond Fort Laramie; and it again appeared, from some unexplainable source, at the Humboldt Sink. More than five thousand emigrants are believed to have been its victims. Of its ravages in the moving column of the emigrants the Hon. F. A. Chenoweth, an eye-witness, has written:

Very soon after the assembled throng took up its march over the plains the terrible wave of cholera struck them in a way to carry the utmost terror and dismay into all parts of the moving mass. The number of the fatally stricken after the smoke and dust were cleared away was not numerically so frightful as appeared to those who were in the midst of it. But the name of *cholera* in a multitude — unorganized and un-numbered — is like a leak in the bottom of a ship whose decks are thronged with passengers. The disturbed waters of the ocean, the angry elements of Nature, when aroused to fury, are but faint illustrations of the terror-stricken mass of humanity, when in their midst are falling with great rapidity their com-rades — the strong, the young and the old — the strength and vigor of youth melting away before an unseen foe. All this filled our ranks with the utmost terror and gloom. This terrible malady seemed to spend its most deadly force on the flat prairie east of and about Fort Laramie.

One of the appalling effects of this disease was to cause the most devoted friends to desert, in case of attack, the fallen one. Many a stout and powerful man fought the last battle alone upon the prairie. When the rough hand of the cholera was laid upon families they rarely had either the assistance or the sympathy of their neighbors or traveling companions.

There was one feature mixed with all this terror that afforded some degree of relief, and that was that there was no case of lingering suffering. When attacked, a single day ordinarily ended the strife in death or recovery. A vast amount of wagons, with beds and blankets, were left by the roadside, [which] no man, not even an Indian, would approach or touch through fear of the unknown, unseen destroyer.

While there were sad instances of comrades deserting com-rades in this hour of extreme trial, I can not pass this point of my story without stating that there were many instances of heroic devotion to the sick, when such attention was regarded as almost equivalent to the offering up of the well and healthy for the mere hope of saving the sick and dying.[46]

The year is rich in dependable narratives of the Trail. Major Osborne Cross, acting quartermaster, who hur-ried forward from Fort Leavenworth and overtook Colo-nel Loring's regiment of Mounted Riflemen on its march to Oregon City, wrote a valuable account of the expedition. Captain Howard Stansbury, detailed to survey the Great Salt Lake region, also wrote a report of exceptional value. William Kelly, an observant and not too captious Englishman, gave his experiences in a well-known book, *Across the Rocky Mountains* (originally published as *An Excursion to California*). Alonzo Delano, in his *A Life on the Plains,* and William G. Johnston, in his *Experiences of a Forty-Niner,* made notable contributions to our knowledge of the time; and F. A. Chenoweth, who has already been mentioned, has left a number of vivid pictures of incidents of the journey.

Cross, who reached the vicinity of the Oregon Trail on May 24, records that he then began to note evidences of the cholera, and later that it was raging with great violence and that many families were returning. At Fort Kearney, where the noted Colonel Bonneville was in charge, he records that the Pawnees had been suffering from attacks of the Sioux, who were crowding them severely. On June 6, on the march to Fort Laramie, he notes that desertions of men eager to get to California had begun; and on the 9th that he had just passed a party of Cherokees, originally fourteen, some of whom had died and the remainder of whom were dying, of cholera. On June 10, at a crossing of the South Platte only sixteen miles above the forks he writes of the immense number of wagons seen and says that four thousand wagons had passed Fort Kearney by the 1st of June, not counting those that went by the north bank of the Platte. A company or two had been left at Fort Kearney, and at Fort Laramie, which had just been taken over by the Government, another detail was left. At Fort Hall he saw the first establishment in that region of a United States army post. Here, early in August, a small garrison was left, and the remainder of the regiment passed on along the Trail to Fort Boisé and the Grande Ronde, whence it proceeded by the Umatilla and the south bank of the Columbia to Oregon City.

Stansbury followed the Trail to Fort Bridger, thereupon with the aid of old Jim breaking a new but wholly impracticable route through the Wasatch Mountains to Salt Lake City. Such of his report as has to do with the Oregon Trail has many references to the suffering of the emigrants. At first the cholera; later the exhaustion of supplies, the failure to find grass for the stock, and the breaking down of wagons claimed his attention. Sometimes it was the breaking *up* of their vehicles; for many of the emigrants, despairing of getting their wagons through, broke them in pieces, using the available parts for making pack-saddles.

At Fort Bridger it was noticed that most of the emigrants for California took the northern route by way of Fort Hall, instead of the route by Salt Lake City. The tragic story of the Donner party, which had become everywhere known, prompted the travelers to avoid its route across the Utah and Nevada deserts. Nevertheless the emigration suffered increasing privations as it struggled onward. Along the Humboldt many of the oxen perished. More wagons broke down or were abandoned, supplies grew scarcer, and by the time the Sink was reached thousands were in a destitute and emaciated condition. Aid was sent from California, and the travel-

worn and hunger-weakened pilgrims moved on. In the
Sierras snow fell early and massed in gigantic drifts,
adding further hardships and further delaying the journey. The first party of horsemen with a pack-train arrived in Sacramento on July 18; the last party of the
wagon trains did not get in until late in November. Of
the 42,000 persons who, according to Bancroft, reached
California by land this year, 33,000 were Americans
(some 9,000 being Mexicans), and 25,000 of these went
by the Oregon Trail. Oregon, however, was well-nigh
forgotten, for only four hundred persons made their
way to the Northwest.

CHAPTER IX

THE FACTIOUS FIFTIES

THE growing intensity of the conflict over slavery af-
fected every interest of the Far West. Frontier defense; the protection of emigrants on the Trail; the
location of mail routes, with the providing of adequate
postal facilities; the construction of a Pacific railroad
and the transformation of the eastern strip of the Indian
country into settled and self-governing communities —
all felt the impress of this conflict. Out of it was early
to come the formation of two territories — Kansas and
Nebraska — under conditions that seemed most promising to the cause of the South, but which brought instead
a prolonged guerrilla war, attended by many atrocities.

The decade saw the Trail and its termini attain a
new and wider importance. In 1850 California became
a state, and the great tide of emigration continued: by
the end of 1852 perhaps a hundred thousand persons
made the overland journey. The narrow and sometimes
faint, uncertain track that Father de Smet had traveled in 1841 had now developed into a broad and well-
marked highway. Coming down from the northern
country with an escort of Flatheads and Nez Percés to
attend the Indian council near Fort Laramie, he reached
the trail in the vicinity of Independence Rock, and thus
writes of it:

The 2d of September, 1851, we found ourselves on the Great Route to Oregon, over which, like successive ocean surges, the caravans, composed of thousands of emigrants from every country and clime, have passed during these latter years to reach the rich gold mines of California, or to take possession of the new lands in the fertile plains and valleys of Utah and Oregon. These intrepid pioneers of civilization have formed the broadest, longest and most beautiful road in the whole world — from the United States to the Pacific ocean. On the skirts of this magnificent highway there is an abundance of grass for supplying the cattle and animals appertaining to the caravans which are incessantly traveling on it, from early spring to autumn, every succeeding year.

Our Indian companions, who had never seen but the narrow hunting paths by which they transport themselves and their lodges, were filled with admiration on seeing this noble highway, which is as smooth as a barn floor swept by the winds, and not a blade of grass can shoot on it on account of the continual passing. . . They styled the route the Great Medicine Road of the Whites. . . How wonderful will be the accounts given of the Great Medicine Road by our unsophisticated Indians when they go back to their villages, and sit in the midst of an admiring circle of relatives! [47]

The year marked by the spectacular pageant of the Indian council near Fort Laramie was further marked by the beginnings of an overland mail service as far as Utah. The following year witnessed this service carried into California, and it also witnessed a recurrence along the Trail of the dread scourge of cholera. In 1853 came the first of the five surveys made with a view to the building of a Pacific railway. In the next year came the opening up of the first strip of the Indian Country, the planting of settlements in Kansas and Nebraska and the breaking out of civil war in Kansas; and in the same

EMIGRANTS CROSSING THE SOUTH PLATTE RIVER

From an old Painting

year (1854) occurred the massacre of Lieutenant Grattan's force by Brulé, Oglala, and Minniconjou Sioux, near Fort Laramie — an act which was avenged a year later by General Harney's defeat of the Brulés. During the first six years of the decade there was a steady continuance of the tide of Mormon converts to Utah, a tide which had its tragic culmination in the handcart emigration of 1856, in which so many perished from hunger and exposure.

In 1857 came the break between the Government and the Mormon power, and a small army under Colonel Albert Sidney Johnston started over the Trail to reassert the Federal authority in Utah. It was, however, a brief and bloodless war, for in the following spring and summer it was closed with peace, and the army marched unopposed through the Mormon capital to its station at Camp Floyd. This year of 1858 is further marked by the discovery of gold at the present Denver and the beginning of a rush to the placers by thousands of excited gold-hunters. The year 1859 saw the business of overland freighting, which had had its beginnings in the hauling of supplies to Johnston's army, grow to enormous proportions, and the town of Atchison begin its rise to a commanding, if transitory, rank as a starting place for overland traffic. At the other end of the line Oregon became a state, and from the city of Sacramento had been pushed eastward to the summit of the Sierras a telegraph line which two years later was to join the westward line at Salt Lake City. This year also witnessed the opening of the Lander Cut-off on the Oregon Trail and the beginning of steamboat connection with Fort Benton, Montana, 2,300 miles from the mouth of the Missouri — an event which was to have an important influence on the course of westward migration.

The new communities demanded mails. In the early days there was no Government postal service to the Pacific. Of the few letters that followed the pioneers, some went by sea, in the pockets of ship captains or voyagers; but more by land, carried by the fur expeditions or by persons traveling with them, and often passing through several hands before reaching their destination. It might take ten months or a year or even a longer time for a letter to travel from the Atlantic to the Columbia. Mrs. Whitman, in the fall of 1838, wrote her sister in New York State that they must " calculate on three years' time " for either to hear from the other. In July of that year she had received her first letters from home, one of which had been eleven months on the way and another eighteen months.

With the beginning of the annual emigrations the time transit was cut to from four to six months, and the volume of mail greatly increased. In the diaries one comes across many instances of a personal service freely undertaken. Clyman, with the emigration of 1844, expecting to keep to the old Trail past Waiilatpu, carried letters for the missionaries, but at the Grande Ronde turned aside, with most of the caravan, by a nearer route to the Columbia.

I forwarded [he writes, October 2] all the letters intrusted to my care & directed to Mr [H. H.] Spalding & Dr. [Marcus] Whitman to Mr Gilbert who left us in the grand round vally to go directly to Dr Whitmans & I hope they went to their proper directions

Very likely they did; for one hears much less of delays and losses by this volunteer and haphazard service than by the crude and inadequate methods used by the Government in its early attempts to provide facilities.

The emigrants had their own ways of communicating with one another and with the settlements they had left. Edwin Bryant tells of the manner of leaving messages along the Trail:

A sort of post-office communication is frequently established by the emigrant companies. The information which they desire to communicate is sometimes written upon the skulls of buffaloes, — sometimes upon small strips of smooth planks, — and at others a stake or stick being driven into the ground, and split at the top a manuscript note is inserted in it. These are conspicuously placed at the side of the trail, and are seen and read by succeeding companies.

He says further that near the mouth of Ash Hollow, on the North Platte, he found a deserted log cabin that had been erected the previous winter by some trappers and which had been turned by the emigrants into a general post office. On the outside walls were posted many written advertisements, while on the inside were a large number of letters " addressed to persons in every part of the world," with requests that they should be mailed by persons going east.

Slowly the Government awoke to the fact that a growing population on the Pacific demanded a postal service. On August 5, 1846, President Polk, in his special message to Congress, recommended the establishment of mail facilities for " our citizens west of the Rocky Mountains." He meant the citizens of Oregon, since he did not then know of the conquest of California. In no particular hurry, Congress, on the following March 3, passed the Post Route bill, which among other things authorized the Postmaster General to contract for the transportation of mail by Panama to Astoria or to the mouth of the Columbia at an annual cost not to exceed $100,000. No acceptable bids for the contract appeared, however, and nothing was done. But by another law enacted about the same time, and a contract undertaken by William H. Aspinwall, of New York, a mail steamship set out from New York for the Pacific Coast by way of the city of Panama, on October 6, 1848, and another mail steamship left the same port for the mouth of the Chagres on December 1. The former of these was that famous *California,* which brought the first regular mail to San Francisco on February 28, 1849. The *Oregon,* following in March, sailed on her return April 12 and thus carried the first eastbound mail in conformity with the contract.

For the decade following the discovery of gold the ocean service was the quickest and easiest mode of reaching the Coast. The average time in transit was about thirty days, though one westbound voyage was completed (February 26, 1858) in twenty-one days, two hours and thirteen minutes. But the growing antagonism to the monopoly that operated this service — the Pacific Mail Steamship Company — served in time to transfer it to the cross-country route. In the early years the Government looked upon the land route with disfavor, and in its few and hesitant efforts toward furnishing better postal accommodations gave chief attention to the inter-mountain routes.

Private enterprise sought to fill the gap. As early as

January 15, 1848, a letter express from San Francisco to Independence was advertised, and an express was sent in April, but the gold excitement brought the experiment to a speedy end. A St. Louis company began a mail and passenger line in 1849, but after one westward trip, taking 120 passengers, the service was discontinued because of difficulties. The Mormons did not wait for the Government to act, but maintained their own postal system between Salt Lake City and Winter Quarters.

The military authorities in California had early established a regular service, open to the public, among their various posts, and at long intervals they had sent messengers to Washington. Bancroft says that Kit Carson started east on April 17, 1848, with the first United States mail ever carried overland from the Pacific to the Atlantic. But as he had previously started east with mail which went all the way across, in September 1846, and again in February 1847, it would seem that an earlier date must be given for the event. Certainly in both cases he carried some mail other than military reports.

In the winter of 1848–49 the Government authorized a bi-monthly mail between Council Bluffs and Salt Lake City and appointed a postmaster for the latter city. But the service must have been extremely faulty, since on March 3, 1849, it was resolved in a council of the Mormon brethren that one of their own people should have charge of the mail between the two points.

The first Government contract service from Independence to Salt Lake City was begun on July 1, 1850, by Judge Samuel H. Woodson. The route followed the

Oregon Trail to Fort Bridger and the Salt Lake Trail to Salt Lake City. It was a monthly service, without relay or mail stations on the route, and one team or set of pack animals was used for the entire trip. The time allowed for the service one way was thirty days. The news of the passage of the act establishing Utah Territory, September 9, was brought in on October 15. But the winter mails were greatly delayed by deep snows, and the service thereafter continued to be unsatisfactory. Governor Brigham Young wrote to the Utah delegate in Congress, February 28, 1852: " So little confidence have we in the present mail arrangements that we feel considerable dubiety of your receiving this or any other communication from us." Nearly two years later (December 12, 1853) he informed the Utah legislature that the mail " contracts heretofore would never justify extra expense, consequently the contractor's feeble attempts, of course, prove fruitless, and we have been left without a solitary mail for over half a year at a time." There was to be little betterment for several years.

The first contract for carrying the mails between Salt Lake City and California was made in 1851. Absalom Woodward and George Chorpenning, those dauntless pioneers in the western mail service, were the contractors and the service was to be once a month each way. The first trip was made from Sacramento on May 1. Deep snow in the Sierras caused delays, but by beating out a trail with mauls the party made its way to Carson Valley and thence by the Humboldt-Goose Creek route, around the upper end of Great Salt Lake, to its destination on June 5. Indians proved troublesome throughout the summer, and in November Woodward was killed near the Malade River, in northern Utah. In December and again in January 1852, the eastbound party was forced to return by reason of deep snows. On the February trip eastward the horses froze to death, but the men, though suffering greatly from the cold, safely delivered their mail. The next mail was sent by vessel to San Pedro (Los Angeles) and carried northeast over the Mojave desert; and for the next two years the service alternated between the direct route in summer and the San Pedro route in winter. In 1854 San Diego was made the intermediate point, and not until 1858 was the direct route again used in winter.

There was, however, a lonely station on the winter route that could not be left neglected. This was the post office station of Carson Valley, at the eastern base of the Sierras, in the present Nevada. At Placerville the experiment of sending out carriers on snowshoes was tried and proved successful. The most famous of these carriers was John A. ("Snowshoe") Thompson. He was a Norwegian by birth, and blessed with daring, strength, and endurance. He used a pair of snowshoes or skis ten feet long; he often, it is said, carried a pack of a hundred pounds; he traveled in any kind of weather, and he usually made the downgrade trip in two days and the upgrade trip in three. For some thirteen years he continued to earn fame and money as a carrier and messenger in the mountains, and many are the tales told of his feats. A tablet to his memory was set up at Carthay Center, near Los Angeles, on November 14, 1926.

In all these early years of the decade the great tide of migration flowed steadily along the Trail. Oregon was again a goal of the home-seekers; from only four hundred in 1849 the number rose to two thousand in 1850, and though declining to 1,500 in 1851, reached the approximate figure of 2,500 in each of the two following years. The sudden rise of California had caused the northern colony to be overshadowed, and one of the many consequences was the failure to give it adequate postal facilities. There is no record of a contract for carrying mail along the Oregon Trail beyond Fort Bridger until the growth of population due to the discovery of gold in Idaho compelled the giving of a tri-weekly service from Salt Lake City to Boisé and Walla Walla in 1864. Oregon, subordinate to California, received its mail from San Francisco, at first by steamship and later by stage-coach.

The Far West demanded a daily overland mail by a central route and the construction of a Pacific railroad. The struggle over slavery made both demands for the time futile, and the first was not to be granted, nor the second even authorized, until after the outbreak of the Civil War. By 1852 the movement for a railway had perhaps won a majority of adherents in Congress; but the contest over its location was bitter and unyielding. The South insisted upon a southern route, with an eastern terminus at either New Orleans or Memphis; and the North a central route, with an eastern terminus at either St. Louis or Chicago. The Senate, at the short session of the winter of 1852–53, considered the question in many hours of debate. Senator W. M. Gwin, of California, though in most respects a supporter of the South, reflected the demands of his constituents in favoring a central route. In the apparent hope, however, of satisfying all factions in the controversy, he introduced a bill (January 1853), providing for a trunk line from San Francisco to Albuquerque and thence by way of the Red River to the Mississippi, with branches to various central and northern points. Intended to satisfy all, it satisfied none, and obtained little support. The discussion, however, brought about an amendment to the Army Appropriation bill, in March, by which the Secretary of War was authorized to provide for the survey of such routes as he deemed expedient. On March 4 Franklin Pierce became President. He appointed Jefferson Davis Secretary of War, and the new Secretary sent out five corps of engineers to survey as many routes to the Pacific. The contest over the route to be selected was thus postponed to another time.

The struggle over slavery was now to break out in armed warfare along the eastern end of the Oregon Trail. The Kansas-Nebraska act, organizing two new territories and leaving the question of slavery within their boundaries to be settled by the citizens themselves, was signed by President Pierce on May 30, 1854. It was an annulment of the Missouri compromise of 1820, prohibiting slavery in the Louisiana purchase north of latitude 36° 30'. A previous infringement — that of the Platte Purchase from the Indians in 1836, which added what had been free territory to the slave state of Missouri — had met with much denunciation but nothing more. The Kansas-Nebraska act awoke an immediate urge to resistance. Assuming that the pro-slavery forces would immediately colonize the newly opened region, the anti-slavery forces throughout the country, but particularly in New England, energetically took steps to thwart them. Emigrant aid societies were formed, which organized parties of settlers to move at once to Kansas. Pro-slavery men from nearby Missouri rushed in and staked out claims, most of the men then returning home. " They were men," as some one has written, " who proposed to reside in Missouri, but vote and fight in Kansas. Jubilant and defiant, they threatened with death any abolitionist who would dare to settle in the territory."

Pro-slavery men made the first settlements. On June 13 the Leavenworth Town Company was organized, on July 27 the Atchison Town Company, and a little later the town company of Lecompton. The first of the New England emigrants, a party of seventy-five, arrived about the end of July and on August 1 founded the town of Lawrence. Later the towns of Osawatomie, Manhattan and Waubansee were founded, and on December 5 a settlement was begun at Topeka. The white population of Kansas before the passage of the act had been about 650 persons, nearly all of whom were connected with the trading posts, forts, and missions. By February 1855, a census showed a population of 8,601, of whom 2,905 were voters, and from then on the number rapidly increased. There came an immediate clash of these hostile forces, and the violence then begun, though intermittent, ceased only with the close of the Civil War. It appears, however, not to have disturbed the movement of emigrants along the Trail; and though Independence had lost to more northern towns its primacy, it was still the starting point of thousands every year.

The year 1854 witnessed a tragedy on the Trail that in later times may perhaps have prompted many acts of savage hostility by the red man against the white. This was the annihilation, on August 19, by a band of Brulé, Oglala, and Minniconjou Sioux, of the command of Lieutenant John Lawrence Grattan, six miles below Fort Laramie. In the Great Council of 1851, at the mouth of Horse Creek, the Indians of many tribes had promised to cease depredations on the Trail, had acquiesced in the tribal boundaries designated by the commissioners, and accepted the gifts and annuities of the Government. In a measure the promise was kept; for though the young warriors, eager to win distinction by killing and plundering, were always hard to keep within bounds, the tribesmen generally refrained from attacking the emigrants. After this incident they showed less disposition to keep the peace.

There are several contemporary accounts, and in a number of particulars they do not agree. The main facts seem to be as follows: On August 17 a large caravan of Mormons, making for Utah, passed the Sioux encampment. In the rear was a man driving a lame cow. Frightened by a dog, the cow ran off into the Indian camp, while the man, also taking fright, ran ahead to the caravan. The incident was reported at Fort Laramie, temporarily in command of Grattan, a second lieutenant fresh from West Point. On the following day some communication passed between Grattan and the Indians, and it was learned that the cow had been killed by a Minniconjou and served at a general feast. On the 19th Grattan, with twenty-nine of the forty men under his charge, an interpreter (said to have been drunk) and two field pieces, marched to the camp and demanded the surrender of the Minniconjou. The chiefs consulted with one another as to what was to be done; but Grattan, hearing that the culprit had refused to surrender, ordered his men to fire into the teepee in which he was lodged. This act of unspeakable folly was promptly avenged. Though the chiefs counseled peace, the warriors returned the fire. Grattan and five soldiers fell, and the others, madly attempting to escape to the fort, were all overtaken and killed. The Indians thereupon rushed to the fort, and fearing that the Government would retaliate by withholding their annuity goods deposited in the nearby warehouses of the American Fur Company, broke into the buildings and helped themselves to the contents.

No general hostilities followed, for the Sioux were divided in counsel. In the following year General W. S. Harney, with a force of about 1,200 men, marched into the Platte country with the purpose of suppressing any warlike movements that might be attempted. The wandering bands of Sioux were ordered to show whether or not they were inclined to peace by coming over to the south side of the Platte. Most of them did so; but a large band of Brulés, doubtless suspicious of Harney's intentions, kept to the north side. On September 3 Harney overtook them on the Blue Water, north of Ash Hollow, and in a hard-fought battle defeated them with great loss. In the following year the Missouri Sioux joined in a peace treaty which lasted for seven years.

There were many pitiful tragedies along the Trail in the summer and fall of 1856. All of them were connected with that exceptional incident — the handcart emigration of Mormon converts to Utah. The idea was

Young's.   In a letter to Franklin D. Richards, in 1855, he wrote:

I have been thinking how we shall operate another year.   We cannot afford to purchase wagons and teams as in times past. I am consequently thrown back upon my old plan — to make handcarts and let the emigration foot it, drawing with them the necessary supplies and having a cow or two for every ten. They can come just as quick, if not quicker and much cheaper. Since they will not have to wait for the grass to grow, they can start earlier and escape the prevailing sickness of mid-summer which annually lays so many of our brethren in the dust.   A great majority of them walk now even with the teams that are provided and have a great deal more care and perplexity than they would have if they came without teams.   They will need only ninety days rations from the time of their leaving the Missouri River.   Indeed, since settlements now extend up the Platte, less will suffice.   The carts can be made light and strong, without a particle of iron, and one, or if the family be large, two of them, will bring all that the family will need upon the plains.

With the first emigrants the plan worked well.   Early in the autumn three companies, of nearly five hundred persons each, arrived safely in Salt Lake City, after a walk of 1,300 miles from Iowa City.   Two later companies, however, arrived only after frightful suffering and the loss of many of their members.   No game was found; food supplies ran out, handcarts broke down, wintry weather set in before they reached the Sweetwater, and fatigue, hunger, and sickness took their toll of 250 lives.   Word came to Salt Lake City of the distress of the pilgrims; rescue parties, with wagons and supplies, were at once dispatched, and the survivors were brought in.   Though in the five years, 1856–60, more than four thousand Mormons crossed the plains and the mountains in this manner, the late emigration of 1856 was the only one attended with disaster.[48]

For several years relations between the Federal Government and the Mormon organization in Utah had been strained. Though Young was the Governor of the Territory, the other officials were non-Mormon appointees from the East. The clash between Mormon and non-Mormon became more bitter. The eastern appointees asserted that the Federal authority was disregarded by Young, who ruled the Territory as a dictator, and that an organized band of bravos and assassins, acting under his authority, wreaked speedy vengeance on any one who dared to dispute his will.

Two incidents helped to bring matters to a crisis. In the winter of 1853–54 a Mormon posse, acting under Young's direction, marched to Fort Bridger, then within the boundaries of Utah, with orders to capture Bridger and to seize his trading post. The old mountain man was charged with selling powder and bullets to the Indians, an act which the Mormons regarded as " treason." There is no good reason to suppose that Bridger made a business of such traffic; and there is, on the other hand, good reason to suppose that the Mormons wanted the Bridger region for themselves. The posse could not find Bridger, who doubtless knew of what was intended and therefore kept out of sight; but it seized the post and shortly afterward established two colonies in the neighborhood. The other incident was the transfer of the contract for carrying mail on the Independence-Salt Lake City route from W. M. F. Magraw to Heber Kimball, one of the dignitaries of the Mormon Church. Magraw's contract had expired early in 1856, and as Kimball had underbid him for the new contract the transfer was regular and legal, but it aroused resentment not merely in Magraw but in thousands of others. Magraw was shortly afterward appointed superintendent of road construction in the West, and from the vantage point of this post he contrived to aid in the general feeling of antagonism to the Mormon community. On December 3, in a letter to the President, he summed up the case against the Mormon government in a severe indictment, and in the following March Associate Justice W. W. Drummond, having returned to the East, wrote his resignation to the Attorney General, accompanied with another indictment no less sweeping and bitter.

President Buchanan decided on immediate action. He appointed Alfred Cumming, of Georgia, to succeed Young as Governor, and ordered an army to accompany him to Utah as a posse comitatus, to assure his being seated. From Fort Leavenworth, in June, this army of about 2,500, in a number of detachments, began to stream along the Oregon Trail. General Harney was at first appointed to its command, but was relieved, and the post given to Colonel (afterward General) Albert Sidney Johnston, who was to meet his death while commanding the Confederate army at Shiloh. Captain Stewart Van Vliet, with fifty men, hurried forward to assure the Mormon Governor that the purpose of the army was peaceful and that force would not be used except in self-defense; and after him came the advance column of the troops, under Colonel E. B. Alexander. On September 28 Alexander arrived at Ham's Fork, within twenty-five miles of Fort Bridger. At once the Mormons evacuated Fort Bridger and Camp Supply, destroying most of the buildings and the growing crops. From Governor Young, two days later, Alexander received a letter ordering him to retire at once from the territory, and about the same time a host of Mormon guerrillas was let loose to fall upon the arriving wagon trains in Alexander's rear, seizing the stock and supplies and destroying what could not be advantageously used.

In the face of severe weather, with his front blocked by heavy snows, the forage of Green Valley destroyed, his rear assailed by guerrillas and no prospect of advancing toward Salt Lake City, Alexander held a council of war. It was decided to go into winter quarters, and after much discussion Fort Hall was chosen as the place. On October 11 the crippled command began its slow march westward through the deep snow. Nine days later, when it had made but thirty-five miles, a messenger galloped up from Johnston, then near South Pass, directing the command to turn about and proceed to the vicinity of Fort Bridger. Moving southward, it arrived there on November 2 and 3, and established Camp Scott. Johnston, with the remainder of the troops, arrived on November 19, and the united command, building such shelter as it could, settled down for the winter. To replenish stock and to bring in reinforcements, Captain R. B. Marcy, with a command of sixty-two men, was directed to cross the Colorado Rockies to Fort Massachusetts. The ill-fated expedition started on November 24, but losing its way in the severe snow-storms encountered did not reach its destination for two months and did not return until the following June.

EMIGRANTS CROSSING THE GREEN RIVER

From an old Painting

FORT BRIDGER

*From Howard Stansbury's "An Expedition to the
Valley of the Great Salt Lake of Utah" (1852)*

From the camp during the winter there were desertions of soldiers who slipped past the guard and made their way to Salt Lake City, and also desertions from Salt Lake City of both women and men who found refuge with the soldiers. One of the Mormon deserters, according to Linn, was a woman without shoes and clad only in portions of a skirt, of a man's shirt, and of a jacket, who walked the entire 115 miles in the snow, carrying a babe less than six weeks old. On her arrival some of the soldiers pulled off enough of their own scanty clothing to give the woman and her babe a comfortable outfit.

Along the Trail this summer of 1857 moved a caravan of emigrants making its way toward Southern California. It was known as " Fancher's Company," and it originated in Arkansas, in a neighborhood where, only a year before, the Mormon apostle, Parley P. Pratt, had been killed by the deserted husband of a woman with whom the apostle had eloped. Other members were added to the party in Missouri and farther along the route, until it numbered about 140, of whom perhaps thirty-five were women and forty-five were children. It was a prosperous party; it had forty wagons, two or three carriages, eight hundred cattle, sixty horses and mules, and it seemed well provided with money. From Fort Smith it moved north to Westport, whence it followed the Trail as far as Fort Bridger. Here it turned off on the Salt Lake Trail. It was well ahead of Johnston's army, and it reached Salt Lake City about the middle of August.

The fact that it was from Arkansas was generally known, and at once it found itself in a hostile community.

Instead of turning west, it went forward through the Mormon settlements to the southwest. It could purchase few or no supplies; it could make no trades; it was boycotted. Still it went on, until it came to a pleasant little valley known as Mountain Meadows — the famous Las Vegas de Santa Clara of the trappers — some 280 miles southwest of Salt Lake City and thirty miles south of Cedar City. Isaac C. Haight, President of the Parowan Stake of Zion and lieutenant-colonel of the Iron County militia, decided that as these intruders were heretics and blasphemers, detestable in the eyes of the Lord, they must die; but that as "no innocent blood must be shed," children under the age of seven should be spared. To John Doyle Lee he gave orders for a massacre, and by Lee a band of Paiute Indians was incited to do the deed. An attack was made on the morning of September 13, and seven men were killed or mortally wounded; but the emigrants returned the fire, killing three Indians and wounding several more. Lee, acting as Haight's messenger, had promised the Indians the protection of the Great Spirit, and this loss troubled them. They sent for him; he came up and after some parley promised reinforcements. Departing, he soon started back to the scene with one hundred Indians and seventy-five Mormons, the latter remaining some distance behind. On the evening of the 14th and again on that of the 15th the Indians attacked but were repulsed.

On the morning of the 16th a messenger arrived from Haight to Lee with final orders. Lee later testified that though his spirit revolted at the contents of the message, he felt that he must obey. The Mormons now joined in prayers and asked God's blessing on the bloody work they had planned.   At 2 o'clock Lee and a companion, under a flag of truce, visited the emigrants and told them that if they would leave their arms and wagons and return under a Mormon escort to the settlements, their lives would be spared.   The emigrants, no one of whom was an experienced frontiersman, accepted this treacherous proposal and marched out of their camp.

In front of them, lying in ambush, were most of the Mormons, some of them in Indian garb, and the Paiutes. At a signal they opened fire and then rushed upon their victims with knife and rifle.   In a few minutes all except seventeen children were killed.   These children, several of whom were wounded, were placed in a wagon and afterward distributed among the Mormon citizens of Cedar City.   The property of the victims was also distributed, but the Indians and the poorer Mormons asserted that they received little or none of it, and that Lee and the higher authorities got a disproportionate share.   The only person ever punished for this hideous crime was Lee, by no means the most guilty.   In a Federal Court in September 1876, nearly twenty years later, he was convicted of murder, and on March 23, 1877, was shot to death at Mountain Meadows by a marshal's posse.[49]

But in the spring of 1858 came peace.   A friend of the Mormons, Thomas L. Kane, of Philadelphia, had talked with President Buchanan and had then made his way by Panama and California to Utah, where he arrived early in the year.   He talked with Young, who by now was in a less defiant mood, and then set out for Camp Scott, which he reached early in March.   Johnston was ignored, but an arrangement was quickly made

with Cumming. Kane and Cumming started for Salt
Lake City on April 5 and reached the capital a few
days after, when Young relinquished the governorship.
Shortly afterward two emissaries from the President arrived with the offer of a pardon for Young provided he
would promise no resistance to the new Governor and
the army. Young, denying that he had ever driven any
Federal officials from Utah or had prevented any from
entering, admitted the destruction of the wagon trains,
and on that score blandly accepted his pardon. Back
at Camp Scott the army, reinforced by the return of
Captain Marcy with five companies of infantry and
mounted riflemen and 1,500 horses and mules, set out on
June 13 for the Mormon capital. The 30,000 Mormons,
as a gesture of indignation, temporarily evacuated the
city. On June 26 the army marched through its deserted
streets and camped on its outskirts. Three days later it
moved on toward a place about forty miles south of the
city and twenty miles west of Provo, where it established Camp Floyd, whereupon the Mormons returned
to their city. The episode was closed.[50]

In the spring of 1859 the Trail was again crowded
with gold-seekers. They were headed for the region
commonly known as the " Pike's Peak Country," but
officially as Arapahoe County, Kansas Territory. For
years men had believed that somewhere within its con-
fines gold might be found, and several parties, urged on
by this belief, had journeyed thither. One of these, composed of twenty men of Lawrence, captained by a G. W.
Smith, set out on May 27, 1858. It arrived safely,
though somewhat belatedly; for in the dry bed of Cherry
Creek, which divides the present city of Denver, W.

Green Russell and others had panned yellow flakes and nuggets a few weeks earlier. The information was carried to Omaha by William N. Byers, who in the following year was to found the *Rocky Mountain News,* and as it spread it took on constant embellishments. The discoveries did not warrant the excitement that followed, for the placers were soon exhausted, and it was not until the discovery of quartz gold on the branches of Clear Creek, in May of the following year, that mining became profitable. But it was not in the mood of the gold-seekers to wait for the full authentication of rumors.

A few hardy adventurers made their way to the diggings during the fall and early winter, but with the opening of spring the rush took on enormous proportions. Two main routes were followed; the first was the " Pike's Peak division " of the Santa Fé Trail to the site of old Bent's Fort, thence to Pueblo and then along the foothills northward. The other was the Oregon Trail or any of its eastern feeders to Fort Kearney and the Upper California Crossing and thence farther up the South Platte to the mouth of Cherry Creek. Two other routes, directly across Kansas, were opened. Thousands of men reached the Missouri River towns to outfit and begin the trek. They put to use every kind of vehicle, from the covered wagon to the handcart and wheelbarrow, while some of the more fevered adventurers, loaded down with packs, started afoot. Many of the wagons bore the painted blazon, " Pike's Peak or bust! "

To accommodate those most eager to reach the fields, stages and spring wagons began running in April.

They broke a new trail — along the Kansas River and then along the divide between the Solomon and the Republican, almost directly west. In May the firm of Jones, Russell & Co., composed of William H. Russell (also a partner in the freighting firm of Russell, Majors & Waddell), John S. Jones, and others, started a weekly coach service from Leavenworth along the same route. It was named the Leavenworth and Pike's Peak Express and was equipped with fifty Concord coaches, each drawn by four mules. On the earlier trips the coaches traveled in pairs. The first arrival in Denver was on May 7, nineteen days on the way, and the first arrival in Leavenworth on May 20, after a trip of only ten days.

The route, however, was soon changed. The contract to carry mail between the Missouri River and Salt Lake City was bought by the Jones-Russell firm; to this was soon added the contract for the Salt Lake City-Placerville route; and the new contractors found it more convenient to run both services along the line of the Oregon Trail, detouring the Denver coaches at Julesburg. The last coach to travel the Solomon route, on which Horace Greeley was a passenger, arrived in Denver June 6. By the new route a semi-weekly service to Denver, on a seven-day schedule, was maintained until towards winter, when it was reduced to a weekly service. The coaches carried mail, but only as a private enterprise; for not until August 1860 did the Government grant Denver a service.

No sooner had the great throngs begun their race for Denver than another bonanza was discovered — this time on one of the California trails. Wandering prospectors had found gold in small quantities at the base of the Sierras east of Lake Tahoe and had started the settlement of Carson City. In the spring of 1859 some of them made the first strike in the seemingly exhaustless silver vein of what became known as the Comstock lode. The first to hear of it were the Californians, who trooped in by thousands; but as the months went by the news brought in other thousands from every point of the compass. The settlement of Virginia City followed, and before long the whole region was dotted with mining camps.

Still the contest over the Pacific railroad and the mail routes went on. By the winter of 1854–55 the transcontinental surveys had been reported to the War Department, and Congress had now more material for debate. In January 1855, Senator Stephen A. Douglas introduced a bill for the building of three railway lines to the Coast. After a spirited debate, it passed the Senate on February 19, by a vote of 24 to 21, but in the House was rejected. There was too much rivalry among the supporters of various projects to make agreement possible on even three routes.

The demands for a daily overland mail became louder and more persistent, and to these were now added demands for more wagon roads in the West. In April 1856, a memorial asking for better means of communication and transportation, signed by 75,000 residents of California, was presented to Congress. On this one matter of western policy the national lawmakers found they could agree, and a number of projects were authorized. In July 1856, an appropriation of $50,000 was made for the building of a road from Fort Ridgley, on

the Minnesota River, to South Pass; and in the following February money was voted for the building of three
other roads. One of these was the Lander Cut-off, the
only improvement or extension connected with the
Oregon Trail which ever received a single dollar from
the Federal Government.

Bills for the establishment of a daily overland mail
continued to be introduced in Congress. With the passage of the Post Office Appropriation bill of March 3,
1857, the South won a great victory. The law provided,
with an adequate appropriation, for an overland Pacific
mail; but though it designated no route, it gave, in effect,
the choice to the Postmaster General by authorizing him
to choose the contractor. Buchanan came in as President on the 4th. To the office of Postmaster General he
appointed Aaron V. Brown, of Tennessee, a strong partisan of the South, who let the contract to a company
headed by John Butterfield of New York. Butterfield
may have had his own notions as to what the route should
be; but the one chosen by him corresponded with the one
favored by Brown. It ran from St. Louis to Fort Smith,
Arkansas (where connection was made with the mail
from Memphis), and thence by Preston to El Paso,
Texas; Tucson and Yuma, Arizona, and Los Angeles
to San Francisco. It was 2,795 miles long, and the
great curve it described caused it to be derisively known
as the " horseshoe " and the " ox-bow " line. The appropriation was $600,000 annually, and the require-
ment was for a semi-weekly service " to be performed
with good four-horse coaches or spring wagons, suitable
for the conveyance of passengers, as well as the security
of the mails," within a limit of twenty-five days for each
trip.

The selection of this roundabout way of reaching the Pacific aroused a storm of denunciation in the East, North, and West, but Brown was unmoved. The contract, which was let for six years on September 16, 1857, provided that the service was to begin on September 15 of the following year, and on the appointed day the Butterfield Overland Mail began to operate. A coach left each of the two termini simultaneously. The first mail from the East arrived in twenty-three days and twenty-three hours and that from the West in twenty-four days, eighteen hours, and twenty-six minutes. The service, notwithstanding the chorus of disapproval, and in spite of the most formidable obstacles, was regular and dependable, but it was not what California and the northern states demanded. They still contended for a daily mail along the central route (which, for most of its length, was along the Oregon Trail) and ridiculed the southern route.

On this central route the service had been interrupted by the Mormon War, but was restored and improved in the early part of 1858. For the route from Independence to Salt Lake City a contract was let to John M. Hockaday and others, and for the remainder of the route ending at Placerville, to the veteran George Chorpenning. By July the service, which was by four-mule vehicles, was made weekly throughout the route, on a schedule of twenty-two days for the eastern section and sixteen for the western. The appropriation was $190,000 for the former, and for the latter $130,000 — the total a little more than half of that granted to the Butterfield Company.

Speed in the transmission of mails was largely a matter of money. With a liberal appropriation for the service, the contractors could employ drivers and buy horses and equipment sufficient to provide any number of relays and send the mails galloping across the country. With a lesser appropriation they must use fewer horses and drivers and provide fewer relays. It was, in the main, the policy of the Democratic administrations and of their Southern supporters to skimp the recompense for the central route. Thus it happens that while the Butterfield Overland Mail, with an appropriation of $600,000, could furnish a semi-weekly mail over a route nearly 2,800 miles long, on a twenty-five day schedule, the contractors on the central route, with an appropriation of but $320,000, could furnish only a weekly mail over a route of 1,900 miles, on a thirty-eight day schedule. " The contractors are ready and anxious," writes a Salt Lake City correspondent in the San Francisco *Bulletin* of January 24, 1859, " to carry the mails from St. Louis to San Francisco *tri-weekly,* in less time than the southern route, for the same compensation which that gets for carrying it semi-weekly." To make a public demonstration of the superiority of the central route Hockaday arranged relays to carry the President's message of December 1858 through to the Coast in the shortest possible time. An advance copy of the message was promised Hockaday's agent by the President, so it is alleged, only to be refused him when copies were given to agents of the Butterfield and the ocean lines. Later he obtained copies, and the packet containing them reached San Francisco from St. Joseph in the unprecedented time of seventeen days. But the favored Butterfield line won the race by delivering the message on December 26, beating the mail steamer by two days, while Hockaday's delivery was not made until January 1, 1859. "Hockaday and Company," says the San Francisco *Bulletin* of January 4, " are heavy sufferers by some piece of jugglery."

Hockaday had done much to give an adequate service along his route, but he soon fell into financial difficulties. Aaron Brown had died, and the new Postmaster General, Joseph Holt, began in March a policy of retrenchment. The service on Hockaday's route was reduced from a weekly to a semi-monthly basis and the recompense cut from $190,000 to $130,000. This action completed the financial ruin of the contractor, and on May 11 he sold out to the firm of Jones, Russell & Company, which in the following winter was absorbed by the enterprising firm of Russell, Majors & Waddell, under the name of the Central Overland California and Pike's Peak Express Company.

The decade closed with the Trail on the eve of a new era. A continuous traffic was now to stream along its course. Through spring and summer would still be seen the winding caravans of the emigrants; but through all the months of the year would be seen the speeding stage-coach and the long trains of square-rigged, canvas-topped freight wagons. For a year and a half it was to be regularly traveled by the flying steeds of the Pony Express. A telegraph line was to span it from Fort Kearney to Fort Bridger, thence turning aside to the trail to California, and stations would be established; stations also for the stage and the Pony Express. Settlements were pushing out from the Missouri to the mountains; new discoveries of gold were being made, which brought successive waves of prospectors, with all their vicious following, along the Trail. The country through which it ran was to be often ravaged by savage hordes, and soldiers were to set up new camps and forts. Instead of an isolated Trail, peopled for a few months of the year by a moving throng, and then lapsing into virtual solitude, it was to become for a brief time, until the railroad robbed it of its usefulness, a highway peopled all the year.

CHAPTER X

THE STAGE-COACH ERA

THE Central Overland California and Pike's Peak Express Company was organized in Leavenworth early in 1860 and in February received a charter from the Kansas territorial legislature. Its incorporators included William H. Russell (the president of the company), Alexander Majors and W. B. Waddell. It was an outgrowth of the freighting firm of Russell, Majors & Waddell, which had established itself in Leavenworth in the early fifties and had become the leading company in overland transport. A considerable part of the business of the firm was that of carrying supplies to the various military posts; and when, in 1857, it obtained the contract for supplying Johnston's army, its business rose to almost incredible proportions. In 1858, according to F. A. Root, in *The Overland Stage*, it transported 16,000,000 pounds of goods, using 3,500 to 4,000 wagons, nearly 40,000 oxen, 1,000 mules and employing from 4,000 to 5,000 men. Its ponderous wagons, each of which carried from 5,000 to 7,000 pounds of goods, were made to order in St. Louis. At the height of its prosperity it operated about 6,250 wagons, with 75,000 head of oxen. Horace Greeley, in *An Overland Journey*, gives us this picture of the home establishment:

Russell, Majors & Waddell's transportation establishment, between the fort and the city, is the great feature of Leavenworth. Such acres of wagons! such pyramids of extra axletrees! such herds of oxen! such regiments of drivers and other employees! No one who does not see can realize how vast a business this is, nor how immense are its outlays as well as its income. I presume this great firm has at this hour two millions of dollars invested in stock, mainly oxen, mules and wagons. (They last year employed six thousand teamsters, and worked 45,000 oxen.)

The new corporation, energetic and experienced in its personnel, strongly financed and avidly ambitious, planned nothing less than a monopoly of the overland passenger, mail, express, and freight business. It early absorbed competing lines; but to complete its monopoly it must get the overland mail contract for a daily service, and to assure the authorization of such a service it must demonstrate the feasibility of the central route. Russell was in Washington in the winter of 1859–60 and in daily contact with Senator Gwin, the chief legislative proponent of the project. While there he resolved to furnish a striking proof of its practicability. This proof was the Pony Express, a magnificent, though expensive, feature in demonstration. The idea, according to Majors, came from Gwin, who agreed to obtain from Congress a subsidy to reimburse the firm for the expense. On January 27, 1860, Russell telegraphed his brother in Leavenworth that he had determined to establish the service at an early day. On his return he presented the matter to his partners. They objected on the score that it could not possibly pay, but his eager insistence won their consent.

Preparations were rushed forward with the utmost

vigor. Riders noted for their courage and hardihood were employed. Some five hundred horses were bought, after great care in their selection, for they must be strong and wiry and fleet enough to outrun any bands of pursuing Indians. Though some of the animals were California mustangs, most were, according to Root, " really not ponies but American horses." Relay stations were provided; the numerous stations put up by the stage company between the Missouri River and Salt Lake City were utilized, and new ones erected until there was one for every twelve or fifteen miles all the way to Sacramento.

On the announced date, April 3, the start was made simultaneously from St. Joseph and San Francisco. At the former city a delay was caused by the lateness of the Hannibal and St. Joseph mail train. But at dark the train arrived, the mail was delivered to the rider, and at 6:30 he sped down to the ferry, where he was taken across the Missouri. Landing, he dashed off into the darkness. Relays of men and ponies carried the mail forward to Sacramento, where the last rider took it with him onto the boat, and at 1:00 A.M. on the 14th, a matter of ten days, six hours, and thirty minutes, it arrived in San Francisco. From here, ten days before, a rider had galloped to the boat which bore him and his mount to Sacramento. From there a rider had started eastward, covering the first twenty miles, including one change, in fifty-nine minutes. The run to Fort Churchill, twenty miles east of Virginia City, a distance of 185 miles, was made in fifteen hours and twenty minutes and included crossing the Sierras in thirty feet of snow. It is a tantalizing fact that the identity of the first rider out of St. Joseph in this dauntless and spectacular service is disputed. Root says that he was " Johnnie " Frey, one of the most noted of the company, but several others have been mentioned. Mrs. Louise Platt Hauck, in the *Missouri Historical Review* for July 1923, asserts, with what seems to be conclusive evidence, that he was a sailor boy, " Billy " (otherwise Johnson William) Richardson. At the other end of the line the rider who started eastward from the boat at Sacramento was Harry Roff; but as to whether or not it was also Roff who began the journey at San Francisco there is no available word.

The service was at first weekly, but was made semiweekly by June. The time scheduled for the entire trip was ten days. Between telegraph stations, after the line reached Fort Kearney, the schedule was seven days, though with the coming of winter it was extended to fifteen and eleven days respectively. The route followed the well-beaten line of the covered wagons from St. Joseph to the present Horton, where it struck the military road from Fort Leavenworth and Atchison; then by Granada and Seneca to Marysville, where it joined the main Oregon Trail, which it kept, by way of the Upper California Crossing of the South Platte, at Julesburg, all the way to Fort Bridger. From there it followed the regular route to Salt Lake City, and then the Chorpenning mail route of 1859 (south of the Humboldt River to Carson City), and the route south of Lake Tahoe to Placerville and Sacramento. Usually two men were maintained at each station to care for stock and to have everything ready for the relays. At the beginning each horseman rode a distance of from thirty to fifty miles, using three horses and keeping within the maximum of two minutes for each change of mail and mount. Later the distance traveled on each trip was extended to from seventy-five to one hundred miles.

There was, however, no regularity as to the length of the ride. Whatever the circumstances, the mail had to go forward, east or west. If the arriving rider found the next relayman ill, or slain by Indians, he must go forward or return, as the case might be, until a relief was available. On one such occasion young William F. Cody, the " Buffalo Bill " of a later time, made a continuous ride, on the western Wyoming stretch, of 320 miles, which was covered in twenty-one hours and forty minutes; and on another, Howard R. Egan, riding west of Salt Lake City, kept to the saddle for a back-and-forth gallop of 330 miles. A yet longer non-stop ride is sometimes mentioned — one of 380 miles, made by Robert (" Pony Bob ") Haslam along the Nevada section of the route.

For their labor the riders were paid $50 a month and board, though a few of them, noted for braving extra hazards, received as much as $150 monthly. All of them had to face the perils of terrific storms, deep snows, flooded rivers, of losing their way, and of being attacked by Indians. Yet, though often pursued, they usually managed, by their courage and resourcefulness and the fleetness of their mounts, to escape. There is but one recorded case of a fatality from an attack by the savages; though the horse escaped and brought in the mail, the rider was killed and scalped. The savages were sometimes a source of danger even when they were not primarily hostile. Egan, on one of his trips, found himself ambushed by a band of Indians (probably Digger Sho-

shones). With pistol in hand, firing rapidly, yelling
lustily and spurring his horse to its utmost speed, he
dashed through the cordon to safety. Later he learned
that the trap had been set for him merely to find " what
it was that an express rider carried to make him travel so
fast." "I want to say right here," wrote Granville
Stuart, in his *Forty Years on the Frontier,* " that for
nerve, courage, and fidelity there never was a body of
men that excelled the Pony Express riders."

The letters were carried in four small leather bags
called *cantinas,* about six by twelve inches in size, sewed
to a square *mochila* which was so placed on the saddle
that one letter bag was in front and one behind each leg
of the rider. To preserve them from dampness the letters were wrapped in oiled silk. At the beginning the
charges were $5 for a half-ounce or fraction thereof,
for the entire route, and $3 a half-ounce from San
Francisco to Salt Lake City, though with August
quarter-ounce letters were accepted for the entire route
at $2.50 each. The Pacific telegraph, slowly pushing its
way from the two termini to a central meeting point,
added considerably to the mail matter carried. At the
last transmitting station from one end of the route dis-
patches were carried to be put on the wires at the first
transmitting station toward the other end. From
Genoa, Nevada, the arrival of the first westbound rider
was telegraphed to Sacramento, while the eastern pro-
jection of the line was but slowly crawling along the
north bank of the Platte toward Fort Kearney. In
November, from a point opposite the fort, it was carried across the river, and here, on the morning of the 8th,
a dispatch announcing Lincoln's election was given to

a westbound rider. Six days later, at Fort Churchill, twenty miles east of Virginia City, Nevada, its contents were telegraphed on to the coast. The best record made from end to end of the route was in the carrying of Lincoln's inaugural address, in March 1861, the total of 1,980 miles in seven days and seventeen hours.

The Pony Express had been in operation less than two months when the Washo Indians of Nevada began hostilities. In the latter part of May several stations were burned and the stock was driven off, entailing losses of about $75,000. A company of volunteers was raised, the Indians were attacked and pursued towards Pyramid Lake, and the disturbance ceased. With the coming of snow it was foreseen that delays would be caused, and the time schedule for trips was extended to fifteen days between termini and eleven days between telegraph stations. But, as Professor Hafen shows, the service could not meet the new schedule. The average time taken for twenty-two midwinter trips between Fort Kearney and Fort Churchill was 13.8 days. Only one trip was missed. The longest time taken for a trip was seventeen days, and in each of four others sixteen days were consumed. On one occasion the Butterfield line, with fifteen days between telegraph stations, was enabled to telegraph news from Los Angeles of three days' later date than that sent from Fort Churchill. But with the coming of warm weather the service was restored to its former efficiency.

Advocates of a central mail route had continued their efforts with vigor. The withdrawal of the Southern members from Congress in the winter of 1860–61 made possible a long-deferred success. The Postal Appropriation bill, enacted March 2, 1861, provided for a daily overland mail and (until the completion of the overland telegraph) the continued operation of the Pony Express, with a reduction to $1 a half-ounce for postage on letters. It also provided for moving the Butterfield overland mail line to the central route. Compensation was fixed at $1,000,000 a year. The contract was awarded, not to Russell, Majors & Waddell, who had made such sacrifices to obtain it, but to the Butterfield Company. A working arrangement was made, however, with the former firm by which it was to operate the Pony Express and the daily mail-coach service as far as Salt Lake City and the Butterfield Company the remainder of the route. What was left of the Butterfield equipment — for the Confederates had thoroughly looted all that could be found in Texas — was brought north. Though the new arrangement went into effect in April, the daily mail-coach was not to begin running until July 1.

On April 26 the board of directors of the C. O. C. & P. P. Company was reorganized, and General Bela M. Hughes was made president in place of Russell. One of the first questions to be settled was that of giving the new city of Denver a place on the main line. To run the stages by Denver and thence up to South Pass would entail the waste of many hours of travel. The Julesburg-Cherokee Trail line offered an alternative, but Denver was many miles from even its most southern dip. The citizens of Colorado believed that there was an even shorter way to the west, and in May, a party of explorers, with Bridger as guide, set out to find it. They discovered Berthoud Pass, but opinion was divided as to its practicability. At any rate, it had no stations, and for that matter, neither had the Cherokee Trail. Time was pressing; the mail must go forward on the designated day; and so, for lack of a route that was at once shorter and equipped for service, the stages were started along the Oregon Trail.

The coach that left St. Joseph on July 1 reached San Francisco on the 18th, and the service continued regularly and satisfactorily throughout the summer and early fall. Fears that the Indians in Utah and Nevada might attack the coaches proved, for the time, groundless. East of St. Joseph there were occasional stoppages of the mail by Confederate raiders, but along the Trail there were no interruptions.

During the summer and the early part of autumn the line of the Pacific telegraph, aided by new Government appropriations, was rapidly pushed forward from both ends. By September 27 the western extension had reached Ruby Valley, in eastern Nevada. Along the Oregon Trail the eastern section was carried from Fort Kearney to Julesburg, to Fort Laramie, through South Pass, and on to Fort Bridger, whence it was diverted to the Salt Lake route. On October 22 it reached the Mormon capital, and the first dispatch it bore was one from Brigham Young to the president of the company at Cleveland:

Utah has not seceded, but is firm for the constitution and laws of our once happy country.

Two days later the western line was brought in, and messages flashed across the continent. With the completion of the line the historic Pony Express came to an end.[51] Begun with the apprehension that it would prove a financial failure, but with the confident expectation that it would popularize the central route, it brought both success and disaster. Each of the partners lost a fortune, and in another half-year they were to lose even the business they had so energetically developed.

Until the coming of winter, service on the stage line was regular, with an average transit of letter mail in twenty days and of paper mail in twenty-eight days. Then followed a succession of snowstorms in the mountains and of floods in the valleys, causing long and repeated delays. In April 1862, Indian disturbances broke out along the Trail from the Sweetwater to Fort Bridger. Sioux, Cheyennes, and Arapahos were on the warpath, and even some of the Utes lent a hand in the attacks. Soldiers were sent to the region, and the Indians dispersed; but the Government had already ordered the mails sent by the ocean route. Not until after the middle of June were they restored to the stage line.

The great firm of Russell, Majors & Waddell (otherwise the C. O. C. & P. P. Express Company), impoverished by the Pony Express and the failure to obtain the mail contract in its own right, was now tottering to its ruin. For some time it had been borrowing money, and its chief creditor was Ben Holladay, a forceful and picturesque character who had made a success in operating local stage lines in the Colorado region. Late in the winter the firm failed, and on March 21, 1862, its equipment was bought by Holladay at public sale. The organization now took the name of the Overland Stage Company or Overland Stage Line, and the new owner began at once to systematize and improve the service in every detail.

For various reasons, not the least of which was the Indian peril on the Sweetwater, Holladay determined to abandon the South Pass route. The change was made in July. The stages were now run from Julesburg along the South Platte to Latham. From here they followed the Cherokee (soon to become known as the Overland) Trail to Fort Bridger. In September Holladay made the further change of placing Denver on the through line. By reason of the wide detour to the south the route saved no distance, but it had the advantage of running through a more populated territory and of being less exposed, west of Denver, to the attacks of Indians. The month of July 1862 marks the permanent abandonment, as a mail and stage line, of the long stretch of the Oregon Trail from Julesburg, by way of Fort Laramie and South Pass, to Fort Bridger.

Atchison had become, and was to remain, the starting point. From here the coaches ran to Marysville, where they joined the original Oregon Trail, which they followed to Fort Kearney and on to the parting of the ways at Julesburg. It was under Holladay that the overland stage attained the height of its glory. His company was highly organized, its service carefully equipped, and its personnel composed of the most efficient men that could be hired. The corps of staff officers and lesser employees included a general superintendent, an attorney, a paymaster, a number of stock buyers, nine messengers, 150 drivers, twenty blacksmiths, several harness makers and carpenters, and more than 150 stock tenders.

The through line had three grand divisions, averaging more than six hundred miles in length — Atchison to Denver, Denver to Salt Lake City, and Salt Lake City to Placerville — each in charge of a division superintendent. Within each of these longer stretches were three minor divisions, each under a division agent (usually a man promoted from the ranks of the drivers), who had complete charge of all matters within his domain.

Including the two termini there were 153 stations, twelve to fifteen miles apart. The ordinary or " swing " stations were often no more than a square, one-room cabin, with a nearby stable. The more important or " home " stations, about fifty miles apart, consisted usually of several buildings. Here meals were served, an occasional traveler was lodged, and (except between Denver and Fort Bridger) there was telegraphic service. About some of these stations ranches developed, where hay and grain were grown. The roofs of the structures were primitive. Upon rafters closely placed were laid willow branches, then a layer of hay, and then a layer of earth or sod. From this earth, moistened by rain, seeds sprouted, developing often into a luxuriant crop of weeds and grass and giving the appearance of a sloping roof garden. At the division headquarters there were repair shops, and still larger shops at headquarters of the grand divisions.

Next in official rank (though not in public estimation) to the division agent was the messenger or conductor. He was usually, says Root, a man of intelligence, decision and considerable executive ability. He sat with the driver, and his run was the full two hundred miles of a division. He had entire charge of the mail and express until it was delivered and receipted for at the end of his route.

In the public eye, however, it was the driver who was the most important of all the company's employees. Certainly he was the most picturesque. Mark Twain's picture of him, in *Roughing It,* has doubtless something of truth, not only as to how the driver regarded himself but as to how he was regarded by his fellow-employees. It seems, nevertheless, to have been somewhat over-drawn. According to Root the drivers were, in the main, "warm-hearted, kind and obliging." Many of them were competent to fill more important places. Some of them were well educated. All appear to have been fascinated by their work, and none wanted to retire from it. They were of most ages from adolescence up and from every walk of life.

There were, of course, some rough characters among them, but these in course of time were weeded out. Most of them, good and bad, were fond of liquor. Root tells of riding with some of them who were obviously drunk; yet he remembered no incident in which an overcharge of liquor prevented the driver from efficiently guiding his team. They were all experts with the lines. They knew how to avoid obstructions in the roads; to round, at high speed, dangerous curves on the shoulders of precipitous cliffs, and to guide their fleet and powerful horses on the gallop away from a band of pursuing Indians. With the long whip also they were experts; they could cut a fly off the back of a lead horse while going at a trot. They were, as a rule, of great courage, though they rightly drew the line at foolhardy recklessness; the continued Indian troubles of 1864–66 and the failure of the army to give adequate protection caused many of them to refuse to make their runs.

Most drivers developed strong affection for the horses they drove, sometimes feeding and grooming the animals instead of permitting the work to be done by the stock tenders. The drivers usually ran for two or three " stages " or " drives " (twenty-five to thirty-five miles), though occasionally for twice the distance. At the end of the " drive " the horses were taken out, stabled and fed, and within twenty-four hours were started on the return run.

The horses used were the best obtainable. " It was the almost universal remark," writes Root, " of those who made the overland journey by stage . . . that they never saw such fine animals. Holladay was a great lover and a good judge of stock himself." Though Government agents during the Civil War were buying up the horses most suitable for cavalry service, Holladay seemed never at a loss in obtaining the pick of the market. All the teams — four-horse and six-horse — were graded in size, the rear team of " wheelers " being the larger. They were also, in so far as possible, paired off by color.

Most of the teams in use on the line [says Root] were well matched, although among a few there was a decided contrast. Some of them, perfect in build, were the most lovely white, while others, just as nicely built, were of a jet black. Then there were some nicely matched, beautiful bays — both of a dark and light shade; there were also some equally fine teams of a chestnut color; a number of handsome roans; the most lovely dapple-grays; occasionally a team of " buckskins "; and some splendidly matched sorrels and iron-grays.

The Concord coach had been brought in by the Leavenworth and Pike's Peak Express early in 1859. Its use became general on all the stage lines of the West, and no other coach ever supplanted it. It was made by the Abbott-Downing Company, of Concord, New Hampshire, a firm that had its beginnings in a wheelwright business founded by Lewis Downing in 1813.

The body of the coach [writes Hafen] was built of stout white oak, braced with iron bands. It was suspended upon two leather thoroughbraces extending lengthwise of the coach and attached at each end to a standard protruding up from the axle. These thoroughbraces were made of straps of leather placed on top of each other to a thickness of about three inches. This leather swing was used in the absence of steel springs to absorb the jars, and it permitted the coach to rock slightly forward and back. Behind the body was the triangular " boot " for mail, express, or baggage, and at the front, under the driver's seat, was another leather compartment [the front " boot "] for the carriage of similar articles.

The coach had three inside seats, capable of holding nine passengers. The front seat faced backwards, and the middle one was often a mere bench-shaped contrivance that could be removed when the floor of the coach was needed for mail or express. There was room for another passenger (sometimes still another was squeezed in) on the box with the driver and the messenger; and on some of the coaches a further seat was set up above and behind the driver, capable of holding three passengers. An occasional three-passenger seat at the rear of the top was not unknown; and on such a stage seventeen passengers might be found. Root, however, gives fourteen passengers, with driver and messenger, as the greatest number with whom he had traveled. There was frequent crowding, especially when one or more of the passengers happened to be of unusual girth. Raphael Pumpelly, who traveled over the Butterfield route from Tipton, Missouri, to Tucson, Arizona, in what was presumably a Concord coach, gives us this picture:

> The coach was fitted with three seats, and these were occupied by nine passengers. As the occupants of the front and middle seats faced each other, it was necessary for these six people to interlock their knees; and there being room inside for only ten of the twelve legs, each side of the coach was graced by a foot, now dangling near the wheel, now trying in vain to find a place of support. An unusually heavy mail in the boot, by weighing down the rear, kept those of us who were on the front seat constantly bent forward, thus, by taking away all support from our backs, rendering rest at all times out of the question.

But there is testimony to the comfort and even luxury of the vehicle. General Rusling writes: " The Concord coaches quite surpassed our expectations, both as to comfort and speed. They were intended for nine inside — three seats full — and as many more outside as could be induced to get on." " Our coach," writes Mark Twain, " was a great swinging and swaying stage of the most sumptuous description — an imposing cradle on wheels."

The overland stages ran night and day, six days a week. The Monday, or " messenger " coach from Atchison, carried no mail and, as a rule, no passengers, but was loaded down with express packages, besides a strong and heavy iron box containing treasure and the most valuable of the smaller packages. The express rate to Denver was $1 a pound. Sometimes, when there was an excess of baggage, a special messenger coach was run. The regulation time from Atchison to Denver, 653 miles, was six days, but a number of hours were often clipped from the schedule. Root says that his fastest going was five days and eight hours, an average of about five miles an hour, including all stops. A fourteen-mile stretch along the Little Blue was made in fifty-two minutes, a fraction better than sixteen miles an hour. It was a four-horse team that drew the coach, which in addition to the driver and the messenger, carried twelve passengers and nearly half a ton of mail and express.

Fares, as we view them today, seem to have been rather extortionate. Until the summer of 1863 the rate from Atchison to Denver was $75; to Salt Lake City $150, and to Placerville $225. Each passenger was allowed twenty-five pounds of baggage, the excess being charged at $1 a pound. As the currency depreciated during the Civil War, rates were advanced until they reached $175 for the Denver trip, $350 for Salt Lake City, and $525 for Placerville. But the increase of fares apparently made no difference in the number of travelers, for the seats were usually filled.

There were desperadoes in those days, and occasionally a coach was halted and robbed. Root tells of the hold-up of an eastbound coach, supposed to be carrying nine wealthy Californians, about thirty miles from Atchison. But the Californians had taken another coach at Fort Kearney, and the robbers found only three passengers, none of whom seems to have had anything worth taking. Holladay himself, while traveling with his wife, was treated to a hold-up. But though he had an exciting time with one of the bandits, who insisted on holding a gun at his head, and though the strong box appears to have been taken, the $40,000 which he carried in a money belt, the several hundred dollars in his pocket, and his $8,000 emerald ring were overlooked. A singular coach robbery recorded was that by a sneak thief who, at a stopping place, unbuckled a strap on the hind boot and contrived to get away undetected with a sack of mail.

The most eminent desperado along the line, or at least its eastern section, was a man who for some time was a trusted employee of the company. He was Joseph A. Slade, and he is said to have come from Clinton County, Illinois. Root's account of him is confused and in parts obviously inaccurate; and perhaps no one knows the real story of his career. Granville Stuart says that while he was camped with a party on the Trail, at the junction of Ham's and Black's Forks, in April 1860, Slade, with a mule train of sixteen wagons, came along and camped nearby. Hearing a shot fired, Stuart and his companions walked over to the other camp and found that Slade, who was drunk, had just killed one of the drivers. Though Slade specialized in plain killings, he sometimes adorned his homicides with a touch of the picturesque, as in the incident of his rounding off the career of Jules Beni. "Old Jules," for whom Julesburg was named, was a station agent when Slade was appointed agent of the division. Slade, according to Root, finding that Jules had been stealing from the company, forced him to make restitution, whereupon the culprit ambushed the accuser and gave him the contents of a double-barreled shotgun. Slade, who was doughty and tough, appears not to have been greatly inconvenienced by his wounds, and he shortly afterward caught Jules, put a rope around his neck and hung him up. Before life was extinct some one cut the rope; Jules managed to get away, and soon afterward began plundering the company's stores in earnest. Slade, after close search, found him, shot and badly wounded him, tied him up against a corral and cut off and nailed his ears to the fence, thereupon finishing the job by sending bullet after bullet into his body. One of the ears Slade is said to have taken down and worn as a watch charm.

Though greatly feared, he could act at times the courteous and kindly man of peace. Mark Twain speaks of him as " the most gentlemanly appearing, quiet and affable officer we had yet found along the road in the Overland company's service," although at that time he bore the reputation of having killed twenty-six men. Some of them were doubtless desperadoes who badly needed killing, but it is certain that others were inoffensive. For about two years he remained with the stage company; but he took to drinking and became quarrelsome, whereupon, some time in 1862, he was discharged. He turned up afterward in Montana, and after a short but lively career was hanged by vigilantes at Virginia City, March 10, 1864.[52]

Indians ravaged both the Overland and the Oregon Trails a number of times in the early sixties, with exceptional destructiveness of life and property in 1864. As the subject of Indian disturbances will be treated in the following chapter, the raids of the sixties need only be mentioned here. The stage company was a heavy sufferer, Holladay asserting that he had lost some $375,000 worth of property. It was a bad time for any sort of loss, since the service was doomed, and recovery by future profits impossible. From Omaha, creeping along the north bank of the Platte, came the Union Pacific railway, and every mile of its progress brought nearer the retirement of the stage.

As the railroad advanced, running stock as well as rolling stock was taken from the eastern division of the stage line and the service reduced. When, in the late summer of 1866, the tracks reached a point across the river from Fort Kearney, the coaches to and from Atchison were permanently withdrawn. In November Holladay sold out all his interests and retired to a palatial mansion on the Hudson River. The service westward from Fort Kearney was continued by Wells, Fargo & Company, probably in connection with the Western Stage Company, since a change in equipment seems to have been made. In December what remained of the onetime Holladay equipment in Atchison was moved to Junction City and Fort Riley, to be used along a line steadily contracting as the Kansas Pacific pushed its way across the plains toward Denver.

The stage-coach was still to do service in filling the gaps between the approaching ends of the railroad and traveling the lateral trails from half-a-hundred points on the line to remote camps in the mountains. But the great days were gone; and the through overland service from the Missouri to the Golden Gate had come to an end.

CHAPTER XI

RED MAN AND WHITE

THERE was no year in which travelers along the Trail were wholly free from the danger of savages. The trappers had fought an intermittent battle of many years with roving bands of the various tribes, and the emigrants knew from the start the need of vigilance. By traveling in companies large enough to protect themselves, by guarding their animals with care, by showing a bold and resolute front when threatened by superior numbers, the earlier emigrants were usually enabled to escape trouble. As late as 1859 Captain Marcy wrote that a well-equipped company containing seventy-five armed men could count on security. Such a company, by corralling its wagons into a circle, could form a defensive position that even a large body of savages would hesitate to attack.

The earlier emigrants found their first trouble with the savages somewhere about the Kansas crossing. Here were the Kaw (or Kansas) Indians, settled on a reservation. They had been repeatedly humbled by the Sioux, sometimes by the Cheyennes, and had lost their warlike spirit. But though they avoided fighting, they practised begging and pilfering in about equal proportions, and they had an especial fondness for the white man's livestock. Farther along, in the Little Blue Valley, all the way to the Platte, roamed the Pawnees. In their main village, at the mouth of the Loup, the missionaries Dunbar and Allis had settled in 1835, but the results of missionary endeavor were not apparent. The Pawnees were regarded as vicious and treacherous, ever ready to profess peace when in contact with a body of whites strong enough to command respect, but equally ready to stampede and capture their stock or to pounce upon small parties and plunder them. Along the Platte the emigrants sometimes met bands of Cheyennes and of Oglala, Minniconjou, Brulé, and Blackfeet Sioux, who were sometimes apparently peaceful and at other times aggressive and threatening. In the neighborhood of Fort Laramie and further along the North Platte, Crows — the most expert and incorrigible thieves known to Indian history — were occasionally encountered. Though they were most susceptible to the lure of horseflesh, they would take anything that could be lifted. At Major Jacob Fowler's camp near the present Pueblo, in the winter of 1821–22, a party of them pilfered so assiduously as to make even their chief ashamed; and another party, in 1832, in welcoming with hearty embraces Bonneville's men, dexterously cut the buttons from their coats. The Mormon Pioneers who reached Fort Laramie in June 1847, were told by Bordeaux, the factor in charge, that he could not keep horses and mules, since the Crows always ran away with them. Twenty-four had been taken a few weeks earlier, and in the course of a few years upward of two hundred had similarly disappeared.

Parties of Sioux might occasionally be met as far west as the upper Sweetwater. The band that surrounded Dr. Elijah White's party near Independence Rock in 1842 may have intended a general massacre, as Frémont thought, but the accounts of White, Hastings, and Crawford are too conflicting to warrant a judgment in the matter. In later times, from 1862 to 1868, all this region thronged with hostile Sioux, Cheyennes, and Arapahos, the last four years of the period being marked with a great number of atrocities.

From South Pass to Fort Bridger and on to the Bear was, in the main, secure territory. This was the domain of the noble Washakie, head chief of the Eastern Band of Shoshones, an Indian whose well-accredited story reads like fiction. The name, which is stressed on the first syllable and which means " rattle," was given him in his young warrior days because of his habit of using a bladder or gourd rattle both as an accompaniment to his singing and as a means of frightening and stampeding the horses of his enemies. Washakie was born about 1804, in a Flathead village, probably in the Bitter Root Valley, southwestern Montana. " He is undeniably a half-breed," wrote Colonel Lander, who knew him well and admired him greatly. But the statement is evidently an error, for according to his son, Dick Washakie, at present honorary head chief of the Eastern Shoshones, the father was of Flathead and Umatilla stock and the mother a Shoshone. Orphaned by the killing of his father in a battle with the Blackfeet, he lived as a child and young man with the Lemhi band of Shoshones, who befriended Lewis and Clark, and who gave to history Sacagawea,[53] the Bird Woman of that immortal expedition. Later he was for a time with the turbulent Bannocks and still later he joined the Shoshones of the region about the future Fort Bridger.

He came into frequent contact with the early trappers, and tradition makes him the friend and companion on trapping tours of both Bridger and Carson. He is first mentioned, so far as known, in 1840, in Osborne Russell's *Journal of a Trapper*. The Shoshones of the northwest (Northern Shoshones) were then loosely united as a single nation, and Washakie, according to Russell, was regarded as one of their three most prominent warriors. The death of the head chief in the following year and of his brother a year later caused the breakup of the nation into various bands. Within a short time possibly in 1843, Washakie drew together under his personal standard a number of groups, and from this nucleus gradually developed the band ever since known as the Eastern Shoshones.

His policy of friendship for the whites was early formed, and from it he never deviated. It was not a merely passive friendship, but one that expressed itself in many benevolent actions. Colonel Lander tells of his helpfulness to the whites and says that at one time he carried a paper signed by 9,000 emigrants testifying to the aid they had received from him. Travelers, Indian agents, and army officers who knew him have left a volume of testimony to the greatness of his character unapproached by that given to any other Indian. In 1868 the Government granted him and his people the reservation in the Wind River Valley which he had himself chosen; but he rightly refused to settle there until forts were built and garrisoned for protection against the marauding hordes from the plains. When finally,

WASHAKIE (1804–1900)

*Head Chief of the Eastern Shoshones and lifelong
friend of the whites*

after four years of waiting, this protection was given, he led his people to their new home. For many years thereafter he served as an army scout, and with a band of his followers he was for a time with Crook in the campaign of 1876 against the Sioux. He died near Fort Washakie on February 20, 1900, and a military funeral was accorded him.[54]

The California-bound emigrants, whether they turned from the Trail at Fort Bridger or at Fort Hall, found occasional Utes, many Bannocks, various bands of Digger Shoshones and, farther on, Washos, who were at times troublesome. The Bannocks were also frequently encountered by the Oregon emigrants. This Shoshonean sub-tribe or band lived mostly by plunder, and unless the emigrant party was numerous and well equipped it was likely to be attacked. The Bannocks had a long career in crime. According to Alexander Ross they had perpetrated the unprovoked murder of John Reed's hunting party, from Astoria, in 1814, and in the years following they added to their score many acts of savage violence. There were, however, periods in which they were comparatively harmless. One such period followed a battle on the Green River, in August 1826, when William L. Sublette, with 250 trappers, almost annihilated the band; another, in the summer of 1836, also in the Green Valley, when Bridger, with a force of trappers, gave them another severe chastisement, and still another, on January 29, 1863, when Colonel Patrick Edward Connor destroyed their village on the Bear River and killed most of the warriors. But among these incorrigible banditti the lesson of a thorough beating did not last long. Forgetting one disaster, unapprehensive of the next, and recruited to fighting force by hostile renegades from more peaceful bands or tribes, they were soon ready for fresh depredations.

Other Shoshones, usually peaceful, were encountered by the emigrants along the Snake. After the Blue Mountains were passed they found the Cayuses, the tribe among whom Whitman planted his mission in 1836. With these or their next-door neighbors, the Walla Wallas, except for occasional horse-stealing, there was rarely trouble until the outbreak and massacre of 1847. Nez Percés were occasionally met, but were usually peaceful. Along the north shore of the Columbia there were several tribes not indisposed to theft and murder, and those who descended the river by boat and portage had often to guard themselves and their property with the rifle; but those who traveled its south bank generally found a peaceful journey. By military proclamation the eastern region of Oregon was closed to settlers after the massacre, and the Trail was abandoned. In 1859, after the Indians had been subdued, the region was reopened, but the last leg of the route to Oregon had long before been exchanged for one by way of northern California.

On the northern California route, especially in the Klamath Lakes country, many massacres were perpetrated. Here were Klamaths and Modocs, and farther along were the Rogue River Indians, all of them bloodthirsty and treacherous. A number of massacres in July and August, 1852, brought on several punitive expeditions, one of them led by the noted Ben Wright. The Indians were checked for a time, but in June 1856, Klamaths, with perhaps a few Shastas, murdered fifteen miners scattered along the Klamath River. They then fled across the Siskiyou Mountains and joined the Rogue River Indians, and another war began, in which the Modocs also took part. Both California and Oregon sent troops to the region, and the Indians were severely punished. But from time to time other depredations followed, and the Modocs were not finally quelled until June 1873.

Yet on the Trail proper the earlier emigrants managed to get through with small loss of life and property. The threatening demonstration by a band of Sioux toward Dr. White's party on the Sweetwater, in 1842, was at least bloodless. Promises made in the Great Council at Horse Creek, in 1851, not to molest the emigrants, were in a measure kept. The massacre of Lieutenant Grattan's command, near Fort Laramie, in 1854, though arising out of an emigrant's loss of a cow, involved no taking of an emigrant's life. The Sioux were often provocative, and the incident at Fort Laramie given by Parkman is quite in the Sioux manner; but their actual depredations were few. By roving bands of one tribe or another small parties or stragglers from the wagon trains were now and then plundered and sometimes murdered, and livestock was often stampeded and run off. But no great disturbance happened until 1862, when by a sort of common impulse the Indians over a wide range of territory became threatening. The belief of the savages that since the white men were exhausting themselves in fighting one another they were in no condition to fight men of another color; the apprehension among them that the whites were aiming to take all their lands; the realization that game was becoming scarcer with each year, and a growing conviction that the easiest way of making a living was to plunder the whites — all these were factors in the general unrest.

The first trouble of any consequence along the Trail began in April. Bands of Sioux, Cheyennes, and Arapahos raided the telegraph and stage stations all the way from Casper to Fort Bridger, burning the structures, killing men, and running off stock and sometimes rifling the mails. On April 28 President Lincoln telegraphed President Young, of the Mormon Church, requesting him to raise a company of one hundred men for ninety days' service in the vicinity of Independence Rock. The company was raised, but as it found no Indians, it was disbanded thirty days later. Troops from the East were also sent along the Trail. The Bannocks again becoming troublesome, Colonel Connor, with the Third California Volunteers, was ordered to Utah. In October he arrived, and on a hill overlooking Salt Lake City established Camp Douglas, whence he sent out small detachments of troops in various directions.

Though the raids on the Sweetwater had caused Holladay to move his stages to the Cherokee Trail, the telegraph line remained on the South Pass route, and by this route, however dangerous, many of the emigrants continued to travel. There were thus two widely separated lines to guard. On the Cherokee Trail, at the north base of Elk Mountain, the Government established Fort Halleck, and it sent small columns of troops to both trails.

In August of that year had occurred the outbreak by certain Sioux bands along the Minnesota River —

an event that was to have far-reaching effects on the plains. Six hundred and forty-four peaceful whites were known to have been killed and two hundred taken captive. Troops were hurried to the scene, and in a swift and brilliant campaign, under Colonel Henry Hastings Sibley, ex-Governor of the state, they routed the hostiles and compelled the surrender of the captives. Other campaigns in the two following years by Sibley and General Alfred Sully drove the remaining hostiles to the Missouri, where they succeeded in spreading among their kinsmen the war fever against the whites.

To punish the Bannocks and their allies, Colonel Connor, with about three hundred troops, set out on a midwinter day from Camp Douglas. The weather was bitterly cold, and the men suffered greatly. At dawn of January 29, 1863, he attacked the Indian camp on Bear River, near the present Franklin, Idaho, killing most of the three hundred warriors and capturing 160 women and children. For this feat, which brought peace, cleared the Trail, and opened to settlement a region that had been harassed for fifteen years, Connor was made a brigadier general of volunteers. It is said that some of Washakie's renegades returned to the camp of the chieftain after the battle, and that he drove them out. But later in the year the Bannocks signed a treaty of peace at Fort Bridger, and thereafter they became closely associated with Washakie's band until 1870, when most of them were settled on the Fort Hall reservation.

West of Salt Lake City there were several harassing raids in the spring and early summer of 1863, but matters quieted somewhat in July, when certain bands of

Utes and Shoshones and the Goshutes (a band of inter-
married Utes and Shoshones), made peace at Fort
Bridger. Other Utes at the same time began running
off the stock of the stage company and committed other
depredations in the neighborhood of Fort Halleck, and
not until the appearance of new details of troops were
they driven off.

It was along the eastern section of the Trail, however,
that the greatest danger was manifested. In April,
May, and July, General Robert Mitchell, commander
of the Nebraska District, held councils with the Sioux,
but each ended in failure; and in September, Governor
John Evans, of Colorado Territory, sought, with no
better success, to get representatives of the various
tribes to meet him in council. To an emissary who told
them that the Governor wanted them to settle down on
their reservation and live as white men, one of them
replied: " Well, you can just go back to the Governor
and tell him we are not reduced quite that low yet." [55]
The Government established a new post, Fort Mc-
Pherson, on the Platte, about a hundred miles west of
Fort Kearney; but the Indians, far from being over-
awed, continued their threatening attitude.

The Cheyennes, with some co-operation from the
Arapahos, Kiowas and Comanches, began a series of
raids in Colorado early in 1864. An appeal by the
Governor for troops was met by the response that none
were available. A force of militia was organized, but
the savages continued their raids. On June 11,
thirty miles southeast of Denver, a ranchman, his wife,
and two children were killed and scalped. In July
attacks were made on a number of the stage stations on

the South Platte, and five men were killed and 130 horses stolen. The outbreak reached its climax in August, in a series of massacres along a wide stretch of territory from the lower Little Blue to Julesburg. At Liberty Farm, on the Little Blue, in southern Nebraska, the station and a wagon train were destroyed; Joseph Eubanks, the stage driver and station keeper, and eight or nine others were killed and scalped, and Mrs. Eubanks, her two children and a Miss Roper were carried into captivity.[56] During these raids thirty or forty persons were killed, and property to the value of nearly a million dollars was destroyed. For some time the stage service was stopped. A mail coach was brought through to Denver from Atchison on the 25th, but for nearly a month no further effort was made to raise the blockade. The Denver postmaster was ordered on September 2 to send eastbound mail to San Francisco, while mail that accumulated at Atchison was returned to New York, both to be transported by the ocean route.[57]

General Samuel R. Curtis, the victor of Pea Ridge, now in command of the Department of Kansas, made vigorous efforts to quell the disturbance. Troops were hurriedly dispatched to various points on the Trail, and the Indians disappeared. Reassuring news from the disturbed district caused a mail coach to be started from Denver on September 23. It arrived safely at Atchison, and on the way passed a coach which arrived in Denver on the 29th. In October the regular service was resumed.

About the end of August, Black Kettle and other Cheyenne chiefs had made overtures for peace. To

Major E. W. Wynkoop, commander of Fort Lyon, who with his command journeyed to their village on the Smoky Hill River, they surrendered four white prisoners. They then accompanied him to Denver, where, on September 28, they had a conference with Governor Evans, Colonel John M. Chivington (who had rendered valuable service in the campaign against the Confederates in New Mexico) and others. Winter was coming on; grass for the Indian ponies was failing, and soon there would be snow. Having plundered and killed to the best of their opportunities, the warriors now wanted peace, security, and Government rations for the winter. In the spring they could, of course, take the war trail again. The conference was indecisive, since the whites had no faith in the Indians' sincerity. On the same day a telegram was received from General Curtis forbidding the making of a peace without his sanction. The Indians were, however, advised to surrender unconditionally, and Major Wynkoop was suggested as the most available officer to whom the surrender might be made.

The chiefs returned to their villages and with their wives and children and such of their warriors as had returned from the warpath assembled at Fort Lyon. Wynkoop telegraphed to Curtis for instructions, but before a reply was received he was relieved from command and Major Scott J. Anthony was made his successor. Anthony ordered the Indians away from the fort, and they moved forty miles to the northeast and encamped on Sand Creek.

Colonel Chivington, with the Third Colorado and a part of the First Colorado Cavalry, at once marched to

Fort Lyon, where he arrived on November 28. After a council with Anthony, he made a night march to the Sand Creek camp and on the morning of the 29th began an attack. The village was destroyed, and more than a hundred Indians, including many women and children, were killed. The battle has been generally known as the " Chivington massacre " and is still a matter of bitter controversy, based upon conflicting testimony. Eyewitnesses reported that there was indiscriminate slaughter, and that the bodies of the slain were terribly mutilated. Irving Howbert, a participant in the fight, in his *Memories of a Lifetime in the Pike's Peak Region*, denies the truth of these stories and asserts that most of the adverse testimony was prompted by politics and a desire to discredit Chivington.[58]

Other posts were established during the fall of 1864 — Fort Rankin (later to be named Fort Sedgwick), near Julesburg, and Camp Wardwell, at the station known as Bijou Ranch or Junction (the present Fort Morgan, Colorado). Early in 1865, General Grenville M. Dodge was appointed to direct the campaign, and new plans were made for keeping the Trail free from molestation.

A fresh outbreak of hostilities, on an even greater scale, now occurred. The winter, until the middle of February, was a somewhat open one; there was grass for the ponies, and the Sioux, Cheyennes, and Arapahos combined for a general campaign. On January 7, 1865, about a thousand warriors attacked Julesburg. The savages first attempted to lure a party of soldiers from Fort Rankin to the nearby sandhills, and though failing in this attempt killed fourteen of them. The warriors then started for the stage station. The west-bound coach had just arrived, and the passengers had alighted for breakfast. Upon seeing the Indians coming they rushed to Fort Rankin, and all were saved. A paymaster for the Federal troops was among them and in his hurry abandoned his money box. Two discharged soldiers traveling east in a wagon were killed and mutilated. The Indians plundered the coach and the supply stores, carrying away sacks of flour, sugar, and shelled corn. They then leisurely moved off to their camp on the headwaters of the Republican River.

The use of the captured goods was not the white man's use; the Indians dumped the flour on the ground, but they kept the sacks for shirts and breech-clouts. Shelled corn, which neither they nor their ponies would eat, they carried away to be strewn on ice, as the white man strews ashes, to give a better footing. For some of the goods they had purely esthetic uses. A bolt of highly colored calico would be grabbed at the free end by a mounted Indian, who would then gallop away; and as the strip unwound to float in the wind and the bobbin danced and ricochetted over the ground the other warriors would greet the sport with howls of delight. The greenbacks, of the value of which few of the warriors knew anything, were generally thrown aside. One warrior is recorded as chopping a stack of them to pieces with his tomahawk and tossing the fragments in the air for the joy of seeing the wind carry them in flurries over the prairie.

The raid for a time paralyzed traffic. No vehicle moved eastward until January 14, when a train of 105 wagons and three hundred men, protected by a military escort with cannon, left Denver for Atchison, where it arrived safely. On the 28th a concerted attack was made on the stations along the South Platte for a distance of about seventy-five miles. Stations and ranch houses were burned and wagon trains captured. Five days later (February 2) Julesburg was again attacked and this time thoroughly plundered and then burned. There were but two posts at which troops were stationed — Fort Rankin and Valley — and the garrisons were too small to afford protection. Repeated appeals were made by Evans, Holladay, and others to Washington, but the forces sent were inadequate. The Government, in its final effort to end the Civil War, needed all its forces on the southern front. The Indians had swung off to the north, followed by a small column under Colonel W. O. Collins, of the Eleventh Ohio Cavalry, and on February 3 a five-coach mail train, escorted by forty soldiers, started east from Denver. On February 11 General Dodge telegraphed that he was prepared to protect the mail route, and the wagons and coaches again began to move.

The hostiles were now in the upper Powder River country, north of the great bend of the Platte — their favorite game preserve since they had ousted the Crows from the region — and for the summer and fall the pressure on the Overland Trail was removed. But along the Oregon Trail, and particularly about Platte Bridge Station (the present Casper), there was almost constant warfare. Here, at the last crossing of the North Platte, there was a telegraph station, and also a toll bridge, which had been built by a Canadian squaw man, Louis Ganard; and the hostiles chose the spot as a favorable place for killing and loot. A few troops had been placed there in July 1859, but they were withdrawn in the following April. No more were sent until May 1862, and the post was not established until the summer of 1863. The history of Platte Bridge Station during the half-decade following is one of a close siege, with repeated attacks on small parties of emigrants and soldiers; many killings, the theft or destruction of much property and the persistent demolition of the telegraph line.

Root, in *The Overland Stage,* makes the curious and quite erroneous statement that as a rule the Indians, out of some superstitious fear, did not disturb the telegraph. The diary of Sergeant Isaac B. Pennick, of the Eleventh Kansas Cavalry, quoted in Hebard and Brininstool's *The Bozeman Trail,* gives many instances of the breaking of wires and the burning of poles in the North Platte region. The savages tried chopping the poles, but the work was too laborious. Burning them, the warriors waiting patiently till they toppled and fell, was tried; but though time was a thing of no great value to the savage, the task proved irksome. Far more satisfactory was the practice of mounting their horses, looping their lariats over the wires and galloping away to tear the strands from their fastenings. Though repairs were quickly made, the destruction was repeated. Among all the instances of courage in the performance of duty, there are perhaps few so striking as those of the soldier linemen who, night after night, with the hoofs of their horses muffled to prevent any sound reaching the ears of the savages thickly clustered about them, strung new wires and reset the fallen poles or replaced the ones demolished.[59]

With the summer of 1865 the pressure against the Bozeman Trail and that part of the Oregon Trail which passed to the north side of the Platte at Platte Bridge Station became more intense. Across from the station, on July 26, was fought the engagement between a small party of soldiers and several hundred Indians in which the gallant Lieutenant Caspar W. Collins and four privates were killed and twelve privates wounded. On the same day, a few miles distant, a troop train of three wagons was captured and burned and all but three of its twenty-five soldiers and drivers were killed. The hostiles were determined that no part of the country above the North Platte should be traveled by the white man's wagons. It was rightly Crow country, held by the Crows from a time before the white man came, and guaranteed to them by the Horse Creek treaty of 1851. But the conquering Sioux had driven the Crows northwestward, and their allies, the Cheyennes and the Arapahos, eager to be in wherever there was a chance for plundering and killing, made one with them in the contest.[60]

To stop the depredations a new military district — the Mountain District — was formed in the spring of 1865, and General Connor was chosen to command it. A force of three columns, aggregating about 1,600 officers and men, was organized to invade the Powder River country and enforce peace. Connor's column, which left Fort Laramie on July 20, built a stockade named Fort Connor (a year later enlarged and renamed Fort Reno) on the headwaters of the Powder, and penetrating the hostile district to the Tongue, destroyed an Arapaho village, killing sixty-three warriors and capturing 1,100 ponies. But none of the columns was properly equipped; none of the officers knew anything of the country in which they were operating, and after a deal of aimless wandering and much suffering from hunger and cold, all made their way to Fort Laramie in October. Connor was relieved, and new plans were made for a campaign in the following year.[61]

The operations of the Powder River expedition had lessened the pressure on the Overland Trail and to some extent that on the Wyoming section of the Oregon Trail. The covered wagons continued to throng the westward highways. Sergeant Pennick, returning from Platte Bridge Station, writes in his diary that on August 17 he found hundreds of wagons at Julesburg; that in the next two days he met 615 more and in the next three days an additional 705.[62] Many of these wagons were doubtless headed for the Bozeman Trail, which continued, despite the Indian menace, to carry a large emigration into Montana.

The Government now resolved to meet the issue and to open the country above the North Platte. At Fort Sully, in October, an Indian commission held a council with some of the Sioux and drew up a treaty permitting emigrant trains to enter the Powder River country unmolested. But the representatives who signed it were mostly of the tribes that dwelt along the river, while the Oglalas, who spent little time at home, refused to sign, and their principal chief, Red Cloud, openly defied the Government to open the region.

Colonel Henry B. Carrington was put in command of the Mountain District, with instructions to establish and garrison four posts and to protect the emigrant

RED CLOUD (1822–1909)

Head Chief of the Oglala Sioux. From a Government photograph taken about 1875

trails. At Fort Laramie he held a council with such of the Indians as would attend, and he sought to obtain their consent to the building of the forts and the passage of the emigrant wagons. The Cheyennes were half disposed to yield, but Red Cloud and Young Man Afraid of His Horses refused to attend and threatened war if the projected invasion should be attempted. Carrington was not to be dismayed. He moved forward, and on June 28 reached Fort Connor, which he enlarged and renamed Fort Reno, in honor of General Jesse L. Reno, killed at South Mountain, Maryland, September 14, 1863. On the 13th of July, near the mouth of the Little Piney, sixty-seven miles north of Fort Reno, he began the building of Fort Phil Kearney (the name of which, like that of the other Fort Kearney, was officially misspelled). Here, on the 16th, he held a further conference with some of the hostiles, who demanded that he retire from the country. Black Horse, of the Cheyennes, though joining in this demand, was still disposed toward an understanding with the whites, but on so declaring himself to a party of Red Cloud's Sioux after the conference, he and his followers were reproached with cowardice. The imputation brought them around to a determination to fight, and thereafter they made common cause with the Sioux. In August a detachment was sent northwest ninety-one miles to a point on the Bighorn, where Fort C. F. Smith (named for General Charles Ferguson Smith, a distinguished officer of the Mexican War) was established. The plan to build a fort on the Yellowstone was abandoned.

Carrington maintained his headquarters at Fort Phil

Kearney. Near the fort, on December 21, occurred the massacre in which Captain W. J. Fetterman, two under-officers, seventy-six soldiers and two civilians were killed. Carrington, who had done prodigies with a weak force, was wrongly charged with the blame and was superseded. In the following year occurred the two noted battles of the Hayfield fight, near Fort C. F. Smith, on August 1, and of the Wagon Box fight near Fort Phil Kearney, on August 2. In all the history of the warfare of whites against Indians it would be hard to find another battle comparable to either of these two. In the first, a party of eleven soldiers and nine civilians, protected by a rude corral of logs and willow branches, beat off, in a fight lasting more than seven hours, a force of perhaps a thousand warriors, losing but one officer, one soldier, and one civilian killed and three soldiers and one civilian wounded. In the other, a party of two officers, twenty-six men, and four civilians, taking refuge in a corral of wagon boxes, defended themselves for three and a half hours against attacks of a force of Indians estimated at three thousand, with a loss of only one officer and five men killed and two men wounded. Some effort to detract from the credit of the latter feat has been made by asserting that the wagon boxes were lined with boiler iron and therefore impervious to the bullets and arrows of the Indians. But the testimony of all the survivors of the fight who were questioned in the matter is that except for nails and bolts the wagon boxes were solely of wood and that they were riddled and splintered by the shots of the savages.[63]

Indian resistance to the Government's policy was constant and determined. The forts were in a constant state of siege, and travel along the Bozeman Trail was impossible except by parties strongly guarded. The Government was thus faced with the alternative either of abandoning the country or of invading it with a force sufficient to overcome the hostiles. After a time it chose the former. The Fort Laramie peace conference in the fall of 1867 brought no results, and in the following April, at the same fort, another conference was held. On the 29th a treaty was drawn up, pledging the Government to abandon the forts. By August 7 the soldiers had left, and the forts had been burned by the Indians. Until the campaigns of 1876–77, when the Indians were expelled, the country remained closed to the whites. With the abandonment of the forts depredations along the Oregon Trail diminished, though they did not wholly cease. In some measure the Indian menace in this section lasted throughout the period of the general use of the Trail.

CHAPTER XII

DECLINE OF THE TRAIL

THE Oregon Trail has a unique place in American history. It was the longest trail; the paths by which the emigrants of the Atlantic States crossed the mountains into the plains and valleys of Kentucky and Ohio were short stretches by comparison. It traversed regions where often no game could be found; and it presented, over many miles of its length, great natural difficulties — deep rivers, high ranges, and arid wastes upon which the midsummer sun poured blinding heat as the strong winds swept them with clouds of choking dust; while the eastern trails wound through a well-watered, a timbered, and a grass-carpeted country in which game abounded. Among western trails it stands out as primarily the trail of the home-seeker; and among all trails as the one by which were wrought the greatest political consequences. The venturous pioneers of the first three emigrations along this route furnished the final argument against England's claim on Oregon; and the caravans that turned from the Trail into California furnished the man-power that at the critical time of the breakdown of Mexican authority made that province a part of the United States.

The early emigrants were from almost every part of the country. Perhaps most of them were such as had reached the Missouri by a series of removals, trying out for brief periods of settlement a number of stopping places on the way. The adventurous spirit was easily acquired and not easily overcome. But at the Missouri the pioneer faced an alternative greater than any he had faced before. He must halt, or he must go the long way to the Pacific. The country immediately in front of him was closed to settlement, and there was no intermediate stopping. So, as a rule, it was the bravest, though sometimes the most reckless, who went forward. Jesse Applegate, writing of 1843, the year in which he commanded the cow column of the emigration, thus characterizes his company:

No other race of men with the means at their command would undertake so great a journey, none save these could successfully perform it, with no previous preparation, relying only on the fertility of their own invention to devise the means to overcome each danger and difficulty as it arose. They have undertaken to perform with slow-moving oxen a journey of two thousand miles. The way lies over trackless wastes, wide and deep rivers, ragged and lofty mountains, and is beset with hostile savages. Yet, whether it were a deep river with no tree upon its banks, a rugged defile where even a loose horse could not pass, a hill too steep for him to climb, or a threatened attack of an enemy, they are always found ready and equal to the occasion, and always conquerors. May we not call them men of destiny? They are people changed in no essential particulars from their ancestors, who have followed closely on the footsteps of the receding savage, from the Atlantic seaboard to the great Valley of the Mississippi.

The motives that started them on the long and dangerous journey were many. Recurrent panics decided some of them, and the panic of 1837, with effects that lasted on the frontier for five or six years, was assuredly an important factor. Poverty of the individual, that somehow persisted through good times as well as bad, decided others. Illness was sometimes the determining motive, the fever and ague of the early days awakening an eager desire to reach a land wherein, it was said, neither was known. There were invalids, too, who started because they had heard that in the high altitudes that the Trail climbed, throat and lung troubles were permanently cured. Youth went for adventure, and men of abounding vitality went to find a wider field for the exercise of their powers.

It was inevitable that John Ball, of New Hampshire, first to cross the continent and make a permanent home in Oregon, should be a pioneer. In his youth he had listened while Sergeant John Ordway, of the Lewis and Clark expedition and a neighbor of his father's, told of the wonders of the far-away land; and the desire that he then formed tormented him until it was fulfilled. Hall Kelley, earliest agitator for the settlement of Oregon, dated his first interest in the subject from the reading of Patrick Gass' journal. To the father of William M. Case, a member of the 1844 emigration, came a public document with an account of the Lewis and Clark expedition, and over this the boy pored with delight, as he resolved some day to go to Oregon.

Enmity to England had its share in the decisions. The emigrants of the early forties were of a generation that remembered the tales of Indian outrages incited by British agents, and they did not choose to forget. They believed that Oregon belonged to the United States and that England was determined to retain her hold unless enough Americans settled there to thwart the aim. " To plant 30,000 rifles in the valley of the Columbia " was a popular phrase of the time, and the purpose it embodied reached a more direct expression in 1844 with the slogan, " Fifty-four forty or fight! " Minto tells the story of a young backwoods Missourian of the emigration of 1844 who, in order to see what the inside of a ship looked like, boarded a British vessel at Fort Vancouver. To the irritated captain's question, " Where do you come from and why do you come here? " he defiantly replied: " We've come from Missouri across the Rocky Mountains. We've come to settle in Oregon and rule this country."

Some went because fathers or brothers or uncles had taken the Oregon or the California fever. It was a highly contagious fever, and those within its range easily succumbed. There were some who started reluctantly, not certain that they would be satisfied with the new country, first making sure of a safe anchorage for a possible retreat. " Mother consented to come [with us]," writes a woman who went from Illinois in 1854, " providing the old homestead could be kept unencumbered to return to in case we should not like California." The promise of unfailing harvests was potent; a farmer, the father of the woman just mentioned, made his decision when he read that in California wheat and peaches were a sure crop each year.[64] The Rev. Myron Eells, in his *Marcus Whitman, Pathfinder and Patriot,* gave the result of his efforts to discover the immediate motive which had prompted the then surviving emigrants of 1843 to make the start. Of thirty-eight who at one time or another furnished this information, sixteen asserted

that they had started because of something said or written by Dr. Whitman (though of course the anti-Whitmanites generally deny the possibility of such a thing);
eleven because they had read something by Dr. White;
six because they had read accounts of the Lewis and
Clark expedition; three because they had read certain
letters on Oregon by Robert Shortess, and two because
they had heard or read of the introduction of a land-
grant bill in the Federal Senate. Colonel George B.
Currey, in an address before the Oregon pioneers in
1887, declared that the best answer he ever got to the
question of motive was from a genuine westerner who
said: " Because the thing wasn't fenced in, and nobody
dared to keep him off."

Whatever the incidental motive, the adventurous
spirit was there in the breasts of these emigrants, waiting only the call for action. These people were the
heirs, by blood or tradition, of the generations that had
been steadily moving westward since the first colonies
were planted on the Atlantic seaboard. They had come
to feel the sense of common ownership in a great territory that stretched from ocean to ocean. Their youth
declaimed the lines of Sewall's poem:

> No pent-up Utica contracts your powers,
> But the whole boundless continent is yours.

They thought of "manifest destiny"; for though the
term appears not then to have been invented, its content
had been often voiced in the speeches and writings of
the period of the second war with Great Britain, and
after that in a growing volume. Those who could safely
break with their surroundings made the journey.

Rightly the pioneer period closes with the year 1848. The way was now broken for others to follow. Then came the tumultuous rush of the gold-hunters and fresh swarms of emigrants. The Trail rose to a greater importance. In turn it saw the march of an army to the Mormon capital, the advent of long freight trains, the Pony Express and the stage-coach; and all this time the wagons of the emigrants continued to pour along its winding length. Then came the railroad, paralleling its course, and the importance of the Trail began to decline.

Who first suggested a railway to the Pacific cannot be said. Mention is made of a Robert Mills who is alleged to have advocated it in 1819; but as there was then no railroad, in the proper sense, anywhere in the world, it is hard to see how he could have proposed the extension of something as yet unknown. H. H. Bancroft quotes a statement that the suggestion was first made in 1831 by a Colonel Low, then a professor in St. Joseph's College, Bardstown, Kentucky. The reception of the idea in his immediate environment was anything but cordial, for the trustees of the college held a meeting and on no evidence but the pamphlet in which he had published his views declared him insane and his seat vacant.[65] The idea, however, was not so easily to be dismissed. It was again publicly proposed in an article in *The Emigrant,* a newspaper of Ann Arbor, Michigan Territory, on February 6, 1832, and the route suggested was that of the Platte and the Snake to Oregon.[66] Most persons who considered the matter at all deemed the proposal visionary, but by another decade it had won serious attention. Its most prominent early advocate was Asa Whitney, a merchant of New York, who favored the Falls of St. Anthony (St. Paul) as the starting point. Memorials for the construction of such a road, under the direction of the Secretary of War, were presented in both the 29th and the 30th Congresses (1845–49). There was no possibility of the passage of any bill embodying Whitney's proposal; and the opposition of Senator Benton, based on his demand for a central route, started a contest over the choice of an eastern terminus that was to continue until after the outbreak of the Civil War.[67]

The annexation of Texas in 1845 and the acquisition of the Spanish Southwest in 1848 opened up possibilities of southern routes. The South naturally favored a route most advantageous to its own interests, and though conviction of the need of a railway became more general, there could be no agreement as to the route until the slavery issue was settled. There could, however, be agreement as to the need of more knowledge on the topography of the West, and the act of March, 1853, authorizing a number of surveys, was promptly followed by Secretary Davis in sending out five parties of surveyors.

When the reports of the surveys came in, Davis recommended, as was to have been expected, a southern route along the general course of the 32d parallel. The South carried its point in the establishment of a southern mail route (the Butterfield Overland Mail), but the railroad project remained in deadlock. With the resignation of the southern Senators and Representatives in the winter of 1860–61 the way was at last cleared for action. Bills for the construction of a railway were introduced in the summer session of 1861, but the press of other business caused action on them to be deferred until the winter session.   Theodore D. Judah, an eastern engineer who had been brought to California in 1854 to build the Sacramento Valley railroad, now became the most important figure in the agitation.   He had carefully surveyed a route across the Sierras by Dutch Flat and Donner Pass, and had made the subject of an overland railroad his single-minded interest.   He arrived in Washington in the fall of 1861, obtained the appointment of secretary of the Senate committee on railroads and later clerk of the main House committee.   With untiring vigor he pressed the urgency of a Pacific railroad by the central route.

There were now but three contenders for the prize of the eastern terminus — the Chicago group or interest, that of St. Louis and that of Minnesota.   The northern claims were soon rejected; and in the final decision, the Chicago group, backed by New York and New England and financing a railroad already pushing its way across Iowa, was enabled to designate Council Bluffs as the terminus.   A bill providing for the construction of the road and embodying, in the main, Judah's views, was passed by the House on May 6, 1862, and by the Senate on June 20 and approved by President Lincoln on July 1.   Judah was not to live to see his work fulfilled, for he died in New York City on the 2d of November of the year following.[68]

The act created a corporation known as the Union Pacific Railroad Company, with a capital stock of 100,000 shares of the value of $1,000 each, of which not more than 200 shares were to be held by one person.

It provided that this corporation should build a line from the 100th meridian (with certain connecting lines eastward therefrom) to the western boundary of Nevada; and that the western end of the line should be built by the Central Pacific Company, an organization formed by Judah in June, 1861. The course westward was to be by "the most direct, central and practicable route," the curves and grades were not to exceed those of the Baltimore and Ohio railroad, and the whole line was to be completed by July 1, 1874.

The Central Pacific began construction early in 1863. But though large land grants and enormous loans from the Government treasury were provided for, private capital declined to finance the Union Pacific, and the project languished. It was seen that without more tempting inducements there would be no railroad, and in 1864 a new bill was passed, almost doubling the grants and greatly increasing the security of investments. It further provided that either extension, on reaching its designated terminus, could continue to lay track until it met the line of the other. Within a short time the financial response enabled the work to proceed. On November 4, 1864, Lincoln formally approved the plan of the first one hundred miles of track west of Omaha. But the start was painfully slow, and not until September 1865 were the first eleven miles completed.

When the road was begun Omaha had no railway connection with the East. Material had to be brought by wagon and by steamboat. Along the Platte there was no timber except the useless cottonwood. The price of ties delivered at Omaha ran as high as $2.50 each, and the rails for the first one hundred miles cost $135 a ton. Though with the mustering out of the armies labor became both plentiful and serviceable, it was at first scarce and poor. The Indians were hostile, and the construction crew was an armed camp. Surveying parties were sometimes murdered and scalped, and the graders had to work at all times with their guns within easy reach. Soldiers guarded the workmen, but the workmen were also mainly soldiers, admirably fitted to deal with the Indians, and with their rifles close at hand could ordinarily keep the savages at bay. General Grenville M. Dodge, chief engineer of the line from 1866 to 1870, gives this picture of the conditions under which the work progressed:

We marched to work to the tap of the drum with our men armed. They stacked their arms on the dump and were ready at a moment's warning to fall in and fight for their territory. General Casement's track train could arm a thousand men at a word; and from him as a head down to his chief spiker, it could be commanded by experienced officers of every rank from general to a captain.

The engineers, choosing the line in obedience to the requirement of the law for " the most direct, central and practicable route," ignored the greater part of the Oregon Trail. Fort Laramie and South Pass were too far to the north. They also ignored a considerable section of the Overland Trail, because of its dip to the south. In terms of the old trails the route taken was the following: Along the Mormon Trail from Omaha to a point across the Platte River from North Platte, Nebraska, then to North Platte and along the north bank of the South Platte (a course rarely used, except for a few of its stretches, by any of the emigrants) to

Upper California Crossing (Julesburg). From here it ascends Lodge Pole Creek, approximating a way taken by some of the emigrants in the late fifties. " This was the route which should have been adopted," said General J. B. Walbach, for whom Camp Walbach was named, "when the road [of the Overland Stage service] was changed from the Sweetwater and South Pass in 1862." [69] At some point, possibly in the neighborhood of Egbert, Wyoming, the railroad parts from this trail to reach Cheyenne. It continues to Dale Creek, where it approaches the Overland Trail, and for a short distance railroad and Trail are close neighbors. Thereafter the railroad veers to the north, paralleling the Trail at distances of from ten to twenty miles all the way to Little Bitter Creek, when it dips to the south and at Black Buttes rejoins the Trail. Railroad and Trail are then almost identical till they reach Granger. There the Overland joined the Oregon Trail on its southward course to Fort Bridger, while the railroad, keeping more to the west, again crosses the Oregon Trail at Carter and reaches the Salt Lake Trail at Le Roy.

Trail and railroad follow approximate courses through the mountains to Morgan, where the Trail turned southwest to Salt Lake City and the railroad turns north to Ogden. By one of the California routes of the emigrants the railroad winds around the north shore of Great Salt Lake (though the Lucin Cut-off now makes a straight line through the lake and across the desert). Where the railroad reaches the upper waters of the Humboldt is the junction place of a number of the old trails — those from Raft River, Fort Hall, and

Soda Springs as well as that from the south shore of
the Great Salt Lake. Down the Humboldt to the Sink
runs the railroad, and down this river in the old days
streamed scores of thousands of emigrants, many turning to the right for northern California near the present
Winnemucca, but most going on to the Sink and the
Truckee meadows. Of the many entrances to California this was the one most generally used, and it is the
one followed by the railroad into Sacramento.

From Omaha the tracks reached a point opposite
Fort Kearney in the late summer of 1866. With the
new year the work was speeded up. Julesburg was
reached in the spring, Cheyenne in the late fall, Laramie
City in the spring of 1868, Benton in the summer, Carter
(near Fort Bridger) late in the year. Faster and faster
went the line forward, obstructed or halted only by cli-
matic conditions. On some days seven or eight miles of
track were laid. W. A. Bell, in the *Fortnightly Review*
for May, 1869, quotes from an unidentified American
this description of the work:

Track-laying on the Union Pacific is a science, and we,
pundits of the far East, stood upon that embankment, only
about a thousand miles this side of sunset, and backed westward
before that hurrying corps of sturdy operators with a mingled
feeling of amusement, curiosity and profound respect. On they
came. A light car, drawn by a single horse, gallops up to the
front with its load of rails. Two men seize the end of a rail
and start forward, the rest of the gang taking hold by twos,
until it is clear of the car. They come forward at a run. At
the word of command the rail is dropped in its place, right side
up with care, while the same process goes on at the other side
of the car. Less than thirty seconds to a rail for each gang,
and so four rails go down to the minute! Quick work, you say,

but the fellows on the Union Pacific are tremendously in earnest. The moment the car is empty it is tipped over on the side of the track to let the next loaded car pass it, and then it is tipped back again, and it is a sight to see it go flying back for another load, propelled by a horse at full gallop at the end of sixty or eighty feet of rope, ridden by a young Jehu, who drives furiously. Close behind the first gang come the gaugers, spikers and bolters, and a lively time they make of it. It is a grand Anvil Chorus that those sturdy sledges are playing across the plains. It is in triple time, three strokes to the spike. There are ten spikes to a rail, four hundred rails to a mile, eighteen hundred miles to San Francisco. . . Twenty-one million times are those sledges to be swung — twenty-one million times are they to come down with their sharp punctuation, before the great work of modern America is completed.

In the race for the finish the Union Pacific built 1,086 miles and the Central Pacific 689 miles — a total of 1,775. There was some apprehension that the two companies, in their eagerness for subsidies, might keep on building, with no effort to form a junction; and Congress, on April 10, 1869, passed a joint resolution directing that the lines meet at Promontory Summit, a point near the northern shore of the lake. The companies had, however, adjusted their differences while Congress was debating the question; the tracks met at noon of May 10, and the event was marked with a celebration. Six hundred persons were present. The last tie, one of California laurel, was laid. Two spikes — one of gold, silver, and iron presented by Arizona, and one of silver presented by Nevada — were driven in with a silver sledge and then the last spike, of gold, the present of California. Telegraphic wires were so connected that each stroke of the sledge could be indicated in the larger cities throughout the land, and as the blows fell the message was clicked off, " One, two, three — done."

It has sometimes been assumed that when the railroad was completed migration over the Trail came to an end. But the life of the Trail had no sudden close. The covered wagons continued, though in a lessening degree, to move along its course. The average emigrant, faced with the costs of transportation for himself, his family, and his chattels, still kept to the highway. In time, moreover, the journey became more of a jaunt and less of an adventure in hardship and danger. The clearing of hostile Indians from the country and the increase of settlements along the line made possible a journey secure from harm and even from discomfort. At convenient distances supplies could be replenished, repairs made, and stock bought or traded. It is impossible to say when the last wagon traveled the Trail. Here and there, in letters, newspaper items, and frontier chronicles, one comes across mention of emigrant trains making their way westward years after the railroad had been built. James H. Cook, in his *Fifty Years on the Old Frontier,* tells of meeting a train of fifteen wagons in north central Wyoming, in the fall of 1881; and though they were then on the Montana Road, they had evidently reached it by the Oregon Trail. A correspondent in western Wyoming writes that many wagons crossed South Pass as late as the years 1893–95.

To the veteran Ezra Meeker the old Trail, though well-nigh obliterated for most of its length, was still, to the day of his death, an existent fact — a reality of the present hardly less than of the past. In 1852, at the age of twenty-one, he had traveled it with an ox-team as a pioneer to Oregon. In 1906, at the age of seventy-five, fired with the purpose of redefining and commemorating the Trail, he made the journey again. He repeated it with an ox-team in 1910, with an automobile in 1915, and in 1924 he flew along its course in an airplane. In the summer of 1928, well on toward his ninety-eighth birthday, he had started from the East in a Ford car to travel the line once more. On the way he was taken ill, and after two months in a Detroit hospital was conveyed to Seattle, where, on December 3, he passed away.

There is little of the old Trail that on his later journeys he could have found. Ranches and farms have been laid out across it, and its broad channel has been plowed over and sown to crops. Settlements have sprung up here and there and blotted out all traces of the ox hoofs and wagon wheels. Surveyors have marked off the face of the country into square townships; and the new roadways run, not by winding courses to the camping spots blessed with wood, water, and grass, but by a series of right angles from town to town. Yet out of the more thickly settled communities and into the more desolate spaces the traveler may still find the authentic vestiges of its course. The solid rock along the Sweetwater still shows the grooves worn by the wheels, and the loose soil of the plains reveals wide furrows. " Nature herself," writes Chittenden, "has helped to perpetuate this memorial, for the prairie winds, year by year, carve the furrow more deeply, and the wild sunflower blossoms along its course, as if in silent memory of those who sank beneath its burdens."

TRACKS OF THE TRAIL IN WESTERN WYOMING

*From Grace Raymond Hebard's "The Pathbreakers
from River to Ocean"* (1913)

A MODERN HIGHWAY PARALLELS THE OLD TRAIL

*Photograph taken by Professor Charles P. Berkey on
the Sweetwater, near Devil's Gate, in* 1926

APPENDIX

MONUMENTS AND MARKERS

A GROWING sense of the historic importance of the Trail has given rise to a movement to mark its natural features and the scenes of incidents occurring along its course. In the House of Representatives of the 60th Congress a bill was introduced authorizing the President to appoint a commissioner to supervise the erection of monuments and markers and locate the general route; but except for a favorable recommendation by the Committee on the Library nothing came of it. A Senate bill and two House bills before the 68th Congress provided for the designation of the route. Hearings were held before the House Committee on Roads on January 23 and February 13, 19 and 21, 1925, and the statements made were printed in an official document of 205 pages. The document reveals a considerable degree of bewilderment on the part of a number of the legislators as to what the Oregon Trail really was. It also reveals a somewhat aggressive spirit of local pride on the part of certain communities in the demand that various stretches of modern highways be designated as parts of the Oregon Trail, even though they bear no relation to the historic thoroughfare. No action was taken, and no subsequent bills have been introduced.

The movement to mark the Trail has been fostered mainly by state historical and patriotic societies and has resulted in the placing of many commemorative stones and tablets. Ezra Meeker, in his *Kate Mulhall* (1926) says that nearly two hundred of these have been set up. An attempt to compile a complete list of them, however, has so far proved futile.

The Trail has not been marked in Kansas, according to a recent letter from Mr. W. E. Connelley, secretary of the State Historical Society, but he is now engaged in identifying it by determining the quarter sections of land through which it passed, and he hopes that the marking will soon be done.

A number of markers have been placed in Nebraska. The first one was dedicated on February 14, 1910, by the Fort Kearney Chapter of the Daughters of the American Revolution and marks the site of old Fort Kearney. Mrs. Clarence S. Paine, of Lincoln, writes to the author that though an effort has been made to compile a list of the Nebraska markers it has not been completed.

In Wyoming the work has been done with thoroughness, and the record is available to the public in the excellently printed and illustrated pamphlet by Professor Grace Raymond Hebard, *Marking the Oregon Trail, the Bozeman Road and Historic Places in Wyoming,* 1908–1920 (1921). By legislative act, approved February 20, 1913, the Wyoming Oregon Trail Commission was created, and the sum of $2,500 was appropriated for expenses, subsequent legislatures appropriating $500 annually to the fund. Under its president, Captain H. G. Nickerson (recently deceased), and its two secretaries, Mrs. H. B. Patten (1913–15) and Professor Hebard (1915 to the present), the commission energetically prosecuted the work given to its charge.

Before the commission got under way the Sons and Daughters of the American Revolution of Nebraska and of Cheyenne joined hands in setting up a stone on the Wyoming-Nebraska boundary. The dedication was on April 4, 1913. The marker, a block of granite, was placed on the south side of the North Platte, near the village of Henry, Nebraska. The spot is near where Robert Stuart and his little party of eastbound Astorians camped for several weeks in the winter of 1812–13.

From the eastern to the western boundary of the state the Trail has been well marked. In Goshen County, on June 17, 1915, a stone was set up across the river from Torrington, another across the river from Lingle, and a truncated pyramid of concrete, fourteen feet high, at Fort Laramie. In the adjoining county of Platte, in October 1913, stones were erected on the divide east of Badger Creek, on the divide between Little Cottonwood Creek and the Platte and on the old telegraph and stage station grounds at Horse Creek, southwest of Glendo.

In Converse County, in September 1913, stone posts on cement bases were placed at a point south of Wagon Hound Creek; at La Prele schoolhouse (a half-mile from the Trail); at the junction of the Trail with a wagon road, southwest of the S. O. ranch, and at a spot close to the Big Muddy and near the grave of an emigrant's child, Ada Magill, who died July 3, 1864. In the same month was erected a ten-foot monument of red sandstone marking the junction of the Trail with a road to Fort Fetterman.

In Natrona County, a mile and a half west of Casper, a monument was dedicated on July 5, 1920, commemorative of Lieutenant Caspar W. Collins, killed by Indians July 26, 1865, and in the C. and N. W. railway station in the city a monument commemorative of the pioneers of the Trail was erected by the Natrona County Pioneer Association. The west face of Independence Rock was marked with an inscription; on the north face, on July 4, 1920, a bronze tablet was set, commemorative of the organization of a lodge of Masons on the Rock on July 4, 1862; and in the same year another bronze tablet, presented by Mr. Henry D. Schoonmaker, was also set in the Rock. The inscription on the last-named tablet carries the quite erroneous statement that the name of the famous landmark was given " by emigrants who celebrated Independence Day here July 4, 1825."

Farther west in Wyoming Captain Nickerson traveled with a team a total of some eight hundred miles during the summers of 1913–14, in some places marking natural features and in other places setting up inscribed stones. The wording is usually brief, such as " Slate Creek Route Oregon Trail, 1843–1914," or merely " Oregon Trail 1843." The work was attended with hardship and many discomforts, by reason of rainstorms, high winds, deep dust, and especially mosquitoes, which drove him " from the streams out into the hills or plains to camp."

" I aimed [he writes] to mark permanent bluffs and boulders, when found at suitable points on the Trail, often, however, I was compelled to haul rocks a long distance. The marking was done by cutting the letters deep into the hardest rock obtainable (generally granite), then painting the sunken letters with the best black paint. I often found it difficult to follow the trail, as it was fenced in for hundreds of miles along the streams and was obliterated by hay meadows and cultivated ranches."

A giant boulder near Devil's Gate and a bluff near Split Rock, both in Natrona County, were inscribed.

In Frémont County, at Three Crossings, a granite bluff was marked; at the site of St. Mary's Station a slate slab was set up, and another at the site of Burnt Ranch Station. In the South Pass, near Pacific Springs, are two markers — one to Mrs. Whitman and Mrs. Spalding, placed by Ezra Meeker, and the other a stone slab placed in 1916 by Captain Nickerson.

The Trail touches the newly formed Sublette County only in its extreme southeastern corner, and no marker has been placed therein. In Sweetwater County at the Little Sandy crossing, and at the point where the Trail leaves the Big Sandy, slate slabs were placed; on the face of the bluff known as Names Hill, near one of the Green crossings, an inscription was made, and slate slabs were set up at two of the crossings.

In Lincoln County, near Fontenelle Creek, about five miles west of its junction with the Green, a sandstone bluff was marked, and a slate slab was set up on Slate Creek about twelve miles southwest of Fontenelle.

At Fort Bridger, in Uinta County, a pyramid of cobblestones, ten feet high, set in a concrete foundation, was erected by the residents of the neighborhood in 1915. Into a face of the pyramid was inserted a bronze tablet (the gift of the state) carrying an inscription bearing the highly dubious statement that the fort was established as a trading post in 1834. In August 1928, the Fort Bridger grounds were purchased by private subscription and presented to the state.

At Emigrant Springs, in Lincoln County, to which the Trail came up from its southward dip to Fort Bridger, a slate slab was placed, and at the crossing of Rock Creek, about eight miles from Cokeville, was set up a solid granite stone. Cokeville has put up a commemorative stone on the outskirts of the town itself and another six miles northwest, near Border, where the Trail entered Idaho.

Occasionally there is discovered a lonely tombstone, marking the grave of one of the many who died on the way, and a new memorial is erected. In November 1925, three men walking across a hillside near Fort Laramie found a faintly inscribed fragment of sandstone that had evidently been broken from a stone still imbedded in the earth. After some difficulty they found the inscription to read:

MARY E. HOMSLEY
Died June 25, 1852
Age 29

A news article on the discovery, published in the Fort Laramie *Scout*, was followed by an editorial in the Portland *Oregonian*, which asked the question, " Who was Mary Homsley? " The question was soon answered by a daughter of the pioneer woman, Mrs. Laura Gibson, of Portland, who, seventy-three years before, at the age of three, had witnessed her mother's burial. Her father, Benjamin Homsley, a blacksmith, with his two young daughters, had reached Oregon and had settled on a homestead. There he carefully brought up his children, and there, in the fullness of time, he passed on. A reticent, undemonstrative man, he had never talked of the tragic loss, and only through the newspaper articles did Mrs. Gibson learn the place of her mother's death. From contributions by citizens of Wyoming a cement monument, in which the old stone is imbedded, was erected at the grave, and on Memorial Day, 1926, it was dedicated by Professor Hebard.

Farther to the west and northwest many other markers have been placed. In 1906 Ezra Meeker, with a covered wagon, drawn by oxen, journeyed along what was left of the Trail from west to east, determined to awaken an interest in its commemoration. At Tumwater, on Puget Sound at its most southern point, where the first American colony north of the Columbia was planted in 1845, he placed an inscribed stone, and other stones were placed, either by himself or later by local residents, at Tenino, Chehalis and Toledo. From the last-named place he proceeded downstream to Portland, to travel the southern bank of the Columbia. At the Dalles a monument was erected by the local Commercial Club, and at various places between there and Pendleton boulders were inscribed and cedar posts set in the earth. Markers of various kinds, some of them granite shafts, were set up at Pendleton, Meacham, La Grande, Ladd's Canyon, Baker City, Old Mount Pleasant, Durkee, Huntington, Vale, the site of the second Fort Boisé, the city of Boisé, South Boisé, Twin Falls, American Falls, Pocatello, Soda Springs, Montpelier and (as previously mentioned) the summit of South Pass. The most notable monument erected along the western section is that at another Emigrant Springs, this one three miles from Meacham, Oregon. The spot was used as a camping place by Wyeth's company in 1834, which was accompanied by the first missionaries, Jason and Daniel Lee, and was later used by thousands of emigrants. The dedication of this monument took place on July 4, 1923. It was attended by President Harding, who made the principal address, and was a part of a general two-days' celebration, in which an Old Oregon Trail pageant was staged at Meacham before 30,000 persons.

NOTES AND ADDITIONS

CHAPTER I

[1] *Journal of a Trapper*, 1834–1843 (1921 edition, p. 85). Russell's journal, the most intimate first-hand record of the daily life of the trapper that we have, appears to have been prepared for the printer about 1845, but was not published until 1914. A second edition appeared seven years later. See, also, H. M. Chittenden's *The American Fur Trade of the Far West* and the introduction to *The Adventures of Zenas Leonard*, edited by W. F. Wagner.

[2] Charles L. Camp (ed.), *James Clyman, American Frontiersman*, 1792–1881 (1928), pp. 29–32. This exceptionally important contribution to the early history of the trans-Mississippi West first appeared in the *Quarterly* of the California Historical Society, beginning in June 1925. In an article in the St. Louis *Weekly Reveille* of March 1, 1847, John S. Robb (" Solitaire ") asserted that Fitzpatrick led the party through South Pass, and implied that Smith had been left behind presumably because of injuries received in an attack by a grizzly bear. Clyman, who describes the grizzly bear episode, gives no warrant for Robb's statement. The injury had happened several months before the start to South Pass, and Smith appears not to have been greatly disabled. There is no good reason to doubt that Smith commanded the party.

[3] John G. White, typescript, *A Souvenir of Wyoming* (1926), Vol. III, p. xi, in the library of the Smithsonian Institution, and correspondence with the author.

[4] *Clyman*, p. 37. A number of fanciful and absurd stories in regard to the naming of Independence Rock have been

printed. Mr. Camp is probably right in his suggestion that as Fitzpatrick cached his furs near the Rock on or about July 4, 1824, the incident prompted the giving of the name.

[5] Senate Document 39, 21st Congress, 2d session, pp. 21–23. Reprinted in the *Quarterly* of the Oregon Historical Society, December 1903.

CHAPTER II

[6] This date is usually given as May 11. The log of John Boit, edited by Edmond S. Meany, and published in the *Washington Historical Quarterly*, Vol. XII, No. 1 (January 1921), p. 3, makes it May 12. Boit may, however, have been in error. See the *Quarterly* of the Oregon Historical Society, Vol. XXII, pp. 311 and 352, notes.

[7] Three articles by T. C. Elliott in the *Quarterly* of the Oregon Historical Society, Vol. XXI, No. 4 (December 1920), p. 341; Vol. XXII, No. 2 (June 1921), p. 91, and Vol. XXIII, pp. 52–69.

[8] In Hall 9, west of Art Gallery. Nos. 145 and 146 in Catlin catalogue. Chittenden and Richardson, in the De Smet *Life and Letters*, express grave doubt as to Catlin's identification of these Indians.

[9] C. T. Johnson, "The Evolution of a Lament," *Washington Historical Quarterly*, Vol. II, No. 3 (April 1908).

[10] H. S. Lyman, *Quarterly* of the Oregon Historical Society, Vol. I, No. 1 (March 1900).

[11] Myron Eells, *Marcus Whitman, Pathfinder and Patriot* (1909), pp. 46–47.

[12] Elwood Evans, *Transactions* of the Oregon Pioneer Association (1877). Mrs. F. F. Victor's statement, as given by Meek, appears in *The River of the West*, pp. 264–65, 279–81. Bancroft (*History of Oregon*, I, 240–41) also has an account, which varies in some degree from that by Evans and apparently increases the number of wagons to four and the number of male adults in the party to eight. It is not certain, however, that all went together. Joel P. Walker, who was with the Clark party, that preceded the trappers by about a month, was a

Virginian from Tennessee and was accompanied by his wife and five children. According to Bancroft this was the " first family of avowed emigrants that came to Oregon or the Pacific Coast." The Clark party, Walker and his family and others, including Father de Smet (then on his first journey to the mountains), had joined the American Fur Company expedition under Andrew Drips, which left Westport on April 30. From the rendezvous, on Green River — the last of these noted mountain fairs to be held — De Smet had proceeded to the Three Forks of the Missouri, whence he returned to St. Louis to prepare for his next journey; while the others, guided by Newell, went on to Fort Hall. Newell received the two wagons of the Clark party as pay for his services as guide.

CHAPTER III

[13] Accounts of this journey were given by the Rev. Joseph Williams, in a pamphlet printed in Cincinnati in 1843 (reprinted, with an introduction by James C. Bell, Jr., in 1921); by Bidwell in his journal, sent east and published, probably in 1843, in Weston, Mo.; in various reminiscences included in the book by C. C. Royce, *John Bidwell, Pioneer, Statesman, Philanthropist* (1906); in Bidwell's article in the *Century Magazine* for November, 1890; and by Father de Smet, *The Life, Letters and Travels of Father Pierre-Jean de Smet, 1801–1873*, edited by Hiram M. Chittenden and Alfred T. Richardson (1905). A critical resumé of the accounts is given by H. H. Bancroft, in his *History of California*.

[14] Mrs. Mary Young Walker, the wife of Joel P., arrived overland in California with her husband some twenty days before the arrival of Mrs. Kelsey, but came by way of Oregon.

[15] F. G. Young (ed.), " The Journal of Medorem Crawford," *Sources of the History of Oregon* (1897); Miss A. J. Allen (ed.), *Ten Years in Oregon*, etc. (1850); Lansford W. Hastings, *A New History*, etc. (1849). This emigrant party picked up F. X. Matthieu and two others at Fort Laramie, and at Fort Hall Osborne Russell, author of *Journal of a Trapper*,

1834–1843 (1914). All four were former trappers and mountain men who had decided to settle on the Willamette.

CHAPTER IV

[16] Kelley, the pioneer of the Oregon-for-America movement, did not succeed, despite his desperate efforts, in reaching the country until two years after Wyeth's first arrival. He started in the spring of 1833, and traveling by way of New Orleans and Vera Cruz, passed through Mexico and entered California. Here he met the trapper and trader, Ewing Young, who, with the juvenile Kit Carson in tow, had first journeyed to California in the fall of 1829. With Young and a party of ten or twelve followers, mostly adventurers and deserting seamen, he started for Oregon, but on the way became dangerously ill. After a partial recovery, he went on with the party to Fort Vancouver, where he had the mortification of learning that he and his companions had been formally charged by the Mexican Governor of California with being bandits and horse-thieves. Disappointed and embittered, he finally reached home in 1836. He had lost a small fortune and never regained even a competence.

[17] "A Day with the Cow Column in 1843," *Transactions* of the Oregon Pioneer Association (1876). Reprinted in the *Quarterly* of the Oregon Historical Society, December 1900.

[18] Yount was one of the famous trappers of the early days. Born in North Carolina, the son of a Revolutionary soldier, he had been brought at the age of ten by his father to Cape Girardeau, Missouri, in 1804. At the outbreak of the War of 1812 the father and his five sons enlisted. Young Yount served throughout the war on the Missouri frontier. Later he went to the vicinity of Franklin, in Howard County, became well-to-do as a stock farmer and married a young woman whose father bitterly opposed the match. Reverses came through the embezzlement of his savings by a friend. With what he could get together he paid his debts, gave the remainder to his wife and, presumably in the fall of 1825, left for Santa Fé.

He became a companion of Ewing Young, the Patties, Bridger, and other notables of the time, roamed over much of the West and in the winter of 1830–31 accompanied the Wolfskill-Warner party from Taos over a route somewhat north of the Spanish Trail to southern California. Here, after varying experiences, he settled in Napa Valley and became prosperous.

It is evident that he had several times endeavored to return home for a visit, but the opportunity never came. Two children, a boy and a girl, had been born to him before he left home and a girl a few months afterward. What provision he made for them is not known, though it is presumed that from time to time he sent money for their maintenance. But when he saw and talked with Chiles he resolved to have his family brought out to him, and Chiles was commissioned to return and bring them. Going east in 1842, Chiles obtained the consent of the mother to take the younger daughter, Elizabeth, then 16 years old. The older daughter, Frances, who was married, consented, with her husband, to go along. The son seems to have accompanied a later party. But the mother, for reasons unknown, declined to make the journey and never saw her husband again. She died in 1850. ("The Chronicles of George C. Yount," edited by Charles L. Camp, *Quarterly* of the California Historical Society, Vol. II, No. 1, April 1923.)

CHAPTER V

[19] Copies of this work are exceedingly rare. It is, however, available in the series of reprints, *Early Western Travels*, edited by Reuben Gold Thwaites.

[20] C. F. McGlashan, *History of the Donner Party*, etc. (2d ed., 1880); Eliza P. Donner Houghton, *The Expedition of the Donner Party and Its Tragic Fate* (1911); H. H. Bancroft, *History of California*, II and V (1885–86); Rockwell D. Hunt (ed.), *California and Californians*, II (1926). Breen's diary, with a brief introduction by Frederick J. Teggert, appears in *Publications* of the Academy of Pacific Coast History, I (July 1910).

[21] *The Historical Record* [of the Mormon Church], Vol. IX (January 1890).

CHAPTER VI

[22] C. C. Royce, *John Bidwell*, etc., p. 21.

[23] H. S. Lyman, *Quarterly* of the Oregon Historical Society, September 1900.

[24] Letter to James Gordon Bennett, from Linnton, O. T., in 1844. Reprinted from the New York *Herald* in the *Quarterly* of the Oregon Historical Society, December 1902.

[25] C. C. Royce, *John Bidwell*, etc. "Early California Reminiscences," VI.

[26] Myron Eells, *Marcus Whitman*, etc., pp. 117–18.

[27] R. B. Marcy, *The Prairie Traveler. A Hand-Book for Overland Expeditions* (1859).

[28] Ezra Meeker, *Kate Mulhall*, pp. 61–63.

[29] Myron Eells, *Marcus Whitman*, etc., p. 61.

[30] John Minto, *Transactions* of the Oregon Pioneer Association (1876).

[31] "A Day with the Cow Column in 1843."

[32] C. C. Royce, *John Bidwell*, etc., pp. 23–25.

[33] H. S. Lyman, "Reminiscences of Hugh Cosgrove," *Quarterly* of the Oregon Historical Society, September 1900.

CHAPTER VII

[34] "National Aspects of the Old Oregon Trail," *Collections* of the Kansas State Historical Society, XIII (1913–14).

[35] Letter from Mrs. Clarence S. Paine, secretary of the Mississippi Valley Historical Association, Lincoln, Neb., Aug. 25, 1928.

[36] Letters from H. E. Mills (July 17, 1928) and Charles Jackson (Sept. 5, 1928), both of Atlantic City, Wyoming.

[37] "Fort Hall on the Saptin River," *Washington Historical Quarterly*, Vol. VII, No. 3 (July 1916).

[38] Letter from the Adjutant General of the United States Army to Walter R. Siders, Feb. 6, 1925.

[39] Senate Document 1, 31st Congress, 2d session, Serial No. 587.

[40] Letter from the Adjutant General of the United States Army to W. L. Short, July 15, 1927.

[41] Senate Documents 174–77 (Serial No. 461), House Document 166 (Serial No. 467), 28th Congress, 2d session.

CHAPTER VIII

[42] Allan Nevins, *Frémont, The World's Greatest Adventurer* (1928).

[43] C. C. Royce, *John Bidwell*, etc.

[44] James A. B. Scherer, *The First Forty-Niner* (1925).

[45] *Ibid.*

[46] Address in *Transactions* of the Oregon Pioneer Association (1882). Quoted by Professor F. G. Young, " The Oregon Trail," *Quarterly* of the Oregon Historical Society, December 1900.

CHAPTER IX

[47] H. M. Chittenden and Alfred T. Richardson, *Life, Letters and Travels* of Father Pierre-Jean de Smet, S. J., 1801–73 (1905), p. 671.

[48] Levi Edgar Young, *Chief Episodes in the History of Utah* (1912).

[49] There are many accounts of the Mountain Meadows tragedy, some of them extremely partisan. The account here given has been made from a careful study of what are believed to be the most dependable sources. See, in particular, *The Mountain Meadows Massacre*, by Josiah F. Gibbs (Salt Lake City, 1910).

[50] See J. Cecil Alter, *James Bridger*, pp. 244–63 and 274–328.

CHAPTER X

[51] Professor Hafen shows that the Californians did much more than the Easterners to support the line. From the San Francisco *Bulletin* he quotes the statement of a St. Louis cor-

respondent, written on May 10, 1860: "California letter writers have more than half covered the cost of several trips, and if as many letters were sent from this end of the line westward, the express would now pay." Root says that during the last seven or eight weeks before the service was closed an average of 350 letters was brought from the Coast on each trip. The average number carried from the East to San Francisco between November 1860, and April 1861, was forty-one; between April and July, 1861, sixty-four, and from then to the close, ninety.

[52] See N. P. Langford, *Vigilante Days and Ways* (1890), pp. 288–320, and Thomas J. Dimsdale, *The Vigilantes of Montana* (1882 edition), pp. 176–87.

CHAPTER XI

[53] The controversy over the identity of this remarkable woman and the spelling of her name fills a large space in current writings on the early frontier. What may be called the Wyoming School contends that the woman, late in life, came to Washakie's reservation and died there in 1884, and that her name should be spelled *Sacajawe*. In North and South Dakota is found what may be called the Dakota School, which contends that she died in 1812, at Lisa's trading post, Fort Manuel (in the present South Dakota), and that her name should be spelled *Sakakawea*.

The date and place of her death are attested beyond any reasonable doubt, and there is no basis for the Wyoming theory except Shoshone gossip. In the diary of John C. Luttig (*Journal of a Fur-Trading Expedition on the Upper Missouri*, 1812–13, edited by Stella M. Drumm), is a record of a woman's death so explicit that it would leave no room for controversy except that it omits the woman's name. Luttig was Lisa's clerk. On Dec. 20, 1812, he sets down an entry of the death of the wife of Charbonneau, a Snake squaw, " the best Women in the fort," aged about twenty-five years. All the attendant circumstances and all documentary evidence since discovered relating to the woman, her husband and her son show that the person who then passed away was Sacagawea, the Bird Woman of the Lewis and Clark expedition.

The spelling *Sacajawea* was popularized by Biddle in his abstract of the journals of the expedition, published in 1814. There was, however, not the slightest warrant for the form in the journals he edited, and it seems probable that he made the change only on the unexplainable advice of his assistant, young George Shannon, a member of the expedition. The author has made an examination of such of the original manuscripts as are in the custody of the American Philosophical Society in Philadelphia and finds that in every instance of the use of the name the writers (including Sergeant John Ordway) indicated the hard *g* in the spelling. They must have heard the name many times, and their testimony as to how it was pronounced ought to be decisive in the matter of its spelling.

The spelling *Sacagawea* was used exclusively by Olin D. Wheeler, after an examination of the journals, in his *Trail of Lewis and Clark* (1904). Since then the form *Sakakawea* has been introduced, on the ground that the Hidatsa Indians of today so pronounce the word. The form is unbeautiful, and the argument in its behalf illogical and fantastic. The spelling *Sacagawea*, used by Lewis, Clark, and Ordway from their talks with the woman and her husband, and adopted by Wheeler, ought never to have been altered.

[54] A detailed biography of Washakie, based upon original sources, including the recollections of many persons who knew him, is in course of preparation by Professor Grace Raymond Hebard, of the University of Wyoming.

[55] LeRoy R. Hafen, *The Overland Mail*, 1849–69 (1926), p. 255.

[56] Root and Connelley, *The Overland Stage*, in several references; Hafen, *The Overland Mail*, p. 258, quoting from George Bird Grinnell, *The Fighting Cheyennes*, p. 148.

[57] Hafen, *op. cit.*, pp. 260–61.

[58] See Frederic L. Paxson, *The Last American Frontier*, pp. 254–63. One of the Cheyenne chiefs, White Antelope,

declaring that Black Kettle, himself and others had brought on the attack by their raids, refused to leave the field and was killed. Black Kettle escaped and was killed in Custer's attack on his village on the Washita, Nov. 27, 1868.

[59] Grace Raymond Hebard and E. A. Brininstool, *The Bozeman Trail*, I, 134 ff.

[60] *Ibid.*, pp. 155–200.

[61] *Ibid.*, pp. 237–61.

[62] *Ibid.*, p. 58.

[63] There are several accounts of the Wagon Box fight. The most complete account is that in Hebard and Brininstool. See, also, the article, "The Education of Red Cloud," by Doane Robinson, in *South Dakota Historical Collections*, XII (1924), which contains notes on the statements made by General Richard Irving Dodge, Cyrus Townsend Brady and others.

CHAPTER XII

[64] "By Ox-Team to California. Personal Narrative of Nancy A. Hunt," *Overland Monthly*, April 1916. The reminiscences were edited by the writer's son, Professor Rockwell D. Hunt, of the University of Southern California.

[65] *History of California*, IV, 222–23, note 34.

[66] John P. Davis, *The Union Pacific Railway* (1894), p. 13.

[67] *Ibid.*, pp. 19–34.

[68] Carl I. Wheat, "A Sketch of the Life of Theodore D. Judah," *Quarterly* of the California Historical Society, Vol. IV, No. 3 (September 1925).

[69] Hebard and Brininstool, I, 90.

INDEX

A

Adams, John Quincy, denies validity of Russian claims, 29; declares Oregon of increasing importance, 30; recommends establishment of military post in Oregon, 30.

"A Day with the Cow Column in 1843," 73–76, 110–11, 116, 235, 258.

Alexander, Col. E. B., commands advance force against Mormons, 179; harassed by guerrillas, 180; establishes winter quarters at Fort Bridger, 180.

Allen, Miss A. J., 59, 61–62.

Alter, J. Cecil, xi, 261.

American Fur Co., branch established in St. Louis, 13; gains monopoly of mountain trade, 25; obtains Fort William, renaming it Fort John, 42, 133; mentioned, 41 and *passim*.

American Society for Encouraging the Settlement of Oregon Territory, 32.

Applegate, Jesse, leader of cow column of emigration of 1843, 71; quoted on Whitman's services, 73; on a typical day's journey, 73–76; on emigrant courts, 110–11; on Whitman's conduct of a childbirth case, 116; on the character of the emigrants, 235; breaks new trail to Oregon, 86.

Arapahos, 15, 39, 40, 202, 220, 222, 225, 229–30.

Arikaras (Rees), characterized, 9–10; attack Ashley, 16; evaded by Henry, 20.

Arrow Rock Ferry, 23.

Ash Hollow, 130, 167; battle of, 130, 165, 176.

Ashley, Gen. William Henry, sketch of, 12–13; start of his first expedition, 14; second expedition, 14; first overland expedition, 19; holds first rendezvous, 20; sells his business, 20; travels Cherokee Trail, 156–57.

Aspinwall, William H., starts first mail steamship to Pacific Coast, 168.

Astor, John Jacob, establishes Astoria, 9; establishes branch of American Fur Co. in St. Louis, 13; retires from company, 25; mentioned, 28, 30.

Astoria, ix, 9, 28, 30; sale of to North West Co., 27; restored to U. S., 28.

Astoria, by Washington Irving, ix.

Astorians, Hunt's party, 8–11; Stuart's party, route of, 11; at South Pass, 18; camp site marked, 250.

Atchison, founded, 174; rise of, 165; starting place of stage-coaches, 203, 204, 208, 209; stage company abandons city, 212.

Atkinson, Gen. Henry, 20.

Atole, 101.

B

"Bad Hand" (see Fitzpatrick, Thomas).

Ball, John, 22, 236.

Bancroft, Hubert Howe, quoted on emigration of 1849, 158, 162; on early suggestion of Pacific railway, 239; on Joel P. Walker, 256–57.

Bannocks, 215–16; characterized, 217; defeated by Col. Connor, 221.

Barlow, S. K., opens road south of the Columbia, 84–85.

Bartleson, John, captain of Bidwell-Bartleson party, 52, 53, 56.

Bear River, first visited by American trappers, 17; mentioned, 36, 57, 118, 142.

Beaver fur, quest of, 1–6; used in manufacture of hats, 2; collapse in price of, 2.

Beckwourth, James P., viii.

Belden, Josiah, viii.

Bell, James Christy, Jr., vii, xi, 257.

Bell, W. A., prints anonymous de-